A LONG WAY TO
TIPPERARY?

TWO AND A HALF YEARS IN THE TRENCHES OF WORLD WAR 1

THE DIARY OF
MAURICE GRAFFET NEAL

King's Royal Rifle Corps

Edited and compiled by his granddaughter, Stephanie Hillier

A LONG WAY TO
TIPPERARY?

TWO AND A HALF YEARS IN THE TRENCHES OF WORLD WAR 1

THE DIARY OF
MAURICE GRAFFET NEAL

King's Royal Rifle Corps

Edited and compiled by his granddaughter, Stephanie Hillier

MEREO

Cirencester

Mereo Books

1A The Wool Market Dyer Street Cirencester Gloucestershire GL7 2PR
An imprint of Memoirs Publishing www.mereobooks.com

A long way to Tipperary? 978-1-86151-121-8

First published in Great Britain in 2014
by Mereo Books, an imprint of Memoirs Publishing

Copyright ©2014

Cover design - Ray Lipscombe

The address for Memoirs Publishing Group Limited can be found at www.memoirspublishing.com

The Memoirs Publishing Group Ltd Reg. No. 7834348

The Memoirs Publishing Group supports both The Forest Stewardship Council® (FSC®) and the PEFC®
leading international forest-certification organisations. Our books carrying both the FSC label and the
PEFC® and are printed on FSC®-certified paper. FSC® is the only forest-certification scheme supported
by the leading environmental organisations including Greenpeace. Our paper procurement policy can
be found at www.memoirspublishing.com/environment

Typeset in 11.5/16pt Plantin
by Wiltshire Associates Publisher Services Ltd. Printed and bound in Great Britain
by Marston Book Services Ltd, Didcot

Contents

∼

Introduction

The King's Royal Rifle Corps

Chapter 1   A flood of khaki   P.1

Chapter 2   Off to France, September 1914   P.5

Chapter 3   The big attack, spring 1915   P.34

Chapter 4   Battle for possession   P.56

Chapter 5   Home on leave, August 1915   P.72

Chapter 6   The Battle of Loos, September 25 1915   P.78

Chapter 7   Convalescence, 1915-16   P.93

Chapter 8   Back to Flanders   P.96

Chapter 9   The Battle of the Somme, July 1916   P.119

Chapter 10   Delville Wood   P.143

Chapter 11   A walk in the sun   P.156

Chapter 12   Back to the Somme, September 1916   P.159

Chapter 13   A rifleman once again   P.173

Chapter 14   A chilly Christmas   P.201

Chapter 15   The Battle of Arras, April 9 1917   P.216

Chapter 16   Farewell to the front line   P.250

Brief diary of events

The price of victory

Some facts and figures

Wit, humour and verse from the front

Glossary

Introduction

∽

Maurice Graffet Neal was born at The Barracks, Barnet, Greater London on 7th September 1890. He was the second child born to his parents, Louise Anatolie (née Graffet) and Alfred James Neal.

His elder brother, Lance Corporal Alfred Graffet Neal, died in 1908 at the age of 19 years on the island of Malta, where he was stationed with the 3rd Battalion, King's Royal Rifle Corps. He suffered a ruptured appendix playing football whilst based at St. George's Barracks and died of peritonitis a few days later. He was buried in the Addolorata Cemetery in Paolo, Malta.

Louise (b.1864 in Le Havre), who was fluent in the English language, had studied in London and in 1886 found a placement as governess to Colonel Terry's children in Albany Barracks, Parkhurst on the Isle of Wight, teaching French and music. It was here that she met and married Alfred James Neal, who was a Colour Sergeant at that time with the King's Royal Rifle Corps.

Maurice's father later became a Sergeant Major in the KRRs, Service Number 5295.

Maurice joined the KRRs, 1st Battalion, in 1906 at the age of 15 years (Service No: 7229) and served in Crete before the outbreak of WWI. He was 24 in 1914 when he left the Winchester Rifle Depot (Mobilization Dept.) to go to war in France, where he initially suffered two minor injuries, a bullet wound to his right arm and a leg wound. In 1917 he was severely wounded in the lower abdomen by shrapnel, which ended his active duty in the trenches.

He was invalided home and was then taken by rail to the Royal Victoria Hospital, Netley, where he endured five surgical operations. It was there that he met and later married Alice Theresa (née Gray), a nurse with the VAD (Voluntary Aid Detachment) at the RV hospital, whose duties included assisting in the operating theatres with the disposal of amputated limbs.

During his three-year convalescent period, which was predominantly at the Royal Victoria Hospital in the newly-constructed Red Cross hospital complex, he spent some time at Countess Cairns near Romsey, Fareham House, Fareham, the New Forest etc and was discharged from service in June 1920.

Maurice and Alice had a daughter and two sons and lived all their married lives in Netley Abbey, Hampshire. After his rehabilitation, Maurice was advised to avoid any heavy work; however, initially he had no choice but to work as a labourer, finding it very difficult to find a suitable job. Later, he found employment as a valet in Green Lane, Hamble Village, Hampshire and then as a steward on board the ship Majestic of the White Star Line (sailing from Southampton to New York). He was also employed as a crew member visiting the Dardanelles and Gallipoli in 1922 and served on other passenger liners going to South America (Brazil and Argentina) and South Africa. He was finally employed at Southampton Docks carrying out office duties.

As far as I am aware, having served 13 years 314 days as a regular soldier with the KRRs, Maurice neither received a pension when his Army career ended, nor a War Disability

Pension. Owing to the nature of his injuries, he had a difficult time in the 1920s and 30s providing for his children with a lack of suitable work to ensure a reasonable income. My mother told me that they had to resort to pawning their items of value when money was scarce.

Alice died in 1960 at the age of 67 and Maurice then moved to Hamble, to be near his daughter, where he died on 5th January 1971 at the age of 80. He was, by then, a grandfather and a great grandfather to my daughter.

His original account was written with pen and ink in a ledger in the form of a book with his own numerous sketches and detailed maps, plus newspaper cuttings and photographs. Apparently, the only time he ever loaned this book was to a disturbed individual who had experienced the horrors of World War I, like himself, and was constantly reliving the experience by compulsive trench-digging on waste ground at the back of the Netley Abbey Royal British Legion Club. Maurice was requested by people concerned for the poor chap's state of mind to explain to him that there was no further danger and that the war was over. He eventually coaxed him out of the trenches he had been feverishly digging. Later, he loaned him his book to read, hoping it would help.

Writing this book, after he was discharged from the Royal Victoria Hospital, must have served as a therapy for Maurice as the horrors he witnessed first-hand were undoubtedly imprinted in his memory for the rest of his life.

In 1996, an alder tree was planted in the Royal Victoria Country Park at Netley, dedicated to the memory of my grandparents, Maurice and Alice.

A soldier, 1914

Maurice in 1915

Maurice's 1914-18 Medals: 1914 Star and Bar (5th Aug-22nd Nov 1914), British War Medal, Victory Medal with "Mention in Despatches" oak leaf and round shot taken from his right arm.

The "Scrap of Paper"

ARTICLE II.

Her Majesty the Queen of the United Kingdom of Great Britain and Ireland, His Majesty the Emperor of Austria, King of Hungary and Bohemia, His Majesty the King of the French, His Majesty the King of Prussia, and His Majesty the Emperor of all the Russias, declare, that the Articles mentioned in the preceding Article, are considered as having the same force and validity as if they were textually inserted in the present Act, and that they are thus placed under the guarantee of their said Majesties.

ARTICLE VII.

Belgium, within the limits specified in Articles I., II., and IV. shall form an independent and perpetually neutral State. It shall be bound to observe such neutrality towards all other States.

PALMERSTON.
British Plenipotentiary.

SYLVAN VAN DE WEYER
Belgian Plenipotentiary.

SENFFT
Austrian Plenipotentiary.

H. SEBASTIANI
French Plenipotentiary.

BÜLOW
Prussian Plenipotentiary.

POZZO DI BORGO
Russian Plenipotentiary.

The 'scrap of paper'

THE
KING'S ROYAL RIFLE CORPS

"Celer et Audax"

Louisberg. "Quebec, 1759." Martinique, 1762, 1809. Havannah. Roleia.
Vimiera. Talavera. Busaco. Fuentes D'Onor. Albuhera
Ciudad-Rodrigo. Badajos. Salamanca. Vittoria. Pyrenees. Nivelle.
Nive. Orthes. Toulouse. Peninsular. Punjaub. Mooltan. Goojerat.
Delhi. Taku-Forts. Pekin. South-Africa 1851-2-3. 1879.
Ahmed Khel. Khandahar 1880. Afganistan. 1878-80. Egypt 1882-4
Tel-el-Kebir. Chitral. South-Africa 1899-1902.

COLONEL - IN - CHIEF
HIS MAJESTY KING GEORGE V

Prior to the Outbreak of the Great War the disposition of the Regiment was as follows:-

1st Batt'n. Aldershot.   2nd Battal'n Blackdown.
3rd Batt'n. India.   4th. Batt'n India.

5th Special Res. Batt'n. Winchester.
6th Ditto   Winchester.   Rifle-Depot Winchester.

Battalions raised during war. Twenty-Five.

Killed in Action, Died of Wounds, etc. 12.800.

The Battalions took part in the following engagements

Mons Marne Aisne Ypres 1914-15-17-18. Langemark
1914-17. Gheluvelt, Nonne-Bosschen. Gravenstafel.
Frezenburg Bellewarde. Festubert, La-Bassee. Neuve-
Chapelle. 1915. Hooge, Loos, 1915. Somme 1916-18.
Albert. Bazentin, Ginchy, Delville-Wood. Poziers.
Guillemont, Flers-Courcelette. Ancre. Arras 1917-18.
Scarpe '17. Arleux. Wancourt. Messines. Pilkem. Menin.
Polygon-Wood. Poelcappelle. Passchendaele. Cambrai '17-18.
St Quentin. Rosiers. Avre. Lys. Armentiers. Mont-Kemmel.
Bethune, Bapaume. Hindenburg-Line. Havrincourt. Epehy.
Canal-du-Nord. Courtrai. Sambre. Selle.

The King's Royal Rifle Corps

The King's Royal Rifle Corps
"Celer et Audax"

(Swift and Bold)

Louisberg; Quebec, 1759; Martinique, 1762, 1809; Havannah; Roleia; Vimiera, Talavera, Busaco, Fuertes D'Onor, Albuhera, Ciduad-Rodigo, Badajos, Salamanca, Vittoria, Pyrenees, Nivelle, Nive, Orthes, Toulouse, Peninsular, Punjaub, Mooltan, Goojerat, Delhi, Taku-Forts, Pekin, South-Africa 1851- 2 - 3, 1879, Ahmed Khel, Khandahar 1880, Afghanistan 1878-80, Egypt 1882-4, Tel-El-Kebir, Chitral, South-Africa 1899-1902.

Colonel-in-Chief: His Majesty King George V

Prior to the outbreak of the Great War the dispositions of the Regiment were as follows:

1st Battalion	Aldershot
2nd Battalion	Blackdown
3rd Battalion	India
4th Battalion	India

5th Special Reserve Battalion	Rifle Depot, Winchester
6th Special Reserve Battalion	Rifle Depot, Winchester

Battalions raised during War: 25
Killed in Action, died of wounds, etc: 12,800

The Battalions took part in the following engagements:
Mons, Marne, Aisne, Ypres 1914-15-17-18, Langemark
1914-17, Gheluvelt, Nonne-Bosschen, Gravenstafel,
Frezenburg, Bellewarde, Festubert, La Bassée,
Neuve-Chappelle 1915, Hooge, Loos 1915, Somme
1916-18, Albert, Bazentin, Ginchy, Delville Wood, Poziers,
Guillemont, Flers-Courcelette, Ancre, Arras 1917-1918,
Scarpe 1917, Arleux, Wancourt, Messines, Pilkem, Menin,
Polygon Wood, Poelcappelle, Passchendaele, Cambrai
1917-18, St. Quentin, Rosiers, Avre, Lys, Armentiers,
Mont-Kemmel, Bethune, Bapaume, Hindenburg-Line,
Havrincourt, Epehy, Canal-du-Nord, Courtrai, Sambre, Selle

France and Belgium 1914-1918
Italy 1917
Macedonia 1916-1917

a German or any other living thing could live in it, but as soon as our infantry jumped over the parapets they were met with a murderous machine gun & rifle fire, which eventually forced what was left of them to retire & so a complete division was rendered useless in a few minutes & nothing gained. Our Division 2nd line of reserves that day, we dealt with the idea of carrying on the operation: had the 1st div got through. Of course they were relieved out of the firing line & we took their place. We knew we would have to go 'over the top' before long. Over the top' is a slang phrase for an attack, but it did not come off until nearly a week later, on Saturday night. It is a queer experience to go 'over the top' our nerves were strung up to their highest pitch as you can guess. For days previous to the attack a heavy bombardment had been going on round our ramshackle billet behind the firing line. You can guess what it was like with about twenty batteries of our artillery blithering away all day & night, then in the end knowing we has to make an attack. Our commanding Officer gave us a speech before going, he himself came with us, but I'm sorry to say never lived to see the dawn of another day. We had to muffle up all our equipment to avoid rattling. At about nine o'clock we filed up to the trenches. We had a white piece of linen tied to the back of us to avoid any one striking his own men in the confusion. About an hour or so afterwards we were all outside our front line trenches & lying flat on the ground amongst many still forms who had lost their life. Nobody can realize what runs through a chaps mind in those few tense minutes of waiting, when you know that in any moment you may be in the next world. At last the order came to go forward, we would

Letter written by Maurice to his mother from the front line, May 1915

B Coy 1st K.R.R.C. British Ex–Force
21-5-15

My Dear Mother,

I received safely the parcel & post-card a couple of days ago & sent a service card to let you know. I waited until now before writing as we are back for a rest & how much we are in need of one, only ourselves can tell. We have been having a very trying time of it, for both fighting and weather. In fact I believe it is the warmest corner I've been in since the war commenced. The only consolation we have is that we were set to do, we carried out well but at what a cost no one can imagine. You read in the official despatch that so many yards of trenches were taken from the Germans. One must think that if it takes such a large expenditure of shells & heavy casualty lists for so small a gain, whatever will be the price paid to reach Germany. Personally, I have my own views about the allied troops ever reaching the German frontier, & so have many others who have been out here a bit, & they are all of a pessimistic nature. I cannot see how we can keep the offensive movement on for any length of time, without conscription, as we could never keep up with the continual demand for more men. For instance the other Sunday morning a general attack by the 1st Div was made, the first offensive movement on a large scale since Neuve-Chapelle. A terrific bombardment commenced on our part, the like of which I could not describe, you would imagine that not a German or any other living thing could live in it, but as soon as our infantry jumped over the parapets they were met with a murderous machine gun & rifle fire, which eventually forced what was left of them to retire & so a complete division was rendered useless in a few minutes & nothing gained. Our Div was 3rd line of reserves that day, no doubt with the idea of carrying on the operations had the 1st Div got through. Of course they were relieved out of the firing line & we took their place. We knew we would have to go 'over the top' before long. 'Over the top' is a slang phrase for an attack, but it did not come off until nearly a week later, on Saturday night. It is a queer experience to go 'over the top', our nerves were strung up to their highest pitch as you can guess. For days previous to the attack a heavy bombardment had been going on round our ramshackle billet behind the firing line. You can guess what it was like with about twenty batteries of artillery blotching away all day & night, then in the end knowing one has to make an attack. Our Commanding Officer gave us a speech before going, he himself came with us, but I'm sorry to say never lived to the dawn of another day.

We had to muffle up all our equipment, to avoid rattling Etc. & about nine o'clock we filed up to the trenches. We had a white piece of linen tied to the back of us, to avoid anyone sticking his own men in the confusion. About an hour or so afterwards we were all outside our front line trenches & lying flat on the ground amongst many still forms who had done their bit. Nobody can realize what runs through a chaps mind in those few tense minutes of waiting, when you know that in any moment you may be in the next world. At last the order came to go forward. Up would go some German lights & down we'd flop on our faces, but they must have rumbled something *for they put up about umpteen star shells at once & we were spotted. Then there was a hell of a rattling of maxims & rifles, shouts, curses, groans, vivid explosions from bursting shrapnel Etc. & I scarcely remember any more sane moments for a good bit. It being quite dark it made the thing more like a huge stage effect scene like one would see at Olympia or somewhere. We got their first line trench easily & then we pushed on & got their second one & would have had the third only for the order to remain in the second one. We could see hundreds of them rushing away down their communication trench, helter-skelter in their hurry to avoid us. They asked for mercy, but very few were shown any, wounded or otherwise, the same treatment was meted out to them as they had been doing to our chaps. We held on to the trenches for over 24 hours until relieved by another Reg. We had scarcely anything to eat, as what was left of us had to be practically on continuous sentry go, in case they counter attacked, but nothing happened. After they lost their trenches we were subjected to the most hellish shelling I have ever been under. They were deadly accurate & our old trenches and reserves suffered terribly. We timed them once and counted 87 shells of all descriptions in a radius of a couple of hundred yards in 3½ minutes. So you can imagine what we had to contend with. A couple of days after the Brigade was relieved by a Scottish Div. & how thankful we are to get away to this village where one would scarcely believe there's a war on although so near the firing line. I wonder if Italy has declared yet, I hope so, it will be a lift to the troops in the Dardanelles as they are up against a big thing in that quarter. I have seen a none too complimentary article in the papers of Lord K. & his tactics. He is an organizer, but not a leader of men, at least that's how it reads. What with Churchill & Fisher & shells, we are getting in a pickle. *(I know for a fact that the artillery on Sunday the 9th told us they*

could not continue the operations as they had run short of ammunition, so there's fact, the 6 in. guns had run out altogether.) *
I will not write any more of war in this letter, we are now waiting to be made up again to strength, we lost most of the officers either killed or wounded, so this makes the third time I have seen the old regiment in a bad way.

To talk about home things, I had a letter & cake from Auntie, I wish she would not send them, fags are so much better than pastries Etc. Please thank her if you write to her, I must send her a line. Your parcel was most handy, we do not get many fags now, & they are the best to send out, also candles and matches always handy. I have not heard from Barnet or London for quite a long time, daresay I shall get a line soon. Wonder where Jack is now, I'm sorry Mr. O'Neill is going in a bad way it is a pity for her & the kiddies, she is such a nice woman. I hope yourself and dad are quite well. I long to see you both so much, but must wait & trust in God hoping all will come right in the end. Kiss dad for me & God bless you both. With fondest love & kisses From Loving Son, Mon.

Write soon as possible .

I wrote this long letter as you wished me to put something about what we are doing otherwise I doubt whether I'd have entered anything at all. (This was written on the back of the letter)

*Although this sensitive information in Maurice's letter was underlined in red ink, it was allowed to reach his mother uncensored.

A flood of khaki

The now famous war ditty which titles this book was foreign to my ears at the outbreak of war. I confess that I had never heard it, and only became acquainted with it at impromptu concerts held behind the line.

On August 4th 1914 I was quartered at Winchester. I was on the staff. We led a rather indolent life there. About one parade a week and that was our military routine – except for musketry or an occasional church parade or kit inspection.

Winchester was the depot of my regiment and also of the Rifle Brigade and Hampshire Regiment. Here it was that the new recruit was shaped and moulded to be finally sent to join a battalion.

We favoured ones were "on the staff", doing various jobs such as officers' servants, grooms, mobilization stores etc. I was with the latter. Owing to lack of accommodation in the barracks, my particular stores were situated in the town itself, which afforded many privileges.

I had been in the service eight years and considered myself an "old soldier". All the staff "wallahs" could boast two, three and four badges on their left sleeves. These were awarded for five, twelve and sixteen years' service with good conduct. Men who could boast of these badges were, in a good many cases, extremely lucky. They had escaped the eye of the provost sergeant, or had been able to have that soldier-like appearance when returning to barracks "full to the bung"!

The smart and rich coloured uniforms of the Army received their death sentences with the outbreak of war. The drab khaki has been the chief raiment ever since – except, of course, the guards and regimental bands. A glimpse of the glory and colour of the pre-war soldier can now be seen at the Trooping of the Colour by the Brigade of Guards or the Naval and Military Tournament or occasional Military Tattoos. Otherwise, khaki is the usual uniform worn by all units for all duties.

My Regiment, The King's Royal Rifle Corps, wore a smart if sombre uniform of rifle or dark green with scarlet facings, whilst the sister regiment, the Rifle Brigade, were the same, except for scarlet facings – all rifle regiments were nicknamed "The Sweeps" on account of the uniform and black belt and buttons. Another nickname bestowed was a corruption of the German "Jaegers" (hunters) and familiarly known as "Jaggers".

Nobody seemed to fully appreciate what the outbreak of war really would mean. To some it was a nightmare; they could already see the nice cushy job at the depot vanishing and being called upon to face the unknown. Unfortunately, I knew several personally and I hold more respect for the conscientious objector than those "soldiers" who purposely scrounged and dodged active service.

Winchester changed in one night from the peaceful cathedral city it was into a bustling hive of humanity. From August 6th 1914 and the following days, the three depots, i.e. the KRRC, the RBs and Hampshire Regiment, were all working at full pressure. Reservists poured in from all over the country and had to be clothed, fed and dispatched to the various battalions.

I was dumbfounded to meet my own father, who had come from Tidworth in response to the organisation known, in those days, as the "National Reserve". Unfortunately there was no provision made for them, and these patriotic old soldiers were left to wander round quite spare, many without any means whatever. I was mighty pleased when I prevailed upon father to return home again.

In reply to my request to go with the Reservists to join the Battalion, I at first met with blank refusal – but I persisted and left Winchester at 11 o'clock on the night of the 8th August.

We all imagined that Aldershot or Blackdown would be our destination, but when we saw a station named Dorking, then Reigate and finally Gillingham in Kent, we gave up trying to think where we were bound for.

About eight o'clock in the morning the train pulled up at a wayside "Halt" and about 150 of us commenced a tramp to a fort on the coast at the mouth of the Thames. Our duties were to guard the coast against a surprise landing. Every dawn, we crawled off the concrete floor of the wagon shed where we slept and marched out to the improvised trenches in the marshland. At night time so many men had to patrol the same mud flats, with orders to challenge or shoot all suspicious persons. I had a shot now and then, but only at wildfowl, etc.

By about the third week we were all getting properly fed up. We knew that our Expeditionary Force in France had been pushed back to the outskirts of Paris and, what with the monotony of our own lives, anything would be welcome to alter our routine.

On the 8th September we had orders to pack up or, at least, 35 men were required to join a draft at Sheerness that evening. I was more than pleased to be included, but I always remember the words of the Colour Sergeant to me before we marched off. He said "You've been harping at me to send you out, but you'll wish yourself here again before long. Goodbye and good luck". We marched five miles to Fort Grain and crossed the harbour to Sheerness. A few hours' rest and the whole draft, known as the 4th Reinforcements BEF, fell in and marched to the stirring tunes of the band to entrain for Southampton.

Off to France

We were eight to a carriage and it was after 9 pm when we steamed out of Sheerness station. The draft consisted of roughly 350 men under a captain and two lieutenants. All through the night we travelled and in the early morning the train drew up in one of the quayside sheds in Southampton Docks. Temporary canteens had been erected, which were a boon to the troops.

After a meagre breakfast on the dockside, we were paraded and, with details of other units, we embarked on the *SS Armenian*. The ship had recently returned from New Orleans with livestock and, after being cleaned out, it was to take us "livestock" to France. Some five ships made up our convoy. The only other ship's name I remember was the *Minnesota*.

About ten in the morning on the 9th September we left the docks, passed down Southampton Water and headed for Spithead. By this time the jubilation of the troops had died down and the men had settled themselves, thinking to be in France by late afternoon. Night came and the French coast had not shown itself. All sorts of rumours were about – was it to be Havre? Boulogne? Dieppe? It was not to be – we were going to sail up the Seine to Paris. Or were we to land at Ostend? We were going here, there and various other places.

All the following day we saw nothing at all, but I gleaned a little information from a ship's hand, who said that the skipper's orders were to "heave to" in lat. something and long. something - about 130 miles from the Bishop's Light, which I knew was in the vicinity of the Scilly Isles. A strange thing was,

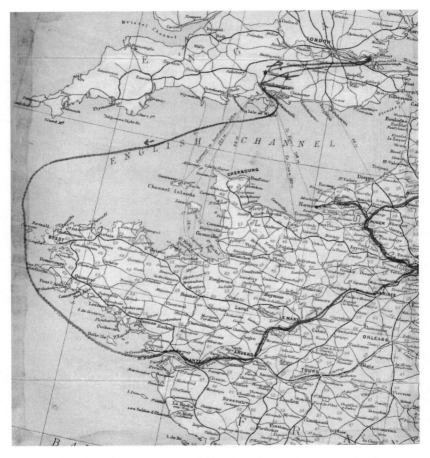

The above map shows the places mentioned in my travels from the outbreak of war.

6

that although five ships left Southampton practically together, we never saw one of them until the second morning when the five were all together with a couple of French TBs as escort.

We eventually berthed in St Nazaire docks and when the five transports were unloaded, there were about 6,000 fresh British Tommies to add to the Army's numbers. We formed up in the streets, representing all arms of the service. Our camp was about two miles from the town and perched on top of the cliffs. A base hospital had been installed and St Nazaire became quite busy. We stayed in the vicinity much longer than anticipated. A rough estimate of the British troops would put the number at between 12,000 to 15,000 men.

In France

It is a remarkable fact that although we were now actually on French soil, we were considerably further away from the conflict than when we had been in England. From St Nazaire to the zone of operations as the crow flies was roughly 300 miles. On the other side of the Channel at Sheerness a straight line from there to the line of the Marne Battle would measure about 175 miles, whilst the distance from Antwerp to Sheerness was only 120 miles.

At this period the Allies had successfully held up the huge armies of Germany and by September 12th 1914 the British had reached the River Aisne. It is practically from this date that the war of movement finished for almost four solid years.

Our life in St Nazaire was to prove a strenuous one. The High Command had become very nervous since the Great Retreat from Mons to the very gates of Paris itself. Men had fallen out with sore and blistered feet. Thousands, unable to keep marching, rode on all kinds of conveyances, and officers even dismounted to let some poor fellows have a ride. They marched with puttees bound round their swollen and bleeding feet. All this led to the most rigorous training for troops like us, just landed.

We had two route marches a day, one of about 10 miles in the morning and in the afternoon about 6 miles. These marches were carried out in full equipment. Our feet were examined regularly and woe betide those who had ingrowing toenails etc. They had to undergo a painful process at the hands of a chiropodist, whose efforts to cure one's feet were rather clumsy and amateurish. Nevertheless, it was a case of feet first and men's feelings after.

We were the first British troops to be seen in St Nazaire and the French folk crowded to the camps to view us. All of our men were of seasoned type, the majority being Reservists who had served their time with the Colours and had seen service abroad. Many were South African War men and they would tell us what it was like to be "under fire". We never quite realized that there was a war on whilst in St Nazaire. Our two route marches a day were through the lovely district where grapes grew in abundance, where everything to our eyes was fresh and foreign and with our bathes in the sea under the cliffs (the bathing was near a village named La Baule). All these things helped to make war and killing very unreal.

The days were sunny and warm, and with the hard training and open-air life we were getting as hard as nails. Odds and ends of drafts from regiments were continually arriving and going, but the numbers increased rather than diminished at our camp. We had the Highland Light Infantry on one side of our tents, rare lads from Glasgow! On the opposite side were the Royal Irish Rifles. Between the two of them we were highly entertained, more so when the respective merits of Scotchmen or Irishmen were discussed.

One day I had a Lance Stripe thrust upon me, much to my discomfort. Some men had to be made Lance Corporals, and why I had to suffer this I did not know. If I had accepted the first step on the ladder of promotion I firmly resolved that it would not upset the tranquillity of my future.

All things have an ending, even two route marches a day, and, after staying for about six weeks in St Nazaire, we had orders to strike camp. This occupied some considerable time and a lot of material and stores had to be loaded up on ships for Havre. Finally, on the 16th of October, we entrained amidst much cheering and flag-wagging for Havre.

The Battle of the Aisne had ceased as a battle and both sides had settled into the earth to growl and fight through winter and summer almost until the cessation of hostilities.

The British Army had now made a rapid move from the Aisne up to the left flank of the French Army. The hand of war was making itself felt right across the face of France. Hundreds of thousands of men were frantically digging the earth for fortifications and protection. Long sinuous heaps of earth marked where the trenches lay. They were like a cankerous sore; they appeared as by magic almost in a night. They spread and twined through town, village or hamlet; over hills and through valleys, across marshland and bog, over downlands, through woods and forests – in fact everywhere from the North Sea near Westende and Nieuport in Belgium, down as far as the borders of Switzerland.

To Le Havre

This railway journey was our first sample of troop train travelling in France. We left St Nazaire at night and went by way of Nantes, Angers, Le Mans, Chartres and Versailles, but did not penetrate into Paris itself; the remainder of the journey was Mantes, Vernon, Rouen and thence to Le Havre. The whole journey of about 350 miles occupied 48 hours. We were eight in a carriage and after the first few hours, some of us felt like jumping out of the window. Fortunately, frequent stops gave us the opportunity of stretching our cramped limbs; this was the cause of some wild scramblings to get in the train again when it commenced to move unexpectedly.

This was not my first visit to Le Havre, for I still retained pleasant memories of my childhood there. My mother used to take me and Alf (my brother who died in Malta) there every year or so. When we detrained and marched to our camp, I remembered this street and that road; this particular building or that one. Here I seemed to be in more natural surroundings. I recalled the days I played with my cousin Robert, our excursions to Honfleur and the mischief we used to get up to. As we tramped up the long hill towards St Adresse, I would dearly have liked to catch a glimpse of them. Still, I resolved to try and get a pass to go and see my aunts, if it were possible, but nothing would be granted. I had forgotten most of my French, so did not send a message to let them know I was near them.

The weather had now changed and there was considerable rain. We had to work hard putting up another city of canvas on the heights overlooking the sea. In between this and military duties, we went down to the docks, unloading transports. St Nazaire had now practically ceased to be a military base and Le

Havre had taken its place. This was to be the largest base camp throughout the war. St Nazaire once again came into prominence when the Americans made it their chief port in 1917.

We were wondering if we had really come to France to fight, or if we had been somehow mislaid. It is a mystery to me, even now, why thousands of troops like us had been left behind simply to build camps, take them down and re-erect them again somewhere else, while up the fighting line regiments were hard-pressed and terribly under strength. We had been in France quite seven weeks – no mails had reached us and the only news we had was from returned sick and wounded or from the continental *Daily Mail*.

On the 29th October we paraded for fatigue as usual and had been busy erecting marquees when the order came to down tools.

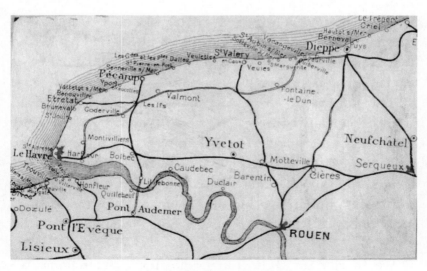

Our route after leaving Le Havre

We leave Le Havre

On returning to our own camp, we received orders to pack up and be ready to move in two hours' time. At last our identity had been established; someone had suddenly had a brainstorm and discovered that there were a few thousand men somewhere in France who had done nothing else but fatigues and gravel crushing. We marched down to the station in high spirits. Everyone was talking and nobody listening – "The war would soon be over, wasn't we going up the Line?" "Hadn't Lord So-and-so said we would all be home for Xmas?" "The Germans couldn't fight – all right in a bunch – useless on their own." "Daren't stand up to our men, can't shoot for nuts", etc, etc. All this silly twaddle was the main conversation. It was only the usual method of bolstering up our own faith in ourselves.

We finally reached the goods sidings, where a wait of several hours elapsed before the train started. However, we managed to bribe some workmen, who at considerable risk, replenished our water bottles – not with coffee! - and a few extra bottles of wine for the journey. In the early evening the train drew out of Havre and that ended my one and only visit for the period of the war.

The journey to the front was very tedious. The train stopped frequently; during these stops we took the opportunity of besieging the engine for boiling water to make tea. The weather was most depressing, rain and the combined chill of late autumn. The flat, rain-sodden countryside, our cramped positions in the carriage and the passing of trains full of mud-caked wounded British and French going the opposite way did not make us any too cheerful.

We stayed near St Omer in a siding for fourteen hours. We were chilled to the marrow, so we improvised a brazier from an old tin, pierced some holes in it and, with the aid of stolen coke, we had a nice little fire when the train restarted. The only drawback was that the only place to put it was between the seats of the carriage, so that we all were half stifled with the smoke and fumes. This forced us to open both windows wide, which let both wind and rain on to us. Finally, after many arguments concerning which was preferable, a fire or a shut carriage, the majority voted for the latter. Much to the disgust of a man who was trying to make toast with some French bread, the offending fire was pitched out onto the line.

The next stop was Hazebrouk on the Belgian border. It was early evening and we could all distinguish a continued rumbling, as of distant thunder. We all gazed in awed fascination in the direction from which the rumbling came and watched the vivid flashing of the guns. There was not much speech – we just kept on staring at this wonderful and inspiring sight. Suddenly, an order came along to don our equipment. We all commenced to hastily gather together our scattered things, when another order came to cancel it and stay in our carriages.

Up the line

The train crawled on once more, and after travelling a few miles drew up in a siding. About ten o'clock we were ordered to prepare ourselves for one more night of agony in a railway carriage. We couldn't lie down, so we alternately arranged our legs between the bodies of our comrades opposite and fell into a fitful sleep.

Before dawn we were awakened by the movement and jolting of the train. It was almost full daylight when we drew up at Poperinghe station. Swarming out on to the platform,

13

our ears were greeted by the sullen and continuous Boom! Boom! And an occasional louder CRRRUMP! As yet we could not distinguish sounds of war, and we neither knew if they were shells bursting or guns firing.

At the back of the platform were the gardens of a row of houses. In every one and in the houses themselves were French troops of the famous Alpine Chasseurs or "Blue Devils". They were all busy removing the marks of war from their clothing and equipment. I gathered from one that "Tings no Goot" up at Ypres. "Allemands pas bon" or that "Ze war it is no goot". Judging by the noise coming from Ypres direction, I was firmly convinced!

Two or three of us wandered to the end of the platform to while away the time. We were looking out on to the roadway, idly smoking and talking, when some French ambulances drew up opposite, by what looked like a school used as a temporary hospital. We had to overcome our curiosity, so went across the road to watch them unload. Shall I ever forget that, my first sight of wounded and dead from the battlefield?

French nurses and ambulance men gently lifted the stretchers out of the cars and we saw what lay on them – men that were once strong and healthy. One poor Frenchman, his blue clothes covered in mud, had head wounds and a blood-soaked bandage round his forehead. The mud and dried blood practically hid his features. He was bearded and it was caked in mud and there was nothing to see of him; Mother Earth had enwrapped him from head to foot. He lay so still!

I craned my neck closer, then a soldier said one word, "mort" (dead). I knew what he had said and told my companions. "Blimey" said one, "strewth" said the other. More stretchers followed, and they all seemed the same, except for the varied wounds – just inert forms. Some were feebly protesting at the unavoidable movement, others were mercifully unconscious and terribly still. Were they unconscious or were they "mort" too?

"Come on" said one of my companions, "Let's get away", and as an afterthought, "Give us a fag". The sight I had just witnessed impressed me a good deal, but strange to say produced no revulsion of feeling. After all, war is brutal to say the least of it. We were inexperienced in its horrors. We were just about to step over the brink and know for ourselves. It wouldn't be long, just up the road that led to Ypres.

We get the order to "Fall in!" A short march and we find our Regimental transport lines. The QM had arranged for tea and a Dixey Stew. We eat this ravenously. I meet an old chum from my Woolwich days, Jock. He greets me warmly and tells me all the news. Billingham, Young, Moore, Barker, Dinger Darton, etc – all dead and all with me at Woolwich. Captain this and Major that, Lieutenant So-and-so – same thing. Sergeants – Corporals too! Wounded or killed. I am sick of his tale of woe, which he rattles off with his usual grin, as though it were some huge joke. He informs me that he is Company cook. He is lucky! He seldom goes further than the transport lines. Tonight, he tells me, we go to join the Battalion at Hooge Château.

At seven, we parade and march behind the ration limbers. We follow the main road to Ypres. There are not too many troops about, and we pass dismounted cavalry who take their places in the firing line like infantry.

There are plenty of civilians still in Ypres itself. Estaminets or wine shops are open and full of French and Belgian soldiers. Ypres had not yet been reduced to a heap of ruins. The famous Cloth Hall was almost intact, as were the majority of the buildings.

Ambulances, limbers, wagons and detachments of British and French were continually passing us. The guns were busy all around. Bang! Bang! Then a more distant boom – Hark!

What's that? Such a queer rushing noise, whining and droning. Suddenly it altered into a menacing shriek and then CRRRASH! The shell had exploded, not near enough to cause any inconvenience to us, but sufficient to cause us to prick up our ears for the next one.

"In South Africa we used to…", volunteered someone, no doubt to put us at our ease.

"Stow it! This is a war this is. Not chasing farmers", was a curt rejoinder.

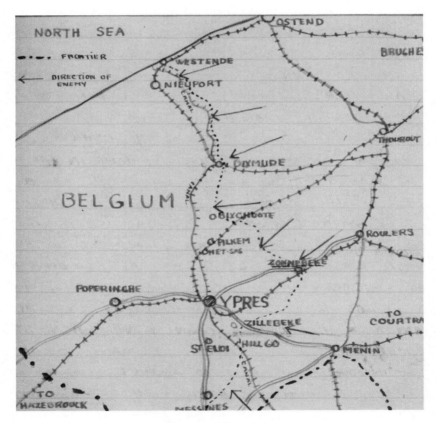

Hooge and Zonnebeke

We pass beyond Ypres and take the road to Roulers. We have now split up with intervals between Sections, this to avoid unnecessary casualties. No smoking! No talking! We hear the whine and rushing shriek of innumerable shells now.

Guns are crashing and hurtling their missiles over to the enemy. At each bang there is a yellowish flash, as of lightning, and the countryside is lit up by successions of these flashes. As though by mutual consent, all the batteries seem to suddenly cease; when they do, the darkness is intensified Then the rattle of musketry is heard, isolated shots, then almost in an instant a crescendo of rifle fire, not unlike the continuous roll of hundreds of kettle drums. Strange lights leapt up to the sky and burned brilliantly for a few seconds during their downward fall, lighting up the ground with an unnatural yellow glare. They were German star shells. I don't think we possessed any at that time.

At last we reach a point where we are halted for some considerable time. We must be very close now. Rifle bullets keep cracking like whips round us. They are dangerous! Other bullets swish through the air – we know they are high. The rifle butts at home were the places that taught us this.

I will always remember the behaviour of a Corporal on this occasion. At home in the depot he was a picture of smartness. He was a member of the "muscle factory" or, in other words, a gymnasium instructor, a terror to the new recruits when putting them "through the mill". He was anything but a brave soldier now! All his muscles, his magnificent chest, his bellowing voice had vanished completely. Instead of maintaining his former dignity and magnificence, he 'ducked' at every crack. He sank to his knees and hid his head in abject terror. "Get up!" yelled one. "Chuck a chest now", said another. The jibe that struck us as most appropriate was from the man who told the cowering corporal, "What about on the hands down now"?

By this time, November 2nd, the British had increased by three divisions and the whole Force was divided into three Army corps, ie the 1st Corps under the command of Sir Douglas Haig, afterwards C-in-C of the British Expeditionary Force, my Regiment being in this.

A tremendous effort had been made by the Germans to break through our troops to gain the Channel ports. Mass attacks had been launched night and day and reached the limit of their ferocity. Their troops had suffered terribly in carrying out the orders of the High Command. As regards ourselves, all regiments were sadly depleted. Our own Regiment had suffered badly! On November 1st, three Companies, 'B', 'C' and 'D' had been holding a line of trenches on the Gheluveldt-Menin Road. During the night of 1st to 2nd November, they were bombarded incessantly, which culminated in an attack at dawn. They were completely overwhelmed and never seen again. The following table will give a little idea of the losses sustained by one battalion, ie 1st Kings Royal Rifle Corps from August 4th 1914 to November 18th 1914. Five officers and 90 men were killed, 23 officers and 417 men wounded and 10 officers and 492 men 'missing' – a total of 1037 who would not fight again.

We are told of this tragedy while we wait in the darkness. Not very cheering, I think. Oh, why did I leave my concrete bed near Sheerness?

Suddenly we are led off to the road again. We are then loaded up with the contents of the limbers, i.e. rations. We proceed in single file over the open. We stumble and curse all the way. Some get hit. They have become casualties without hardly being in the war at all.

We finally get into a trench of the most rudimentary nature, scarcely more than breast high. There had been no time to make elaborate or strong ones. I strongly suspected it of having been a ditch utilised into a defence work. We stayed there for two days and nights and had repeated orders to keep a "sharp look out". However, the Germans never attacked us, though I saw an attack taking place on our right. It was a wonderful sight. Instead of pouring in a rapid fire as per orders, I'm afraid that we newcomers were too spellbound to do anything but gape in wonderment. Were these masses of field-grey men actually our enemies? How steady they came on, wave upon wave, shoulder to shoulder almost. What folly! Bullets and shrapnel cannot miss them. Their ranks break, great gaps appear, but through the smoke they still advance.

We do not have any more time to stare, something is happening more to our front. A great number of Germans have emerged from the cover of a wood. What will they do? We pour a rapid fire into them. I am all excitement, but my nerves are steady. These are my first shots at living targets. We are doing the famous peace time "mad minute" or 15 shots in that time. Shells commence to pitch perilously near us, but we keep on firing into the massing Germans. Quite suddenly they seemed to fade. Had they all been knocked out? There must have been a sunken road or a fold in the ground. Anyway, there was the wood and only occasional groups instead of the hundreds, or was it thousands? The attack didn't come our way, and that was all that mattered to us.

We are relieved by the French and march to a wood. It still afforded good protection. It takes a long time to smother nature with gunfire.

We spend two days in the wood, keeping inside during daylight. Enemy shells occasionally pitch near the wood, and we enjoy watching them burst on the clayey fields.

Some of our new chaps wander away to find fresh water. They are told of a pump in the yard of a battered farmhouse, some 400 yards from the wood. They go directly towards the Germans but are unaware of it. We shout and signal their danger, but they do not heed. They actually reach the pump unharmed and fill water-bottles, etc. Suddenly, fountains of earth and smoke appear with their attendant CR-R-RUMP! CR-R-RUMP! Our water carriers are seen dashing away from the unhealthy spot, their bottles somewhat hampering their speed. Woolley shrapnel bursts above their heads, the geysers of earth fly up around them as the shells pursue them, but the heroic water carriers do not waver from their course. The shells not only chase them, but they are pitching near us! We cannot watch them arrive. We rush to take cover in the improvised dugouts. All the men return unharmed, but are severely told off! The wood we were in was always included afterwards for its dose of high explosive from the enemy.

The Regiment, together with the whole Brigade, are to be withdrawn from the fighting. We are very much under establishment. When we join them, there is only "A" Coy. and HQ left. We are all included in "A" Coy. until the remainder can be formed with fresh drafts. I scarcely recognise the remnants of the Regiment. They all appear to me as strange, fantastic beings. Beards have grown upon them during their terrible weeks in the salient. Neither do they seem to recognise many of us. We must appear too new to them, rather too "peacetimeish", as strange to them in our freshness as they to us in their utter weariness.

Anyway, the few days in the line have begun to alter our appearance – we can boast a week's growth of whiskers, which give us a trampish look, making us feel a little more like veterans. It does not need very much of this life to make one feel and look like an "old stager".

Back to rest

The French come at night to relieve us and make a great commotion – striking lights, calling each other and fumbling around. We leave them to get on with it, lights are dangerous! We follow the track of the Ypres-Roulers railway. Everyone is dog-tired and we trudge on in silence. A halt is made at a small wood. The Cookers are there with the first hot tea since leaving the transport lines. We are told to anchor down for the remainder of the day. It is about 4 am and I settle into the wet undergrowth and sleep to past ten in the morning.

All day we hide and watch the battle from a distance. Ypres is gradually getting reduced. We see the smoke and dust rise up and hear the dull roar of the explosions. Just as darkness is settling, we set off for Ypres. We are put into billets near the canal bridge. It is rather cramped, I sleep on an old kitchen table, that is, when the German shells let me. They are at times uncomfortably close and seem to explode with an extra shattering crash, no doubt due to the buildings.

Next day, accumulated mail bags are distributed. Nothing for me! It is now November 12th – I have been away just two months and not even a p.c. for me, or as a matter of fact, for any of us who were at St Nazaire. There is a great surplus of parcels for those now known to be killed, wounded or missing. These are given to anyone – the letters being returned to the base P.O. beside an issue of cigarettes, also accumulated for weeks! We have all the contents of the parcels, which nearly all contain cigs and bacca. We feel like a walking tobacconist's shop, and what we cannot stow away on our persons, we give to the French and Belgian troops who are continually passing.

We are held in reserve, but beyond an occasional alarm to "stand to", nothing happens. On the fifth day we leave Ypres and take the road for Bailleul. During a halt by the roadside, a staff car pulls up and the Prince of Wales steps out. He tells the men to remain at ease and offers his cigarette case to both officers and men. He talks earnestly with the officers, which we afterwards heard was information concerning the death in action of Prince Maurice of Battenberg.

Nearing the end of our march on the evening of the 16th November we hear of the death of Lord Roberts, familiarly known to all as "Bobs".

Our new abode is the small town of Caestre, not far from Hazebrouck. New drafts from the base join us and in a short while the Regiment is once again up to strength. It is practically a new battalion, as are all those that went out in August 1914. We do intensive training, route marching, drilling, including saluting by numbers!

We line the roads about this period to welcome the King on his first of several visits to France.

The Germans having been troublesome with the native Indian divisions round La Bassée, we are moved from Caestre by motor buses to Bethune on the 21st December. The long rest had done us good and we would miss our coffee and rum in the estaminets of Caestre.

I was now in charge of a Section and was very fortunate in the loyal friends that formed it.

On arrival at Bethune we leave the buses, or rather they leave us. Plenty of wounded are in ambulances on the way to rail head further back. There is a good sprinkling of "Jocks" – they look rather gruesome and wild. Their khaki is muddy and torn, likewise their kilts, and blood is oozing through bandages on heads, arms and legs – they tell us it's "murder up yon". This is quite right, I think to myself, for what else is killing but murder!

We leave Bethune, which is practically untouched by shellfire, and march to Beuvry. Here we bivouac in a field. It is cold and raw. We can see the firing line a long way off down the poplar-lined road that leads to La Bassée. To the right there loom up great pyramid-like heaps. They are slag heaps by the coal mines. This part of France is all coal mines and mostly industrial and farming. It is fairly flat to the left of the La Bassée canal all the way to Armentières, but on our right, although a mining district, it is not unpleasant. The country is more in gentle slopes and chalky – black and white as it were. More still to the right rise the slopes of Nôtre-Dame-de-Lorette.

When darkness settles we march off in sections towards Annequin, a village about 2½ kilometres on this side of the trenches. We are met by guides from the regiment we are to relieve. We go in single file, tripping and cursing – there were no duck boards on the trench bottom then. The sticky mud retard our feet and they become glued to the earth at each step. We do this follow-the-leader business for hours, so it seems. After all, the guide had only done what all guides were apt to do, and that is lose himself and us!

We are finally shepherded into a trench and the Connaught Rangers are glad to leave such an unhealthy spot. Later, my Section is moved to the extreme right and touching the main La Bassée Road.

Our neighbours are the French and I believe my Section has the distinction of being the extreme right of the British Army. We get on very well with the French. They obligingly fetch us red wine from a seemingly inexhaustible stock. This makes us rather excitable – Corporal Moss says there are Germans creeping in our entanglements. We all blaze away at the dark figures, which appear to move. This sets the whole line ablaze and panicky. When dawn breaks, we see what we had been scared of. Just a heap of corpses which the French said had been there for a week or more.

One Frenchman is smoking a pipe on sentry, with his body, from the waist upwards, above the trench. He must have had too much 'vin rouge'. He talks loudly, but a well-placed bullet sends him toppling to the trench bottom. They bury him and place the pipe in his hand – the 'poilu' and his beloved pipe are not parted in death.

We spend Xmas Day in supports – the 2nd Battalion pass us on their way to the trenches. Once it was Blackdown and Salamanca Barracks, now it is the La Bassée Road "somewhere in France"! Had there been no war, many of us would have been home on Xmas leave. We could not make merry, even though our pockets had been full of money – there was nowhere to spend it! So we made the best of a bad job, eating our small portion of Xmas pudding and an extra swig of rum.

Richebourg

I had forgotten to mention that whilst at Caestre, the long-delayed mails arrived. I received about nine letters and pcs, also parcels. The latter had been spoilt by the length of time in transmission and bore the marks of rough handling and successive soakings. We also received parcels from organizations at home. In each was a request to write to the sender. I did so and was under the impression that the sender was a nice young lady! When one day a parcel came with a letter mentioning that her father was a retired colonel of my Regiment, I promptly dropped the correspondence.

On the 29th December 1914 we left the La Bassée road and went to billets near Festubert. Our particular abode was an isolated group of farm buildings, in the centre of which was a stagnant, slimy pool heaped with garbage and dung. Round this were grouped the barns in which we slept. It was here that we each received the Queen's gift box with pipe tobacco, etc. This billet was very depressing. The flat, rain-sodden countryside, the leafless trees and the dull days all combined to lower one's outlook.

We go up the Line again; it is a quiet place. We hear our opponents are a Saxon division. There is not much firing either side. We are all too concerned trying to make ourselves as comfortable as possible. This land is flat and intersected with numerous ditches. The weather is unkind. It alternately rains and then freezes. The waterlogged ditches overflow and the trenches fill. We flop about in icy cold water and mud throughout the long winter nights. Then it freezes hard and we are converted into human icicles – our overcoats are like boards, our feet swell in the sodden boots and both socks and boots have to be cut away.

It was during this trying period that many cases of S.I. wounds occurred. S.I. means "self inflicted". The common method of these men, driven to desperation, was to shoot at the foot or fingers. This method, not only being extremely painful, made a bigger mess of things than the men imagined;

not only by the nature of the wound, which in many cases meant the amputation of the hand or lower leg, but the court martial and punishment.

The floods eventually forced us to abandon the Front trench and redoubts were built at intervals on the top. These afforded an easy target for the enemy, but strange to relate, they never touched them whilst we were there. We began to live on the top, especially at night. The Germans were in a similar plight – a mutual understanding existed between us. "If you don't shoot, we won't" sort of style. This did not agree with some of the higher officers, but in spite of their efforts to "disturb the peace" we managed it all right, until the Germans put up a board on which was written in chalk "Keep low. Bavarians coming tonight".

The conditions of life being so bad, we could only manage 48 hours in the Line and the same out. So many were being sent down to the base with frostbite, rheumatism, pneumonia, etc that all those suffering from frostbitten feet or "trench feet" in a mild form, had to undergo treatment in billets. This consisted of vigorous massage with some grease and laying down with the offending portion of one's limbs in a raised position. We were never at any time really dry, in billets or out! The barn roof was minus its covering of tiles and the straw on which we lay, being damp, used to steam with the heat of our bodies. How I escaped pneumonia I do not know to this day.

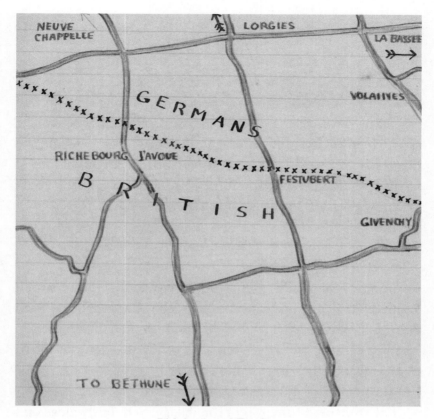

Richebourg and Festubert

On the whole, the period spent at Richebourg was most depressing – casualties from the enemy were slight, but the elements were our greatest foe. When I look back, it seems nothing else but a time of absolute misery, in which the weather contributed more than its share.

The troops from India had now arrived, making the British up to eleven Infantry Divisions and five of Cavalry, of which two of each were Anglo-Indian. Allowing for the shortage of men, I could never agree to the use of troops (native) from our colonies. Not only did this tend in some quarters to lower our prestige by utilizing them, but it was heartrending to see the poor devils dying by the score from cold and exposure.

During our occupation of the Line at Richebourg we had two four-days rest periods back at Hinghes, a village untouched throughout the war until March 1918, during the Big Push. We were very glad to get orders for a change of sectors. This took place about the third week of January 1915. The new position for us is Givenchy.

Givenchy

As the war progressed, so did the activity in this sector, and it ultimately became a spot to be dreaded. The trenches passed right through the village, which stood on a slight eminence. The procedure of occupying the Line was generally two Companies in the Front Line and two in support in billets, and the change about was every four days.

The trenches at the top of the village were fairly close and a sunken road ran between them, but the portion which I was accustomed to with my Company was a considerable distance from that of the Germans.

By this time we were all possessed of "livestock". We hadn't had a bath since leaving Caestre and in spite of repeated washing of shirts, etc, the filthy parasites increased and multiplied. Sometimes a garment would be "combed out", washed and left out all night in the hopes that the frost would complete the work of destruction, but once the heat returned, so did our "bosom friends"!

Hundreds of dead bodies lay in front of our wire, most of

them Indians. They had been there since December 1914 and they were still there in the summer of '15 when we returned to this sector! Our chaps were keen on souvenirs and these were from dead bodies. I remember one night on patrol, hunting for the knives the Gurkhas used.

We came across some dead Indians and I thought I saw the hilt of a knife. Grabbing hold of it, I saw that I had hold of the dead man's thumb and that my pulling was raising his stiffened arm upwards. Needless to mention, I hastily let go my hold. I often had my leg pulled over the affair. We did bury a few that lay handy – one or two were huddled up in a sitting position. It was impossible to straighten them out, so they had to be laid sideways in the hastily dug grave.

My Section remained the same, with hardly a casualty. We always, or nearly always, performed sentry, listening post, patrol or working parties, together. One night, I and two men were on listening post - the usual time to be out being 3 hours. On this night it froze like the very devil. We lay out in front of the wire on the ground. If anything untoward happened, such as an attack, etc, there was a wire running back to the Front Line, on the end of which hung some tin cans. The violent jerking of the wire caused the cans to rattle and this gave the alarm. I do not remember this signal ever being used.

Besides myself, I had Richardson and "Peter" Dean. I was always pestered with Peter! For some time we lay and talked, but drowsiness kept creeping over us. The intense cold soon numbed our fingers and toes. We kept guessing at what time it was, or how long we had lain there. I lost count of things and just lay like a log; of course, I never realized that we were freezing slowly. Peter and Richardson made no response to my efforts to rouse them. I realized the penalty should I also be found asleep, so I got the wire between my teeth, my hands being numbed and useless. I then managed to twine it round my elbow and by this means tugged at the alarm. Soon I heard voices and saw men approaching. They soon got us back in the trench. With the aid of hot tea and rum and a vigorous rubbing, the circulation began to flow again through our frozen limbs. None of us were any the worse for the unpleasant experience.

When in reserve, our billet did not offer much in the way of recreation; it was too near the Line, which perhaps was fortunate. It prevented any movement by day and, incidentally, stopped the officers from holding any ridiculous drill parades. As an alternative, inspections were resorted to: inspections of feet, rifles, ammunition, clothing and equipment, etc. Nevertheless, it all helped to pass the time and gave us occupation.

Our billet was a farm once. In the loft, which ran the whole length of it, were stored thousands of onions – the same as sold by the Breton in England. We partook of them at every meal, chiefly fried or boiled, same as eggs, until we reeked of onions. However, a continued onion diet gets monotonous and I believe that towards the end of our stay in Givenchy, if anyone had suggested onions as an item on the menu, he'd have got his block knocked off!

I lost two of my chums from the Section – both killed by snipers' bullets whilst occupying a sap at dawn. Our casualties were not heavy by any means. A few were killed, some wounded, others were sick. Sometimes there was not one casualty for 24 hours. On the other hand, another 24 hours may result in several.

I could never imagine myself amongst the casualties. It never struck me that way, that I was just as liable to get a clout as the next man was. No doubt it was very fortunate that I did look at things in this manner. We used to say that bullets and shells were harmless unless they touched one. This was quite true! A hundred thousand bullets could come your way and miss you, but the hundred thousandth might end your earthly career.

We went to Bethune for hot baths and a change, but did not stay – we were back again in Givenchy.

In the course of a few hours, we had left many "bosom pals" behind at the baths, but we were quickly aware of their brethren, which irritated our skins worse than those we left

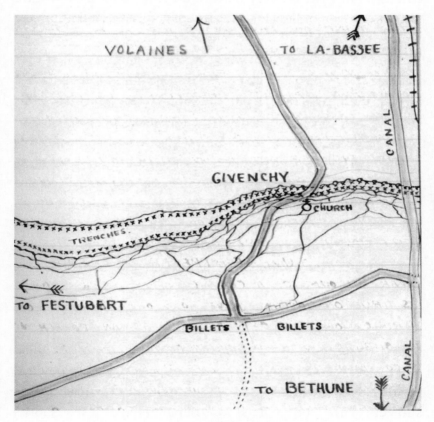

Givenchy and district

behind. A wag said he 'saw them chats [body lice] a-following behind us, all the way from Bethune'.

On March 2nd 1915 our Commander, Colonel E. Northey left us to take over command of the 15th Infantry Brigade. We were all sorry to lose him, he being an ideal Commanding Officer. He was succeeded temporarily by Major Shakerley, DSO.

About this period, trench warfare was developing. Hand grenades, or bombs were needed badly - we, of course, never had any, but Fritz did and he was not slow to let us know. We were not slow to follow his lead; if the factories could not make them – we would!

One favourite type was made from old jam tins, filled with powder and old iron or glass. A primitive affair, but it made a noise if it did no damage. Another bomb our chaps made was called the 'white-wash brush'. It consisted of a flat piece of wood fashioned to the shape of a white-wash brush. On this was placed a slab of gun-cotton and bits of iron, nails or glass were then bound round by wire. A fuse was then attached and the bomb was ready. Sometimes the fuse took a long time to burn, so Jerry simply used to pick them up and sling them back to us, when they promptly exploded. These crude implements must have caused great amusement in the German lines.

Neuve-Chappelle

We heard rumours of a coming offensive, but we did not know if they were true or not. We did not have long to wait for verification. The C-in-C had had many conferences on the subject with the chiefs of departments. The Corps Commanders and Divisional Generals debated on it. They, in their turn, handed the news on to the Brigade staff and Battalion Commanders. The Company Officers were instructed and they, in their turn, informed Platoon Officers and senior NCOs. The whole thing was an absolute "secret". The artillery knew all about it weeks ago! Ammunition columns, transport and despatch riders, who were some kilometres further back, discussed it freely in the estaminets – so that beyond being "secret" officially, everyone knew of it for certain, except us infantrymen who, being cut off from outside life, knew but little until informed definitely by our seniors.

At this time we had the 5th Liverpool Regiment attached for instruction in trench warfare. They were a territorial unit and an admirable body of men. Many a rum ration did I have from them, too.

The big attack
Spring 1915

The Great Day was fixed for the 10th March. We all received our instructions and were impatient to get it over and done with. Not because we were brave and sought to "get at" Jerry, but simply because we realized that the 10th of March would mean RIP for some. This is the worst of knowing a date beforehand. It becomes a fixture and an obsession; it means that our earthly career has a good chance of ending on that day. However, I think that a good many felt as I felt. I had no dread of being "sent west". It was more nervous excitement at the thoughts of my first attack, or what became a familiar phrase known as "over the top".

The order of the assault is "C" Coy on the left flank, "A" Coy on the right and my Coy "B" extended behind both, a second line or "wave". "D" Coy and the 5th Liverpools to hold our original trenches.

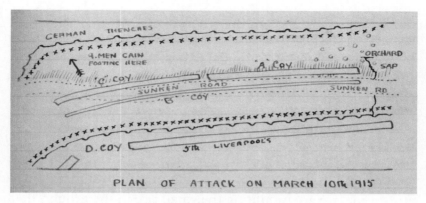

Plan of attack, March 10th 1915

We spent the eve of battle in billets, "D" Coy and the
5th Liverpools holding the Line. Rum was given to us and
everyone was excited, discussing the events to happen on the
morrow. The way we carried on, one would have thought we
were going on an outing instead of into a scrap. Songs were
sung with great fervour and pathos. One Irishman sang "Bold
Robert Emmett", another about "A young man cut down in
his prime" and still another of "Laying him down on the
hillside". All this singing was abruptly ended by an order to
keep quiet 'and get some sleep'. I forget if I slept or not, but at
dawn when we fully realized what was to take place, there was
not much gaiety. We all had that queer void sort of sensation
in our middles, something like one has when leaving home for
the first time. We could not eat, but swigged off the hot tea.

Hastily, we don our equipment and "fall in". Up we go in
single file; in the communication trench a tree has fallen across
the top. It has a horseshoe-shaped twist which is arched above
us as we filed through. Some say this is an omen of good luck!
Already the guns are busy and one or two 'planes are about.

The enemy is nervous – his machine guns keep on spraying across to our Lines.

We file out quickly through the gap in our Front Line, and things are not so leisurely now – everyone is nervous and agitated. Our guns have increased their fire. We see them explode on Jerry's parapet and barbed wire. There are sharp orders yelled, we duck and run along the sunken road to get in extended order. Whistles are blown – "Over boys!" is shouted and in the space of a few minutes from filing out our Front Line, we are mounting the small rise in the ground that concealed us.

We are atop now in full view. I see a jumble of wire and wooden stakes 50 yards ahead. There is much yelling and confusion. It is only a short distance, true, but we are barely half way and no-one is in front. Where is "A" Coy? They are leading.

A voice yells "Get down!" and automatically I fling myself flat on the ground. There are dozens of our fellows lying in front by the barbed wire. They are "A" Coy.

A voice on my left informs the world in general that its "B——- murther". It is Paddy who, the previous evening, had sung "Bold Robert Emmet, he died with a smile". I look cautiously at him but he hisses to me to "Be still!" Obeying his instruction, I keep my head turned in his direction.

Suddenly, a convulsion shakes him from head to foot and he lies still. The blood rapidly drains away from his face and hands. He turns ashen grey, and I realize that no more will Paddy sing to us in billets.

I look to the man on my right, who has partly turned on his side facing me. He is making a gurgling noise and blood is oozing from his mouth – he does not live long.

What are our orders? Are we to lie like this until a bullet accounts for us all?

I look ahead; a dead German lies about five feet in front, his head towards me. I must drag myself a little closer to him. There will be a little more cover behind him, I think! Ever so stealthily, I creep nearer. A hundred whips seem to crack in my ears – they have seen me move. I resolve to lie still again. The dead German has been lying out for a long time. His skin is nearly black with exposure. His hair is cut short and there is a large hole in his skull. I notice the grey uniform going rotten – the tarnished buttons and mildewy leathern equipment. I am not interested a bit in this German's corpse. The details impress themselves upon me only because it seems to be an eternity that I lie here staring at the hole in his skull.

Some of our chaps are lying in their wire. Major Shakerley's brother, the Captain of "A" Coy, is suspended on the barbs. He is dead.

Someone tugs my boot, and a voice says, "Get back!" This is no easy matter – if I stay much longer they will get me. What is saving me at point blank range? The dead German I suppose? One or two attempt to rise and run back, but the Germans are waiting for this to happen. They immediately fire on the retreating men and drop them. What shall I do – get up like the others and take a chance, or lie here until darkness hides me? How long have I been here? Two, three, four hours perhaps? Or only ten minutes? My throat is parched, I see my hands are yellow – what's up with me? Of course, it's lyddite from our shells.

The Germans are lobbing bombs at us now. I must get back, I think – they are after my body. Slowly I retire. I am trying to move and to appear to be still at the same time. My equipment slowly works itself up under my armpits – I keep my nose glued to the earth. The whip-like crack of bullets never ceases. How far must I travel in this fashion? Ought to be near the slope of the sunken road, what a journey!

A voice says, "You're all right now". I see that I have wriggled back far enough. I am safe!

After getting under cover in our trench, I ask the time. It is twenty past eight, and the whole business since leaving our billets has only taken an hour and five minutes.

The attack had failed, but this did not perturb the High Command. The real business was at Neuve-Chappelle; ours was just a "side show". It was a very dear "side show" or bluff attack for us. "A" Coy suffered most. "C" Coy fared a little better, nine of their men getting into the German trench. Naturally they couldn't possibly stay there. They were very lucky to get back to our lines at all. We lost, wounded or killed, 157 - four of them officers and 96 wounded, a total of 253. One can imagine how destructive this engagement was, when the killed outnumber by almost two to one that of the wounded.

My Section lost five, but I still had "Peter" Dean and Moss with me. Peter said "These attacks don't agree with me, I shall tender my resignation". He always made a joke of everything. But it was impossible to be cheerful. We had learned our lesson. Trenches were bearable so long as one got reasonable luck, but you had to keep in them. Once either side commenced getting frisky and trying to grab the other side's trench – then, look out! "A" Coy could barely muster one platoon – they must have lost nearly a hundred men.

The whole preceding five or six weeks, the battalion had, perhaps, about 15 killed during ordinary trench duty. Yet in a few minutes, more than ten times that number had met their death - for a "side show".

About the 12th March we were relieved by the Guards Brigade and went to rest at Bethune.

We are all in a disused factory. It is a haven of a place to us after Givenchy. We can go out in the evenings and visit the estaminets. We can sit and drink and smoke, crack jokes with all and sundry. The war seems a long way off, although it is but eight kilometres away from us.

All shops are open and everyone seems to be following their normal occupation. It is hard to believe that the horror of the trenches is so near. Not many buildings are damaged, so few in fact that they are unnoticeable. Bethune never did get properly strafed until the German 'push' in 1918.

New drafts join us to make us up to strength. The General pays us a visit to compliment the Regiment on its recent behaviour – these little speeches are simply rot! We don't want to hear smooth, honeyed speeches – it doesn't help to restore the 157 dead that lie at Givenchy. Of course, the General can't help it, we realize that; all the same it is galling to have to parade and listen to any of it.

A second stripe is given to me; Vice Corporal for somebody accounted for at Givenchy. It is so simple in wartime to get promotion. No learning of books and sitting for exams. No classes for this or that. Just so long as one escapes being 'hit' and has a little common, he simply cannot help himself. Naturally, it is just as simple to lose stripes. It all depends on temperament and luck!

Although I was now Corporal, I never broke away from my chums. I could never understand why a stripe or two should alter some fellows. In normal times, there was no question whatever about it. An NCO was I.T. He must not be seen out in company lower than his rank. An NCO was even forbidden to go out with his brother, should that brother not be of equal rank.

It does not need iron discipline to rule men in war time. If they are treated the right way, fraternized with, respected and made to feel that they are not common Privates. Anyway, I never relied upon stripes to get an order obeyed. Neither did I alter my general outlook, mannerisms or ways with the men. They were my comrades in the trenches and they would be the same to me in billets.

I found that this method proved to make things twice as easy, not only for me, but for us all. I hardly ever needed to detail men for any particular duty. More so, if I happened to be detailed as well. They simply used to say "I'll make one", "And me", "And me too", so that I never had unpleasantness in that direction.

War is bad at its best, therefore an arrogant or tyrannical NCO only tends to make life, in general, a perfect hell for the men under him. This type of non-com sometimes did not reign long. He became a casualty, either through the action of the enemy, or from our own side! Many a score have met their end at the hands of our men. They might have lived to see the armistice had they had less regard for their stripes and more for the men. Personally, I have known instances of NCOs and even Officers being earmarked for early doom by their subordinates. It is very seldom, once the men had selected a victim, that he lived to "get away with it".

We did not stay in Bethune long, but were for some months continually in its vicinity. The sectors from Neuve-Chappelle down to Vermelles were to be the limit of our travels.

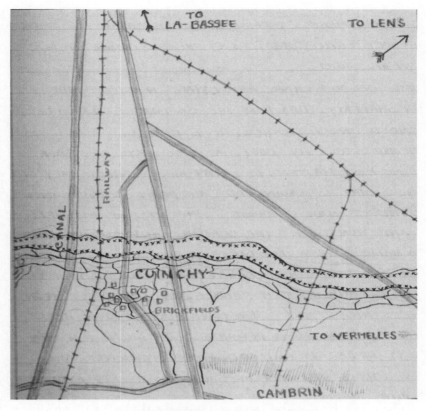

The Brick Field Sector - La Bassée Road

Our next spell in the trenches was the famous Brickfields before La Bassée. Sometimes we would be on the left of the La Bassée road, up to the canal, and sometimes on the right of the road, known as "Bomb Alley". The trenches actually passed through a brick-making area, hence the name. Huge square piles of bricks were dotted about. They were about the size of an eight-roomed house and made excellent cover from shells. Naturally, great holes and gashes were made by the explosions and bricks were displaced and scattered by the thousand. Nevertheless, the piles still remained, although repeatedly battered by artillery.

The order for occupying the trenches were generally as follows: four days Front Line, four days in Support and four days in Reserve at Bethune, making twelve day periods in all.

The Guards had been occupying the brick stacks and the trenches had been strengthened and deepened. Many were named after famous London thoroughfares. For instance, the main communication trench was "Harley Street". There were others named "Bond Street", "Piccadilly", "Regent Street" etc. It was rather comical to see a board with a name such as "Shaftesbury Avenue" and then another that says "To The First Aid Post" and an arrow pointing the way. Or, a little further another notice telling one to "Beware! Keep Low, Under Observation".

Naturally we soon became accustomed to our new trenches. We ate when we could and as often as we could. We slept by day and prowled about from dusk to dawn. The minimum of sentries were posted in daytime. They worked in pairs and in every other bay of the trench. One gazed vacantly through a periscope while the other sat beside him and scratched himself. They each shared two hours of this, then they were relieved by another two men and so on through the day.

At dusk the order was given to "Stand To!" This means that everyone must take his place on the fire-step and keep a sharp look out. When darkness had settled we would "Stand Down!" Keeping swords fixed on our rifles and then afterwards through the whole night, double sentries were posted every few yards. Besides sentries there were rations to be drawn from the "Dump" and working parties to dig and strengthen any weak spots. Others might have to carry barbed wire, wooden stakes, sandbags, timber and a host of other things under the supervision of REs. A popular rhyme used to say:

God made the bees, the bees made the honey,

The infantry do the work and the REs get the money.

Then, besides all these things, "Listening Posts" and a patrol or two were out in "No Man's Land". Sometimes things were quiet, and there was no special activity by either side. However, casualties were occurring just the same. Splinters from shells or "minnewerfer" (trench-mortar) and snipers' bullets all took their toll. We had no dug-outs worth mentioning. Our so-called 'shelters' were hollowed out of the trench wall, and afforded no protection whatever. Still, we felt more secure from the splinters, etc, if it were only beneath a strip of corrugated iron and a waterproof sheet. We imitated the ostriches, I think, in that respect.

To be in Support in this Sector was quite to our liking. We were billeted in much-battered houses just by the communication trench. Here the money-grabbing civilians still hung on to the remnants of their homes, knowing that so long as the "Anglais" and fate permitted they would reap a rich harvest by selling muck to the 'Tommies'!

Following on this four days, we would go to our factory billet in Bethune – four days of imitation 'peacetime' with a bath and change of underwear – but not always. There was a considerable shortage of shirts etc then, and we had to 'strafe' our undies for lice and wash them ourselves.

For nearly two months we carried on with the same procedure in the trenches, support and reserve. I had my photo taken with three chums at Bethune. All three of them were afterwards killed. Their names were Richardson, Cook and Bayliss.

Spring was now well advanced and we heard of rumours about another offensive. There were the outward signs of this by the information given by all and sundry, including French estaminet proprietors and the unusual activity of the staff.

On May 7th 1915 we were told all about it. Our Division (the 2nd) would be in reserve to the 1st Division near the Rue de Bois in the region of Richebourg.

The battles at Festubert

On May 8th 1915, we moved to the area immediately behind the zone of the impeding operations. We were bivouacked in the open among the orchards, which were thick with blossom. The weather was ideal; all nature was one mass of flowering blooms. It was hard to realize that on the morrow men were to die by the thousand.

We heard that a lot of cannon were massed for the occasion. In those days, two to three hundred guns concentrated on a front of perhaps three miles or so was considered the last word in artillery support. Unfortunately, we still pinned our faith in the use of lyddite and shrapnel shells. It took the War Office a long time to forget that we were not up against Boer farmers or 'nigger chasing'! Our enemies were the last word in military efficiency. They laughed at our deluge of shrapnel – they were fairly safe in their dug-outs and trench shelters. The wire was not even cut. High explosive shells (known as H.E.) were the only things that would destroy wholesale, and we used such a small percentage of these that they were negligible.

We receive orders that we stand to arms at 5 am on the ninth. It is an ideal May morn: the Front is very quiet, the sun is just coming up and the shafts of light pierce the mist that is hanging over meadow and orchard. Birds are chirruping gaily and fowls are contentedly clucking and scratching for food. Who could possibly imagine here beneath apple, pear and cherry trees that, not two kilometres away, thousands of men are going to do their best to exterminate each other in an hour or so?

At 6 am the boom of the guns commences. First on our left, then on our right and again, directly in front. Gradually, the fire gets more brisk until all else is smothered by their dominating voice.

We stand about in groups speculating on the luck of our comrades in the 1st Division. We do not have very long to wait. The first fury of the bombardment has died down and the staccato of the machine guns has abated.

Walking wounded come straggling along, making for the Dressing Station, while others are piled into horse ambulances or any vehicle going in the right direction. We make enquiries such as, "How goes it chum?" One tells us "A1, doing fine!" Another that "Not one of us got as far as their b..... wire".

So the day wears on, full of false hopes and alarms. We do hear, at last, that the whole attack was a complete failure. The irony of the whole thing is that our misguided General Staff had issued orders about the drinking of water during our advance to Lille and beyond, in case the Germans had poisoned the wells! Did they fondly cherish the hope that shrapnel and two divisions of men would break through the enemy's defences?

Just as dusk is falling, we receive the order to go up to the trenches. There is not far to go, but quite far enough, as the Jerries are bombing rather heavily with 5.9s, this particular size of shell being the most effective and accurate projectile they use. At least we thought so! And when an infantryman passes his judgment on such things, you can bet your boots on it that he's right!

The trenches are shallow in some parts, not reaching above my shoulders. I notice a number of our dead lying between our Front and Support Lines. They must have advanced from the Support trench and been mown down by machine guns. What tragic folly to order an advance from such a position! The poor fellows met their end before they could reach our own Front Line.

We relieve a Welsh regiment – they are anxious to get away. They are quiet and have little to say to us. We know why. So many of their chums are lying dotted about and must be left behind for ever.

Darkness comes quickly. We get orders to attack at 10 pm that night. What a farce to try and launch an attack with troops just in the line! The trenches are strange to us, neither officers nor men know the ground in front at all and have never seen it by day. We are told a stream runs between the trenches and is about four foot deep on the average and six to ten feet wide. The REs, with the assistance of infantry, placed duck boards across at intervals last night. In all probability they were smashed up during the morning and will be of little use. My Platoon Officer is not very optimistic about it. Still, an order is an order and, if we all get wiped out, it has to be carried out.

I will confess that I do feel nervous – I remembered Givenchy, so did the others!

Half an hour before the attack is due, the order comes to cancel it. What a relief! We are now told to get on top and bury the dead as quickly as we can. This is cheerful, too! I go with some of my Section and commence the unpleasant business. There are so many lying around, so we go to those that are nearest.

The enemy is nervous. Rocket lights keep shooting up from his trenches. Machine guns keep traversing across No Man's Land. Have they seen us? Or can they hear us as we mutter and pant, dragging bodies into handy shell craters? There is no time to bury them decently; it must be done as speedily as possible. Some bodies are warm, and I think that perhaps they may still contain a spark of life, but I am reassured when I see their faces. I have seen so many before! We grope for their Pay Books and identity discs and these are handed over to an officer.

At long last the gruesome work is finished. They are not really buried; the only difference is that, instead of them lying on top of the earth, they are now heaped pell-mell in craters with just a sprinkling of earth over them.

It is near midnight, and a patrol has been out in front. They report that the Germans have already placed knife-board (knife-rest) barbed wire in and near the stream, no doubt in anticipation of a fresh attack. Our artillery are told of this, but they remain silent. In fact, the guns have scarcely fired at all since the morning's bombardment - why is this, we ask?

The night wears through and with the breaking of dawn, news reaches us that at seven o'clock we are to make the postponed attack. An artillery bombardment will precede it, of short duration, but of great intensity. We wait anxiously for this to take place, but wait in vain. It is quite seven and our guns are inactive. We hear that once again we are reprieved!

Something is seriously wrong. We are all fidgety and filled with a feeling of dread. Our Company Officer is just as wise as us. What is taking place in the minds of the General Staff? We await the next order impatiently – let's get it over, whatever it is.

At last, we get the news we are to attack for certain at 2 pm, whether the wire is cut or not. We curse and blaspheme. Why the hell didn't they poke us over last night and done with it?

The Germans are evidently on tenterhooks. They plaster our parapet repeatedly with machine guns. This is unusual in day time; at night there is occasion for this, as a good deal of movement takes place on top. What hopes will we have once our heads show above the trench?

As two o'clock draws near, we assemble by the short ladders, the mounting of the first rung which may mean "finis" to some of us. We are now thoroughly "strung up". None of us has eaten. It's impossible when that gnawing in the pit of one's stomach is going on. The same sensation one has if one is leaving home for the first time, that "wind up" feeling.

The guns are slow, why don't they begin? An occasional shell or two come over but nothing that stands for a bombardment.

"Keep where you are" is the order suddenly passed along. What is wrong now, we stand and crouch in the trench waiting for what? Our Platoon Officer comes along - he looks rather relieved. He tells us that for the third time we are reprieved from attacking. Furthermore, the native Indian troops will be taking our place at 10 o'clock that night.

The gnawing feeling of nervousness gradually leaves us. We nibble at dry biscuits, brew tea and smoke, talk and speculate on the why and wherefore of the happenings of the last 48 hours.

When darkness has once more settled down, we prepare to leave. At 10 o'clock the Indian troops file in; they immediately fix swords, mount the fire step and commence to blaze away into the void! Poor fellows, they are not fitted for this kind of warfare. They are nervous and excited; they do not see their enemy. It is all grovelling in the earth and shelling from invisible guns. This western method of warfare is beyond their comprehension. Much better had they been left east of Suez in their own element to deal with the "Johnny" Turk.

We now go back to billets in about the same spot as where we were held in reserve to the 1st Division among the scattered farm buildings amidst the orchards round the Rue-de-Bois district. We get into conversation with artillery men whose batteries are near us. Why, we ask, was there no bombardment and no attack by us? Why aren't they firing as they are accustomed to do?

"No b...... shells!" they tell us – batteries down to four shells per gun per day! No reserve supply either for emergencies! If the Germans had only known, they could easily have crushed us with their own guns and practically walked through to Calais.

Afterwards, back at rest, I wrote home describing these things and, by a miracle, the letter was uncensored – it is now in this book as a memento of those days.

Our General Staff must have been chagrined by the events of the last few days. The operations of the 9th May were on the whole a debacle; to add to this, our artillery were practically without ammunition – nevertheless they would not admit defeat, although it was so! In military operations anything undertaken with a definite plan and which fails is nothing else but defeat.

Neuve-Chappelle was the first offensive since the Marne. The main objective was Aubers Ridge; we failed to get it and lost something like 2,500 killed. The village became ours and a few lines of battered enemy trenches. This did not affect the general contour of the 350 mile front by a decimal fraction.

The 9th May was our second attempt. It fizzled out even more tragically than Neuve Chappelle and cost us perhaps

1,500 deaths. Even so, these lessons were unheeded and in spite of shortage of shells, etc a further attack without artillery preparation was fixed to take place on the night of the 15th May. We went into training for this every night, on the 11th, 12th, 13th and 14th.

The whole Brigade, which I have forgotten to mention before, was made up of the 1st Battalion KRRC, 1st Battalion King's Liverpools, 2nd Battalion South Staffords, 1st Battalion Royal Berkshires.

For four nights we practised what we were supposed to do when the real thing took place. Of course, everything was according to plan. White tapes represented trenches, whistles blew, we lay down, advanced, rushed the last few yards and the supposed enemy were all killed or captured and nobody was hurt. All the brass hats were satisfied, so on the 15th May, after our dress rehearsals, we were shepherded up to the trenches at Ferme-de-Bois to try it on "Jerry". As you will see later, Jerry took a distinct dislike to it.

The night attack

Everything depends on silence; nobody must talk. We have strips of white linen on our backs, to prevent us from shooting or sticking one another. The handles of mess tins are secured to prevent them tinkling.

We file out of the Front Line like long strings of ghosts. It is very eerie and uncanny, so very quiet! Across an old trench and a stream, past our own wire entanglements, then we extend and lay flat. At 11.30 pm the advance is to begin. It is horrible waiting, but so far the enemy is not suspicious. He sends up star lights every now and then, his machine guns give short splutters, an occasional shot from a rifle and that's all.

Suddenly we are off! We do not go far at a walk. Star shells leap up to the sky in quick succession. Red, green and white rockets as an S.O.S. to their artillery. The machine guns no longer splutter, they pour out beltfuls at us. Vivid flashes behind their lines let us know their artillery are not slow to respond.

From an ordinary walk, our advance has by now lost all semblance of order, or silence. We shamble on, stumbling, cursing, some going headlong to earth, others yelling "stretcher bearers!" "This way!" "No, that way!" "Keep up!" "Christ 'elp us!" - "My leg, my leg!" "Me arm, me arm!" It is just wild confusion.

I suddenly come into their wire, and my puttees and clothes get ripped by the barbs. A big German looms up in front of me. His hand is raised as though to fling a grenade. In a wild panic I loose a round off from the hip at point blank range. I do not pause to look at him – there are others to be dealt with – some are in shirt sleeves, showing how sudden our attack has been.

"60th this way!" yells an officer, and we go on until a trench is reached behind their line (support trench). The Coy S.M. sends me to round up all our stragglers. This is a lively job! I bump into men of the Munsters, Staffords, Berkshires and of course our chaps and Peter. I ask him where he's been? He replies "B......d if I know, but the CO's killed". I tell Peter to remain with me. Stragglers keep coming over from all quarters and I round ours up as best I can. These I guide to the captured trenches.

I am told to hold a portion of trench against a possible counter-attack, but nothing develops directly in front of us. At dawn Jerry's artillery gets to work in earnest. All the day, until dusk, they send over a tornado of steel. Luckily for us, he vents his spite on our old line at the back, no doubt thinking his own troops are hanging on in parts which we now occupied.

The South Staffords held our old line during the attack and they suffered terribly from artillery fire. So intense was it, that we were practically "cut off" from them by a curtain of shells. On the night of the 17th May we were relieved and went into support behind breastwork defences. We lost 307 killed and wounded, including our CO, Major Shakerley, whose brother was killed at Givenchy.

On the whole, these operations were successful, as some ground was gained and our losses were not heavy.

We remained 24 hours in support and marched back to a village, well behind Bethune. A new CO was appointed, Col. Jelf DSO. Fresh drafts joined us and once more we were up to strength.

I was made L. Sergeant Vice; someone had been a casualty. Moss was made a Corporal, but Peter remained in the Ranks.

The extreme penalty

Whilst in the Bethune area, we were unfortunate enough to have to be present at the 'promulgation' of the death sentence on one of our Regiment. In the Service, I believe, they always use that word in such cases, i.e. "the finding of the court will be promulgated in due course, etc". In any case, if I am mistaken in the meaning, 'promulgate' or 'no promulgate', a man had his life taken for next to nothing.

As far as we could ascertain the start of all the trouble was one day in 'the line' at the Brickstack sector. Unusual activity on the part of the Germans caused a 'stand to' in our trenches. The victim of this story was before the war a Special Reserve man, or a one time Militiaman. His idea of soldiering was confined to annual training of about 28 days, a two pound bounty and plenty of ale. The war had dragged him into its net, and therefore, he hardly realised how dreadful his crime was when he refused to leave his 'shelter' and 'stand to' with the others.

He was put 'in arrest' and nothing more was heard of the case in my Company. We were in billets on the canal bank almost, near Beuvry. An order had been given one night (I was Orderly Sergeant), that the Battalion would parade at 5.15 am drill order and all companies to rendezvous at a point marked so-and-so on the map. There was a considerable amount of speculation amongst us as to what was to happen. "It's an attack", "It's a big fatigue somewhere." Or we were a Guard of Honour to some bigwig. Yes, we were indeed a Guard of Honour - or shall I say, Dishonour!

The following morn after an early drink of tea, we parade at 5.15 am. Orders were given that any man caught talking or looking about would be duly punished. We marched off, still wondering what it was all about. At the end of the village, we were marshalled in two long rows and led into a large gravel pit. Once inside, we were faced towards one of its sides. We were told to 'stand easy' but no talking.

We whisper, 'What's the great idea?' 'Stuck here like a lot o' b........ fools'! etc. After some time, we are called up to attention. Who or what are we standing to attention for and why? 'Stand still!' A rooster is crowing somewhere near, a deep boom now and again drifts from The Front. Someone gives a smothered cough here, a clearing of the throat somewhere else, a shuffle of a foot, rustling of dead leaves.

CR-A-A-ACK! We all are taken so completely by surprise that instinctively we turn our heads towards the sound.

"Look to your front, damn you!" bawl the officers. Too late, dear officers, too late! We have seen in one fleeting glimpse enough to know why we are here so early in the morning. The lone huddled figure in khaki lying on the ground. The two or three figures walking towards it. The half dozen men with their rifles just lowering from the aiming position. We know now!

"Present Arms!" We do this automatically, but not smartly, we have not recovered from our surprise.

"Order Arms!" "Stand Easy!" Any man who does not stand still will be Court Martialled, etc, etc. A procession of officers then mount the bank that we are facing. The Brigadier General and Staff, the Commanding Officer, Majors, Adjutant, etc. A "Brass Hat" then produces a sheaf of documents and reads to us, something like the following: -

"On the ——— inst' a Field General Court Martial was held at so-and-so on No.———Rifleman *Blank*. That he was charged with the offence, that whilst on active service he did (here is read the charge) and that the said Court found him guilty on all counts, etc. and under para umpteen, section umpteen, he was sentenced to be shot. The findings of the aforesaid Court Martial had this morning been duly carried out, etc."

Another officer then takes his place on the 'platform'. "Men" he says. How terribly grieved he was, but discipline must be maintained in wartime, etc, etc. What a disgrace to the glorious traditions of the Regiment (groans), what dishonour to the battalion (more groans).

We are getting restive, and the men swear audibly. A few raspberries are emitted. The speechmaking ends hurriedly. We are exhorted to refrain from talking about the morning's doings and given the remainder of the day off.

Poor Rifleman *Blank*! Poor Special Reservist! Poor wife and children of Rifleman *Blank* back in London!

A cross is erected with just RIP and the date.

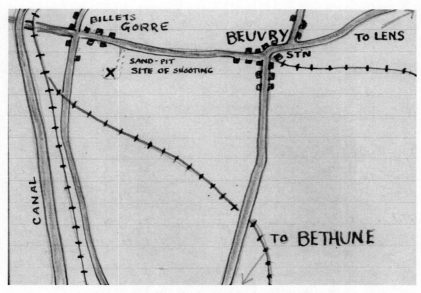

Location of the 'Extreme Penalty', April 1915

Battle for possession

In and out the line

Following our rest at Allouange, near Chocques, we once again go up to Bethune and on to the Brickfields sector. We are fated always to be in this part of the Line for the greater part of the summer. I suppose it was simpler to keep divisions in one particular group of sectors, in case of sudden emergencies, as the men knew all about them. Unfortunately, as time wore on, the war increased in its intensity. What were once considered quiet parts had gradually developed into 'hot corners'.

The usual programme is gone through – Front Line, Supports, Reserve. Some days we are in the brick-stacks, other days Cambrin and so on. I seem to click for being out in front a good deal, wiring, patrols or covering party. This last job is not too bad – all you are required to do is lay out in front of any working party at night to prevent a surprise attack by the enemy.

One particular night I go out with five men, including the renowned Peter. We are to cover a wiring party of REs and our own men. After selecting a likely shell crater for cover, we lie flat with rifles and hand grenades ready for instant use.

Jerry is not too bad so far, just the ordinary night noises break the peace. Behind us our chaps are busy. Work must be done quickly. Every time a star light is shot up, everyone stays perfectly still in the position he happens to be in when the lights are fired. I have been caught thus countless times – it used to strike us as ludicrous and, in spite of the seriousness of the thing, it looked so comical, we had to laugh. It was for all the world like the variety turn of old; living statues. Here a man with mallet upraised, another with arms spread out like the limbs of a tree or a scarecrow, others crouching; standing bolt upright; in the act of walking; and all manner of postures.

We hear the muffled BOMP! BOMP! BOMP! of the padded mallet, the checked coughing and low talking of the men, the louder curse as someone gets hooked up in the barbs. You may imagine what it's like to try and erect barbed wire on a dark night in front of people, a bare hundred yards or so away, who would cheerfully kill you if they could!

The work proceeds for some time undisturbed and I think that it will all be finished in peace. I am sadly mistaken! Without a word of warning, the whole German line flares up into a bedlam of noise. Star shells turn night into artificial day. Machine guns and rifle fire are like the roll of huge kettle drums. Minnewerfers are lobbed up and over to us by the dozen, it is difficult to watch where they may pitch. They leave a trail of sparks behind them in their flight, but they seem to criss-cross in the sky, so all we can do is lie still and chance it.

Shells now come shrieking over us to burst behind. What must we do – lie here or bolt back for cover? I decide to stay where we are, for if we get up we're sure to get hit. We are fairly safe in our shell hole – the only thing to fear is should a minnewerfer or shell land on top of us. We wonder if the Germans expect an attack from us or vice-versa.

I don't know how long this affair lasted, but when the ferocity of the bombardment had abated, I told someone to go back and ask for orders. Peter went, and I heard later that when he approached our trench, he yelled down to those on the fire-step, "What's all this b——y noise about, eh?" He told them we were safe and returned to us to tell me that we must go back and bring along any wounded we could of the working party. We half lifted and half dragged three men in, only one is alive. I noticed a messy shambles and asked for sandbags. We went back and scooped up the remains of one of the REs. All his limbs were severed – no doubt a minnewerfer had caught him.

I had the greatest respect for these dreadful things and I honestly think they were more demoralizing in trench warfare than anything else. They were fired from a miniature howitzer or mortar. They were simply trench-mortars, minnewerfer meaning 'mine thrower'. Our chaps nicknamed the shells thrown by them as 'rum-jars'. They had this appearance when in flight. Later on in the war, the Germans had improved on them and they lobbed over shells about three feet long. They were filled with high-explosive and the casing was of thin steel. This used to split into pieces, the edges being as sharp as a razor blade.

The concussion from the 'minnewerfers' was terrific and as they descended at a steep angle, they were more dangerous than shells. They would throw about 400 yds, but the most deadly range was about 200 to 300 yards. At this range they would descend at a very steep angle and inflict great damage. We used to have the devil of a time with them.

During the day, sentries had to keep one eye cocked in the air all the while and blow a whistle to warn us. The Germans soon tumbled this manoeuvre and instead of one blast on the whistle, we would hear two, three, four or perhaps six blasts at once. That meant that perhaps that many minnewerfers were sailing through the air to pay us a visit. This would mean a wild stampede up and down the trench to try and dodge them. As they were usually sent over at different angles, this was extremely difficult and it was only pure luck if we dodged them – many poor fellows were unfortunate enough to run away from a descending mortar, only to be blown to pieces by another which had come from a different direction. Up to this time we really had not got anything effective enough to reply with, so we simply had to put up with it.

Mining was also just beginning to develop. This was simply burrowing a shaft from our Front Line, then tunnelling out towards the Germans, the whole being prevented from caving in by baulks of timber. When the tunnel or shaft was reckoned to be somewhere under the German trench, dynamite or some other high-explosive was packed in and the charge detonated with an electric current. If all went well, a large portion of the German trench and its unlucky occupants were blown sky-high.

Another form of mining was named 'counter-mining'. This was blowing in the German tunnel before they could complete it. On the other hand the Germans were doing exactly the same thing to us and it was pure luck as to who would be the first.

Miners were specially recruited into the REs for this work – they were known as Tunnelling Companies. When a tunnel was practically completed, or when nobody was actually working in it, we (the infantry), had to go to its furthest limit and listen. On several occasions I did this particular job. Generally, three of us went down. A supply of candles was given and we had to stay perfectly quiet.

I was always greatly relieved if I could hear the Germans

at work, as they would not explode a charge whilst their own men were underground. To have to stay for an hour or more in this condition was a great nerve strain. Everyone had a particular dread of being buried alive!

On one occasion we had to work at blocking up the tunnel after the dynamite had been placed ready for use. We were working against time, for the enemy was thought to be on the point of exploding his mine. Had that happened, I wouldn't be writing this! Because the sandbags, which were filled at the tunnel's entrance, had to be carried well into the tunnel itself, I had to remain at the business end (where the charge was laid) and supervise the plugging of the passage. Well, I must say our chaps did the job in record time. RE Officers helped, with the perspiration pouring off them, urging our men on to work faster, so as to beat Jerry and, incidentally, save our own skins. An Officer at last told me and the men to "Get!" as quickly as possible – this we carried out with the utmost haste. In fact, so eager were we to reach the open that we got in each others way a good deal, thereby causing much confusion – cursing and laughing at the same time. A few minutes later, the mine was blown up. Whether it had successfully counter-mined the German mine, we never knew. There followed afterwards the usual ding-dong scrap for possession of the newly formed crater, but as it was more on Fritz's side of No Man's Land, he eventually had it.

Later on, we got a welcome move towards the Vermelles district. It was now late June and beautiful summery weather. We were taking more line over from the French. The country was not unpleasant for a coal mining district. The only things that marred it were the hideous slag heaps in pyramid form dotted about near the pit heads and the steel towers that worked the pit shafts. The country was chalky and is not unlike open downs of moderate undulations. Poppies were everywhere. They showed up so vividly against the chalk. Our billets were the best we had struck so far. We sampled Mazimgarbe, Grenay, Bully, Noeux-les-Mines, etc, all mining places and with excellent wine, too!

Once in Noeux-les-Mines the Billeting Officer had selected a wine brewery for us to domicile in. What a three days we had! Peter was permanently 'fogged' and, as a matter of fact, so were a good many of us. However, nobody seemed to worry particularly, because so far we hadn't been caught actually taking the wine, which was quite easy once 'look-outs' were posted. On the evening we left to go to the trenches, we had all made doubly sure of our wine supply. All day and at every opportunity, we were mopping it. Water bottles had been filled and many a pack held emergency wine in bottles. At night we paraded all right and marched off, but unfortunately, it must have been 'singing' wine.

Silence was the order within a couple of kilometres from the line. There was neither silence nor order. One or two began to sing, which quickly affected all the others. In fact it wasn't singing by any means. They yelled out popular choruses and ditties, emphasizing any blasphemy ten times louder – there was much laughter and cat-calling.

Suddenly, we are halted by the roadside. It reminds me of a goods train stopping rather abruptly – they all pile up, rank on top of rank, then slow back again. The CO takes drastic steps, all water-bottles are inspected and if it is wine, it is unceremoniously tipped out on to the road. The CO is real mad about it and after he has gone, our Company Officer severely lectures all of us and ends up by calling us "a b——y lot of drunken fools". As most of us are 'one over the eight', we can't be very well punished. Nevertheless, two men cannot contain their high spirits and they disappear from our Front Line that night – it is presumed they got on top and wandered over to the enemy.

It was fortunate for us that this new sector was extraordinarily quiet. It was a regular holiday for us compared to La Bassée Road. We are quite 700 yds from the enemy – this entails less vigilance in the matter of sentries, but requires extra patrols, etc in No Man's Land. A small mining village is behind our lines, but quite close. The rows of typical miners' cottages get their daily dose of crumping, for what reason we don't know, unless because they stood on a slight rise and were an eyesore to their gunners. The name was Maroc, which used to remind me of Morocco. Three or four times a day, poor Maroc was reduced a little more and more. If a house boasted a few rafters or a whole side still upright, the Germans would persist until it had been bashed down. We often used to think their gunners had bets on their respective batteries' shooting.

At another time, we were in a different sector in front of Loos. Behind the German line were two huge towers, which in normal times formed a pit-head. Our chaps called them The Crystal Palace. Whenever shells strike them, there is a resounding CLANG! Of metal against metal.

We are engaged in sapping at night; "sapping out" means digging directly forward from our Front Line. This is done at about 250 yds intervals. When these saps are considered to reach far enough, each party then commences to dig right and left, until they meet. By this manner a forward trench is formed at any distance required out in No Man's Land. Naturally, this work is not done in one night by any means. Other regiments began the work, we carried on where they left off and, no doubt, after we have gone others will carry on until it is completed. We don't know what the "big idea" is (we found out afterwards that it was preparations for the coming offensive). This night work is all right as long as one is left in peace to get on with it, unfortunately this is not the case. The enemy can spot the new earth mounds in daylight. His gunners then get busy to try and level it flat, and with a goodly amount of success. His main object is to get it 'well taped', then at night-time, having the range to a nicety, he will proceed to 'crump' the poor infantryman, who is digging, with his well-known whizz-bangs!

This is the peculiar pet name we have given to his field-gun shells or 77 mm. They come so swiftly that they are on top of you before you have time to get to cover. Moreover, they are very effective, being mainly shrapnel. The first object, therefore, of a digging party is to get well down first where each man works – this is for his own safety. If he can dig a hole deep enough, he has a sporting chance of escaping the splinters. After the hole is deep enough, he can proceed to connect up with the next man and so on until a continuous line is made.

On our right, the French are having a hell of a time. The slopes of Nôtre-Dame-de-Lorette rise up clear above the surrounding countryside. All day and night heavy artillery duels are going on. Carency, Souchez, 'The Labyrinth' are all in this district. A pall of smoke hangs over them by day and at night the sky is vivid with bursting shells.

A great battle for possession was going on at this time. It was a terrific fight that the French and Germans waged, and it took place when both sides were still fresh and full of fight. War weariness had not yet made itself felt.

The French certainly had a cause to fight for. Not only were the Germans on their soil, but the war of 1877 had not been forgotten by any means. The loss of Alsace and Lorraine and the humiliating terms imposed by Bismarck. Why Germany was now still eager to overwhelm France once again, I do not know. Anyway, there they are now, in the year 1915, just a few kilometres from here on the slopes of Nôtre-Dame-de-Lorette, Teuton and Poilu, hammering away at each other with bomb, bullet and shell!

This war so far was a bit of a mystery to the majority of us, and nobody seemed to be very clear as to its exact origin. We had a hazy idea that it was something to do with Belgium and that's about all. It came like a tropical storm, before we scarcely realized it.

I have heard some queer arguments amongst us concerning the war. Each man's own particular theory, when whittled down to bare facts, was simply his own version of what he was doing before and since the outbreak of the war. Politicians, international agreements, treaties, etc, all took a back seat in these conversations. We could never tackle the subject at all with any reasonable solution as to its cause – all we knew or realized was that there was a war on and we infantrymen occupied the orchestra stalls from start to finish.

Well, it wasn't such a bad war at times. We always had the knowledge that a few days in billets awaited us, provided we didn't become a casualty whilst in 'The Line'.

We did not remain as long as we would have liked to in the new trenches, they had been fairly quiet and a regular 'cake-walk' to some places. The rest area was much nicer too! I went down a coal mine in Mazimgarbe, it was all very strange to me. This particular mine had a shaft and cages, but one other I visited had steep gradient tunnels from ground level to the seams. All the electric plant and machinery was German and supplied just previous to the outbreak of war. We always used the miners' baths to have our 'dig out' when we were handy to the mines.

About the first week in July, we found ourselves at Locon behind Festubert, but we only stayed a short while. Givenchy was the next sector we had to take over and a very changed Givenchy, too! We had left it about the 12th March, but three months or so had entirely altered it. Mining had been the chief cause, and it was all at the village part of the trenches and on to the canal bank. It was very hot and we had the job of helping the REs as usual with their blessed tunnelling.

At one part a tunnel was being driven out from our line. My chaps had to help drag the sandbags of earth to the shaft head. Others had to wind them up on a winch and still more to drag them along the trench and dump them. If it rained, an unpleasant job became a nightmare – slimy bags, slimy hands, slimy trench, in fact sticky, wet, slimy everything and everybody. When it was like this, three words fitted the occasion, "b——— the war!"

There were many such mines at Givenchy and we always felt on tenterhooks, not knowing when Jerry would blow one up and us with it.

One hot afternoon, desiring to sleep before anything else, I retired to my primitive shelter, a little cubby hole scooped out on the trench side, the outer portion being draped with old sacks etc to hide the candle light from showing during darkness. Along its inside wall were placed a few boards to serve as a bed. I was very thankful for even such a rough and ready shelter. It was quite natural for us to fall sound asleep, anyhow or anywhere, at very short notice. Guns and the general collection of war noises did not affect us, but should anything threatening take place, our subconscious self instantly responded; our bodies would act, in spite of us not being fully conscious.

This is what happened to me on my stretching out to snatch a sleep. Previously I had noticed some pieces of rotten blue cloth protruding out from the wall side, just like wallpaper that is peeling off, but never thought much of it at the time, although there was a nasty stench on warm days. Smells of all kinds were common – it could not be avoided – stagnant water in shell craters where perhaps a corpse was rotting, or the exposed dead that lay out for the sun, wind and rain to reduce to a skeleton. Anyway, we never laid the blame on the dead – the most common remark on these smelly occasions was, "Whose bin an' left the (toilet) door open?"

I had scarcely lain down before I was sound asleep. How long I had been like it I don't know, but perhaps ten minutes at the most. Quite suddenly I came to full consciousness, to find myself standing bolt upright. What was happening? The ground trembled violently, like it did in Crete once, during an earthquake.

At the same instant I realized the cause, a deep muffled boom came from the direction of Jerry's line. I rushed outside, grabbing up my rifle, etc and saw a huge column of smoke, together with a geyser of earth, stones, timber, etc, mount in a leisurely way up to the sky. Then, like a fountain, the debris, after reaching the apex of its upward flight, described a graceful arc before descending to earth. I could not help but notice how some things, such as timber, kept turning over and over in the air.

Somebody shouted, "Stand to! Duck your nuts!" I passed

the order on to the others and stood watching the rush to earth of the debris. It came down with a swishing rush, great baulks of timber, millions of stones, huge clods of earth and dust. How we shouted to each other - "Billo!", "Look out!", "It's going over us, no it ain't, run quick!" and various other things until all was again quiet. No damage was done to us or the trench, but a crater fifty-foot wide, had made its appearance just in front of our barbed wire. Jerry had either miscalculated the distance or had tried to blow in one of our tunnels.

Our artillery now got busy – and so do Jerry's! Trench mortars and machine guns joined in and we got a hot and noisy half hour or so. Gradually the rumpus subsided and I had time to visit my roosting place – I had left some cigarettes there.

But, alas! My poor, old rickety shelter had collapsed. The roof of timber and tin was now mixed up with the earth. The rough bed of boards was covered with soil and lying on the top was a dead French soldier, much decomposed. The upheaval had forced him out from the earth wall of the shelter. It was his faded blue uniform that had been showing through in places.

We made a rough, wooden cross, and reburied him at night. The only inscription on the cross we could put, was "Here lies a French soldier, mort pour la patrie".

The shelling of the mine crater continues intermittently for some time, neither side disputing its ownership until darkness settles. Battalion bombers aided by bayonet men go out to reconnoitre the crater, and simultaneously the enemy decides on the same game.

We all 'stand to arms' during these operations. It is rather quiet considering, but we'll soon get plenty of noise. Neither side is sending up many lights, so we guess that they also have a party out in No Man's Land.

Suddenly we hear the dull explosions of many bombs. This goes on for some time, until each side realizes that the other is at the crater, too. So, to give them light, up go several from both front lines. There follows immediately a fierce exchange of grenades from the opposing sides, who are on the edge of the crater facing one another.

We are now told that we must help some other 'crowd' to dig a trench out to the lip of the crater. All spare men are requisitioned, led on top and told to "dig like hell". This they do, but panic takes hold of them and they down tools and bolt for the protection of the main trench.

I see them coming and wonder if the enemy is hurrying them on, but no, they are like sheep. They tumble into the trench pell-mell on top of each other. I then see two or three officers loom up out of the darkness looking for the digging party. I am standing on the fire-step. Where are those ———— —! men? I tell the men the officers are seeking them. They begin to clamber up again. I hear them laughing at their own foolishness. The officers rave and curse, but the men do not heed them.

"I'll shoot the next man I catch running away!" says the exasperated officer to everyone in general. He receives his answer with derisive laughter and threats from the mouths of many.

During all this commotion, the occupation of the mine crater is still in dispute. First one side will get in, only to be driven out again by the other party.

The result of the night's work is that neither side is able to hold the crater against the other. Our chaps manage to dig a sap up to its lip. This is reinforced with sandbags and barbed wire, but it is eventually made untenable by combined artillery and trench-mortar fire. Several casualties are the only result of this affair.

We were pleased to get a move away from Givenchy again. There were too many mines altogether for our liking. The day previous to our leaving, another one exploded, but more on the right of the previous one and not on our battalion front.

We got back to Bethune for a few days and then to Cambrin on the right of the La Bassée Road. We stayed in this region for a few weeks, sometimes in the Brickstack Sector and sometimes at Cambrin, which was as far as we got away from the Line. Annequin, another village, was a reserve billet. We went back as far as Bethune or Lillers or Choques only when the whole Brigade was withdrawn from the Line. Formerly, Bethune was included in the area of a Brigade holding the Line.

Bethune was not as inviting as formerly. Too many staff there, also Red-caps. We were really better off in billets near the trenches, as these offensive individuals did not worry us and being under enemy's observation, not much movement could take place, such as those irritating parades all COs seemed to delight in. On the other hand, we clicked for night work in or near the trenches. The infantryman's bogey was the everlasting carrying parties. If an infantryman wasn't loaded up with his own things, he was pressed into service to carry someone else's, generally the RE's! It was not uncommon to be relieved one night from the trenches and the following night, instead of a good sleep, to be going up to the same spot with a duck-board on your back, or a 60lb "toffee apple" or sandbags, barbed wire, etc and various other things that the REs love to give us.

In spite of all this we got a good deal of fun out of it at times. More so when we had any cash and had been in the estaminets with "vin rouge" and "vin blanc" to keep us cheerful. The usual time to parade for REs fatigue was about 10 pm. All according to the time of year, of course!

The O. Sergeant would come round the billets with the usual "Any of these men here?" and then spin off a string of names. Some would dissent. "Me again, Sergeant?" or "What about so-and-so, he dodged it last time?" etc.

A carrying party was anything from a dozen to a hundred men at times. If it was a large party, it would be split up into smaller ones, each under a sergeant, with a lieutenant in command.

First thing was to parade in drill order with rifles, etc, then march in single file to the RE dump. Here everyone would load up and with an RE as guide, set off to wherever the stuff had to go. Sounds very simple but remember it was pitch dark so, unless the moon is visible, it was a very uncomfortable journey. It was not uncommon for a so-called "guide" to lose himself. In the event of this happening, he was cursed well and truly by all. Should it be dry weather, we got along in fine style compared to wet weather, but wet or fine, it was a beastly job to perform. There were innumerable obstacles to beware of all the way. These orders were continually travelling down the long line of perspiring men: "MIND THE WIRE!", "LOOK OUT, DEEP HOLE!", "KEEP CLOSED UP!", "DUCK YOUR NUTS!" "EASE UP IN FRONT!" "WHERE THE 'ELL ARE WE?" "BLASTED FOOL'S LORST ISSELF AGIN!" "'OW MUCH FURTHER?" Naturally, all these remarks were punctuated profusely with uncomplimentary language.

Sometimes we were held up for some cause or other, the men leaning against the trench side having an "Irishman's Rest". If the delay was too long, they dumped their loads and it was ten to one that no sooner had they done so than the order to move on was given. Then the men's personal opinions of everyone and everything connected with the war would make good reading for stay-at-home critics.

Home on leave
August 1915

All through the warm days of August 1915 we fluctuated from Reserves to the Front Line and vice-versa. To say that we were fed up was putting things mildly. We were kept too long in one area; we wanted to be continually on the move to fresh sectors, we had had enough of the La Bassée front. Too many minnewerfers and 5.9's, too many "whiz-bangs" and rifle grenades, too many mines! What a variety of death dealing things there were! We who manned the trenches got the benefit of all of them. Even out in Reserve we were not safe, by any means. One had to go back at least half a dozen miles to feel safe to any degree. How we envied those whose jobs took them right away back out of danger. The Gunners who served the guns had a risky job, but rifle-grenades, trench-mortars, etc couldn't reach them. Those on the ammunition columns were better off, they only came up to the Batteries by darkness. The cavalry were miles and miles behind and had been for some time. The Army Service Corps dwelled in peaceful valleys. They brought supplies so far and no further. The Ordinance Corps (commonly referred to as 'the Audience Corps') were at the base camps. The medicals were mainly at railheads and base hospitals. A minority did find themselves right in the thick. They were the various unit doctors and an assistant. The regimental Aid Post was their abode, generally in a handy position by a main communication trench. Other small parties of medicals were a little further back in "Dressing Stations". There were some mounted field ambulances, but their chief work was the conveyance of wounded to the nearest C.C.S (Casualty Clearing Station). The men of the long-range guns were also the object of our envy. We often used to say, "Why the hell did we join the b——- Infantry?"

Even our own regimental transport were several kilometres away most of the time. How quietly they would come up at night with rations, but as soon as these were dumped from the limbers, what a clatter of hooves and iron-bound wheels as they hurried away out of range, back to transport lines.

One early morning (about the 22nd August) I was down a hot, stuffy dug-out. We had just "stood down", that is been released from the usual dawn stand to arms. Peter was busy making tea for us both. We all suffered from the overpowering inclination to sleep at this hour. Our neighbours, the Boche, were very fond of trench-mortaring us at meal times and we heard some resounding explosions up in the trench. We paid little heed to them – if one landed on top of us, it was all up. On the other hand, if one didn't, what was the use of worrying?

We supped our combination of tea and grit and had a smoke before dozing off. I was for trench duty at nine. Someone came down the few steps and shouted my name and Peter's. "What's up now?" we enquired sleepily. He told us we were for leave that day and to get all instructions now from the Company Officer's dug-out, at once.

Nothing during the whole of my life has ever made me so deliriously happy as that news did on that August morning. Peter flung both his arms round me and kept repeating, "Today! Today!" We were so happy that I really thought we would start howling tears of joy.

I cannot forget easily those unlucky mates of ours. They looked the picture of misery that morn. One or two I never saw again. Poor chaps.

We seemed to have new life in us, Peter and I. By 10 am we had received all instructions and with "good luck" ringing in our ears, we made a bee-line for Blighty. On no other occasion have I got out of the trenches in such a hurry. I was fearful that at the last minute, death might rob us of our few days happiness. Peter kept saying, "Faster, faster, put a jerk in it". We did put a jerk in it. Whizz-bangs were coming over and bursting in front of us. "They b—— must know we're going on leave" said Peter. At last we reached Annequin in safety. We were both dry so went into a nearby wine shop and sported some 'vin rouge'.

Thinking it easier, we trudged on towards Bethune. A convoy of empty lorries was also going that way. We jumped in and were soon at our destination.

At one o'clock I was to meet Lieutenant X—— at the Hotel de Something or Other. He paid us our leave money and gave us the required pass to each and final instructions. At 2 pm we got into M. lorries (by this time we had been joined by men from other units) and went to Lillers to entrain. About 4 pm we left Lillers for Boulogne. We had sufficient wine and my head was ramping a bit. Some tried to sing, others dozed off. The train slowed down to a crawl at St. Omar.

We took the opportunity of standing on the foot-board to

ease ourselves. The train jerked when Peter was in this precarious position, and he fell on the line. He was up like a jack-in-the-box and running alongside, and we stretched down and lugged him into our compartment amidst cheers from the others.

At last, Boulogne and the sea! We thankfully dumped our ammunition and went aboard, making ourselves comfortable on deck. The motion of the ship and the swish, swish of the water gave us absolute contentment. We simply lay silent, but perfectly happy.

The hills behind Folkestone stand out black and solid. Blighty, at last!

A train awaits us on the jetty. Dawn is just beginning to break; it is 3.30 am. By 5.30 we glide into Victoria Station. What a contrast. Yesterday in the Front Line, this morning, London!

Ladies guide us to stalls and buffets. We eat and drink, free, smokes are pressed upon us, too!

After refreshments we seek out the cloak-room. Here we indulge in a preliminary 'wash and brush up'. Feeling a little cleaner, we sit in the saloon-bar of a pub, just outside the station, to celebrate. Double whiskys, too! I cannot manage more than one. Peter and another two are for the Midlands and North. A taxi is hired and I see Peter off at Euston and the other two at King's Cross. I am now alone, so I go by bus to Waterloo. I am uncomfortable, full of lice, cannot go further in this state! Down the New-Cut I buy new underclothes and go to the U.J. Club and have a first bath in Condy's Fluid and another in good, hot soapy water. Leaving behind all my old gear and wearing the new underwear, I feel a different man.

Unfortunately, I 'fall in' with a couple of chums and we go to the pub again. I lose my pack or valise somewhere. It isn't the amount of drink that beats me, it's the excitement and general change of life in so short a time. I can always say that I always knew when to say 'enough!' when I was home. The happenings during the brief stay with my parents won't be of interest.

Needless to mention, the day of my return to France came all too quickly.

At 5.30pm on September 1ˢᵗ, I stood with hundreds of returning 'Tommies' on Victoria platform. This well-known London terminus was the last link between the troops and their loved ones. Scenes unparalleled before the war took place under its broad arched roof, when every evening at about 5.30 the 'Leave Special' was due to go. There were several besides Mother to watch me off. The platform was packed with relatives and friends. Some were demonstrative, some pathetically silent, others cried openly, whilst a few cracked jokes and laughed. It was always a mighty relief to both those that are going and those who remain when the train got in motion.

About 8 pm we were in Folkestone. I noticed a pack left on a seat and took it to replace the one I lost. We were soon shepherded aboard a waiting steamer and by 11 pm we are once again in France. We are marshalled by divisions on the platform of Boulogne station. Ammunition is doled out again and by midnight we packed away in railway carriages and off to the Front.

About 5.30 am, twelve hours after leaving Victoria, we alighted from the train at Lillers. Again, RTOs (Railway Transport Officers) marshalled us into our Brigades, etc. I was told that my Battalion was at a place about eight kilometres distant, Norrent-Fontes. We would have to march it, without breakfast, too!

We trudged on for some little distance, exchanging reminiscences of our few days' leave. Peter was blinding everybody and anything. We were all different somehow, our going home had unbalanced us a little. We did not care what happened now!

An estaminet came into view. Madame was brushing the doorstep, we told her we were hungry, could we eat? She was dubious at first. She brought along her husband, and we explained as best we could that we had travelled far. Upon displaying our ready cash, we were admitted. She soon brought out coffee, and by bribery a bottle of Cognac was brought to light. Then eggs and fried chips (a favourite dish), and French bread supplemented by various delicacies unearthed from our packs and haversacks. The food and other things soon began to clear the air of dejection that hung over us.

Madame and her husband got quite friendly. We managed more Cognac by the gift of Army socks. The pack I picked up at Folkestone was inspected. It belonged to a man of the Royal Irish. The coat was too small for me, so in a spirit of generosity, I presented it to Monsieur. We got, in exchange, a bottle of Malaga. We stayed there until nearly 11 o'clock, then marched on to our destination. Nothing was said about us taking six and a half hours to cover eight kilometres!

Norrent-Fontes was not much of a place, something between a large village and a small town. Our beds were of straw and our rooms were barns. We heard that we were back so far because a rest was needed before a coming attack. No wonder they gave some of us a leave!

We stayed a few days only and made a move towards the Front again; it was the usual place – La Bassée! Things were getting livelier and there was that ominous quietness that precedes a storm. We were busy making preparations, endless working parties for everlasting carrying and digging.

The Battle of Loos

September 25th 1915

I do not know whether I ought to tell you of an incident that happened to myself, Peter and Moss about this time. If things had followed their normal course the affair might have ended seriously for us, but war plays queer pranks at times with us pawns, pushing us hither and thither on the chessboard of fate.

As I mentioned before, our leave had unbalanced us a good deal. We no longer regarded anything with the same equanimity as previously. Therefore, any chance we had of a 'flare up', we at once indulged without further thought of its consequences.

It was whilst in billets at Annequin that we went out on the 'tiddley'. We carried out this part of the programme so well that we forgot who we were or why we were there! The next early morning three very much surprised British Tommies awoke cold and stiff with parched throats and throbbing heads to find themselves out in the open. How or why we had slept there I shall never remember.

Realising at once the mess we had got ourselves into, I

plumped for returning to our billets at once, but Peter said, "May as well be shot for a big fat crime as for a small lean crime". We could see how frightful we looked with our unwashed faces and matted hair, so we decided to wash ourselves first. This we did at a small running stream. Feeling considerably refreshed, we decided on some grub, and this we manage to get from the very place that had been our downfall the previous night; we had not been scarcely more than 200 yards from it all through the night.

One point was clear to us; we would be 'adrift' from our unit from overnight to whatever time we reported back. Oh well, I thought, what was done can't be undone, we were absent and that was it and all about it. We were not deserters! If we didn't get shot for it, in all probability the Germans, in due course, would do it. So we made up our minds to return to our Regiment.

I made straight for headquarters, and how the fellows stared at us! I wondered what they imagined we had been up to. If we had risen from the grave it couldn't have caused more astonishment amongst our own chaps.

The Adjutant appeared from a doorway. He stared hard at us. I saluted and reported our return. He looked at his wristwatch and at us and asked "What's the reason?" I invented a yarn at once – "Must have been drugged or something", I told him. He was puzzled and asked "Where?" I reply that we 'came to' in a field that morning, with the loss of two watches, one ring and all our cash.

The RSM was requisitioned, also the Second-in-Command – we abided by the same tale. We were told that, under the circumstances, we were 'in arrest' until such time as the matter was sifted out, but most fortunately the matter was never sifted. I heard later that the Adjutant and other Officers were discussing the affair at night and that the Adjutant did not want the thing to go any further. As he explained, in all probability we had been drinking vile stuff from somewhere or other and had simply flopped out until the effect had worn off, returning to report, sadder but wiser.

The Captain of our Company then emphasised the point that we had returned to our Units voluntarily so, therefore only 'absent' could be brought against us as a crime. However, things of greater importance were to happen, so that our foolish escapade was entirely submerged during the days that followed.

Every night we carried up to the Front Line cylinders of poison gas. The Germans, for the first time, were to have a sample of their own medicine, which they had used against us the previous May, near Ypres. Two men to a cylinder and goodness knows how many there were. Besides these, there were articles innumerable to be carried. Cases of small arms ammunition, rifle grenades, bombs, sandbags, short ladders (for mounting the parapet), trench or duck boards, rolls of barbed wire, etc etc. All these entailed many journeys through tortuous trenches during the hours of darkness.

We gradually gleaned information from various sources about the coming offensive. It was to be on the 25th September and would stretch from the La Bassée canal southwards to a point somewhere by, or opposite, the village of Loos. Demonstrations would be made at other points further north; the French would attack also. Thousands of cavalry would then ride clean through the breach and chase the routed enemy. The mining town of Lens was our main objective.

We listened to all these tales of paper strategy and laughed it to scorn. "Who'll break through, us? Don't run away with those ideas; What's Jerry doing playing at darts, while we proceed to capture Lens and La Bassée, etc? No, we were not pessimistic, neither were we optimistic. We sized these affairs up quite logically, knowing full well the gigantic job it would eventually be to break the enemy's defences.

On 23rd September we moved up to immediate supports. We crammed into cellars, all that remained of the houses they had once supported above them.

The S. Staffords and Royal Berks of our Brigade were to assault in the Brickstack Sectors. We and the Liverpools were to support, if successful. There was not much sleep for us, for we could not remove our equipment, or boots, or any part of our clothing.

September 25th was heralded by the preliminary bombardment by our guns. The morning was thick with the usual September mist. There was also a fine, drizzly rain. The gunners were shooting 'blind'. How could the observers see anything beyond a few hundred yards?

As the fire from our artillery increased, we gathered on top of the cellars to see anything we could of the affair. Much better to be out of cellars while a big 'strafe' is on. Besides, a shell may knock the remains of the building down on top of us. The poison gas would be loosed off, too. There was scarcely any wind, just a breeze – the gas would drift about aimlessly. The firing of the guns was now general all over the Front, even, I suppose, to those parts not directly affected by an assault.

Runners or messengers rushed to and fro from various HQs. A motorcyclist rushed past, avoiding shell-holes and shrapnel, as by a miracle, with his despatches. How were we faring? It was impossible to even guess during the first couple of hours.

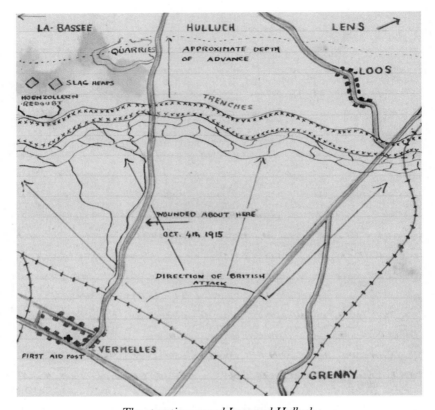

The operations round Loos and Hulluch

A trench gained here or there, or a complete set-back? Presently, the first walking wounded appear. Some tell us it's all OK. Others, that it's perfect hell and no luck.

As the time goes on and we are not called out, we surmise that the assault in our part is a frost. The fury of our guns has abated, but Jerry is plastering our lines and back areas with huge 'crumps' and 'whizz-bangs'. Should we have to go, we shall in all probability go over the open and will make a good target.

At last we hear definite news. The S. Staffords and Berks of our Brigade were completely repulsed without gaining a footing in their trenches. The poison gas we sent was a fiasco. There was not sufficient breeze to move it. The stuff hung like a green pall over our lines, moving in no particular direction until it was finally dispelled. The enemy was evidently quite aware of our intentions as regards the use of poison gas, because he at once lit prepared fires all along his parapet. The flames from these, which were chiefly oil soaked, rose up many feet, lifting any gas that came along well above the trenches. On our right, Scottish troops made the attack. Unfortunately, our own gas was responsible for the failure. The poor fellows were half choked and demented even before the assault was launched. It was here that a piper gallantly played his bagpipes on the parapet to rally the men and was awarded the Victoria Cross.

All day long on the 25th we are kept penned in by our cellars. We were not allowed to stir or to take off any of our equipment. Rumours came and were quickly squashed by fresh ones. The cavalry were through by Loos! We had captured Lens! The Germans were giving up in their thousands! All this and several more yarns. The point that struck us most forcibly was that the Germans had not lost an inch of ground on our immediate front. Why then should things be different elsewhere?

As night draws on, we hear the incessant gunfire on our right, whereas our part had simmered down to the ordinary trench routine. The King's Liverpools relieve the S. Staffs and two reserve companies of the Berks relieve their other two companies in the Front Line; we still hang on to our cellars.

We try to sleep at night, but it's impossible, there is nowhere to stretch out in comfort. Heaps of brick rubble doesn't tend to help one to lie soft! On these occasions we half lie and half squat, and doze a little, and swear quite a lot. It is remarkable how much a good all round cursing will ease us.

It is just turned midnight and we are ordered out and formed up in the cobbled road. Bullets keep coming over from the front trenches. Some swish as they travel high. Some hit the hard 'pave' of the road with a loud 'clop!', only to ricochet with a loud buzzing, like a monster bee. Others pitch into bricks or knock yet another tile off the shattered houses.

Finally, we march off through Annequin and reach a place by the ruins of Vermelles. We stay in a big open space with a couple of batteries of 60-pounders for company. As dawn breaks we get the 'lie of the land' and see barbed wire cages for the reception of German prisoners. We breakfast in the open and then stroll across to view the prisoners, something like viewing wild animals instead of men. Some of the men are fine specimens and retain the Prussian dignity and complete contempt, even though in such an inglorious position. Some speak a smattering of English and are eager to give 'souvenirs' in exchange for cigarettes, etc.

It is whilst here awaiting orders that I see my first real shell-shock case. I suppose I notice him because there is nothing particular to do. He is standing at the rear of a horse-drawn ambulance and every time a 60-pounder gun from one of the batteries near goes off, he collapses to the ground and shakes as with ague. This rather amuses some of us. We cannot make it out at all. We think it is just a case of 'wind up' – we little think that he will be one of thousands to be ruined and shattered for life by this dread disease of the nerves.

Later we receive orders to move. The Battalion is now temporarily amalgamated to a Brigade in the 7th Division. We move up the Hulluch road and occupy our old system of trenches. There is plenty to be done and no chance of sleep. The German artillery are working overtime and we get plenty of 'strafe' from their guns. We are quite strange to this part and are ignorant of what is really taking place, until we suddenly find ourselves in the open. We are in an attack! And it's broad daylight, too!

All I remember distinctly is heaps of rusty, twisted wire and stakes, explosions, smoke and corpses. Then a trench with green sandbags and steel loopholes and German equipment and field grey living and dead.

The Worcesters are with us. We are mixed up a good deal and it takes time to re-organise and sort units out during an attack. At nightfall I have to go with a party of men for fresh water. We go out over the top to our old trench line amidst a hail of bullets and shrapnel. It is an awful journey and more so in strange trenches. I think we took over four hours and it was not more than a mile to go! There is a drizzle of rain and quickly everything becomes wet and slimy.

The Germans are not easily shaken – they worry us a good deal and repeatedly counter-attack us. We have blocked up their old communication trench, but they come along it in large bombing parties. I cannot help noticing how some of them show complete disregard for death. They come on in such a cocksure manner, big men with their 'pickelhauber' helmets, flinging their 'stick-bombs' and shooting with revolvers.

Once they almost succeed. I watch them approach as usual, the dull detonations from the bombs growing nearer and louder, then from out of the curtain of smoke they loom up like giants coming straight for us. They had overwhelmed our advanced posts. I shoot frantically straight into them (with what success I don't know), and the stick-bombs come sailing through the air right on top of us. I notice one big man in particular; his helmet is without its cover of field grey. The black patent leather and brass fittings look out of place in these surroundings, but the wearer has a horrible leer on his face. He is so near that, in spite of the noise, I distinctly hear his guttural speech as he seems to be urging the others on. I aim at his head, at his legs and his middle but he comes right up to me, then twists round and drops. If I've killed him, it can't be helped, besides, I think, how can one be sure, I wasn't the only one trying to bowl him over, was I?

In between these counter attacks we have to work hard. Being in the newly-won trenches, the parapet and parados are facing the wrong direction. So we have to build up and strengthen the one-time support German trench into a fire trench for our own needs.

During the days we spend here, we live on 'bully' and biscuits with nothing but brackish water to drink, and very little of that. The weather is unkind and the nights very cold. All of us have that clammy, grey pallor that resembled death; even our lips are blue. We look ghastly, more so in the hour of dawn, that hour which in ordinary times seems uncanny until the full light of day supervenes.

At last we receive the welcome news of being relieved on the night of the 30th September. As we file out on top of the trenches and make our way rearwards, we see the result of the last few days. Hundreds of corpses lie by the old German wire. They are both German and British. Nearly all are wearing gas masks. The moonlight reflects from the glass eye-pieces of the dead with a horrible glare. They are like dead from another planet, the gas masks having robbed them of any normal appearance.

We are silent. Physically we are beat and our brains are dulled for want of sleep. Myself, I have not had a sound sleep for a week, so it is not to be wondered at.

Bethune, billets, it is 11 pm. Hot tea, bully stew, letters, parcels, then sleep. How nice those hard dry boards are after slimy earth.

Next morning I am very much taken aback to learn I must appear before the CO. During the last few days I had forgotten about our little escapade. We are all there, that is myself and Peter (I never set eyes on him in the trenches), Moss was wounded, so he's out of it. Adjutant gone, CO gone too.

The temporary CO doesn't know what to make of it all. He says we've all been in action since the 'affair' and behaved splendidly, so he very thoughtfully remands Peter and myself. We spend the remainder of the day cleaning our very muddy clothes, boots and equipment. I feel much easier in mind, the CSM having told me I would 'get away with it' (the absent business).

About 9 pm we prepare for another night's rest and are scarcely asleep when a gruff voice rouses us, "Roll blankets in bundles of ten, parade in half hour's time, full marching order!"

The task of getting a battalion together at night is no easy matter. Nevertheless, we are all assembled out in the street in the required time. The first thing that happens on these sudden rude awakenings is a voluble amount of cursing from everybody, concerning everything in general appertaining to the war.

We have no need to wonder why we are called upon. Jerry has either attacked, or is going to attack. If he has already done so, we have either been knocked out of our trenches, or are hard pressed; if no attack has yet developed, then we are being rushed up in case of emergencies. Oh well, it can't be helped, if we've got to go, we cannot help ourselves in the matter.

The roll is called by Section Commanders, who report to

the Platoon Sergeant, who again report to Company S.M. The 'skipper' of the Company then reports to the Adjutant. The whole Battalion then moves off by Companies towards the flashing skyline. As huge electric signs advertise the nightlife of London, Paris and other cities in peacetime, so do the guns and star shells and the Boom! Boom! in war time.

We are going to the same place! Something's gone wrong, but what it is we don't particularly care. We are simply mad and venomous towards the troops who relieved us a bare 48 hours ago. Why can't they hold the line like us? If we could, so should they! This is the general spirit shown on these occasions, with no thought to the cause or circumstances that have made the 'High Command' dig us out of our billets.

As we approach Vermelles, we are halted. There are many halts on these night journeys from one cause and another. Everybody seems to be about as soon as darkness sets in. Every unit's transport is on the move, going or returning from the Line. Long lines of artillery ammunition supply columns. Infantry Transport, Army Service Corps horse and mechanical, REs with limbers and G.S. wagons loaded with materials. Added to these are company upon company and battalion upon battalion of pack-laden infantrymen. There are several roads that lead to the trenches, but all this mass of men, horses, mules, limbers, motor lorries, etc must eventually converge as they draw near 'The Line'.

This is what is taking place now at Vermelles. The road to Hulluch is the only outlet towards the communication trenches and 'Fritz' knows this too. He can enfilade a good deal of the road from the left, and he sends shrapnel over every few minutes in the hopes of catching anything or anybody.

We fall in again and move off in the usual manner, that is,

'artillery formation'. We are now split up at intervals between platoons and march two abreast. This is to avoid unnecessary casualties by shell or bullets. A young lieutenant and I take the lead of the platoon. He enjoys himself as I recount to him the 'night out' I had and tells me I was a fool, but that it was practically certain nothing further would be heard of it. I tell him that I hope to 'get one' as soon as possible as I'm fed up. He replies that it's a foregone conclusion with us all, if the war lasts long enough.

We are now well along the Vermelles-Hulluch road; it is elevated a little, so there is no cover whatever. We concertina up in bunches, then slack out again repeatedly. Bullets are whipping across and down the road. Shrapnel shells come with their menacing scream, then burst, the splinters droning or going 'Thop!' into anything soft.

We are at a standstill again; a pair of mules attached to a limber are by me. The driver is cursing them for their stubbornness. Suddenly one mule throws up its head and grunts, then pitches forward, dead. It falls almost on me and its mate is tripped up too, driver and all! We move on once more, we cannot stay to help.

The call 'stretcher-bearers!' has been heard more than once since we left Vermelles. Some of our chaps have been caught with shrapnel. I wish it was me!

Then I get what I was seeking. My rifle is on my right shoulder and I feel a mighty numbing blow on my elbow, just like a kick. I spin round and drop, but am quickly on my feet again. The young lieutenant stops as the men file by. "Whereabouts?" he asks. I tell him in the right arm. "You've got what you wanted" he added. "I must be off, goodbye and good luck" and he vanished. That was the last I saw of a perfect little gentleman.

The pain makes me feel sick, but the relief of mind is worth it. I stand holding my right forearm with my left hand, watching the boys file by up to the trenches. I have a feeling of regret, to see them going away from me perhaps for ever. It was the splendid pals one had, not the war that we are sorry to lose.

I turn about and make for a Dressing Station. If I stay any longer, I may catch another 'packet'. A little distance along, a group of artillerymen are standing. One asks me have I got a 'Blighty'; I say to him I don't know. He then invites me into a shelter by the gun pits to inspect the wound. He notices that it has not got a 'first field dressing' and sets to work to cut away my blood-soaked sleeve and put on my own field dressing, which is carried on the bottom inside of our jackets. All the time he is talking about my nice little 'Blighty', another one gives me a sup of tea – they are good fellows; never seen me before in their lives, perhaps! Still it makes no difference in this war – we're all comrades and that is all that matters.

A blast of a whistle is heard, and my friends hurriedly bid me cheerio and tell me to follow the road to Vermelles. I am scarcely clear of the gun pits and can hear the megaphoned orders to the gunners. "Three thousand, seven hundred, two minutes left, etc, etc, battery fire!" Six bright flashes, followed by the six loud bangs and the whistling rush of the shells.

Other batteries are joining in, and the 60 pounders behind Vermelles crash out their deeper note – shrapnel is coming uncomfortably close behind me. I glance round and see the trenches lit up by leaping Very lights and hear the rattle of rifles. Something is happening up there, or perhaps it's only a nervous flare-up, it often happens at night for quite a long time after an attack.

I am in Vermelles, or strictly speaking in what *was* Vermelles.

I am directed to an Aid Post and see the dilapidated Red Cross flag hanging limply from its staff. Several stretchers are outside, some empty, leaning against a wall, others on the ground with still, khaki forms lying on them.

Inside, I report to an NCO of the 'Medicals'. "Sit down, mate" he said. "Now let's have your number, rank, name, company, regiment, brigade, etc, etc". Following this rigmarole, I am inoculated against possible tetanus. The wound is re-dressed, a label is tied to me and, with more hot tea and bread, I await the coming of the ambulance convoy.

The MO comes in, eyes us all and addressing the NCO says "How many now for evacuation?" "Fifteen, sir", replies the NCO "Any fresh cases?" adds the MO "One not long been in, a sergeant of the KRRs" and he points to me. The MO says to me, after examining the wound, "Nothing serious so far, you'll probably go to England with it". This information cheers me up wonderfully.

The MO then walks to a still figure on a stretcher. He asks the NCO "How long ago?" The NCO looks at his watch and replies "About twenty minutes".

"Take him outside with the others, they'll have to be buried before daylight", says the MO, stifling a yawn. He slowly proceeds to fill his pipe and to hum a ditty.

By 1 am the motor ambulances were taking us down the poplar-lined road to safety and the CCS (Casualty Clearing Station). I believe the name was Gisnay or Fouquiers. We are in tents and the place was in low-lying meadows split by a narrow river and hard by the railway. Being October it was thick with mist and cold. Next day, or rather the same day (as we got there at 2 am), we were redressed and labelled and entrained for the base hospital. Etaples was our destination and I was sent to the 3rd Canadian General. I was not kept long and was soon on my way to Boulogne and home. On arrival at Dover we were once again sorted and put on a train. I thought that perhaps I might get to a hospital in London, but was much disappointed to get hauled out with others at Canterbury station.

CHAPTER SEVEN

Convalescence
Winter 1915-16

I was in the Military Hospital but a short while, 17 days; following on this I had 10 days' sick leave and by the 1ˢᵗ November 1915, I was at Sheerness after an absence from home of about fourteen and a half months, during which time I had gone through many trials and vicissitudes. I therefore determined that I would make up for it, if it were at all possible.

I shall not dwell too long on my stay in Sheerness. For some weeks I was a Category man, and as such had to be seen by the MO fortnightly. I was attached to the 5ᵗʰ Battalion. This was a feeding unit for service battalions overseas. The 6ᵗʰ Battalion was also there and used for the same purpose. Besides training fresh drafts for the front, all ex-sick and wounded were sent to either of these Battalions before proceeding overseas again. I and another sergeant were put on a job supervising the digging of trenches on the sea-front by Minster and Eastchurch. Every day we went out by motor-bus or train from 8 am to 4 pm. A hot meal was served on return to barracks.

The restrictions in Sheerness were very severe indeed for the civil inhabitants – everyone going or entering the town was held up, be they in a train, motor-bus or on foot, and the town being so placed that there were only perhaps three routes of ingress or egress. A good deal of friction existed between those men known as "Expeditionary Force" and those of the permanent staff. More so in the sergeants' mess and corporals' mess than in the canteen, this perhaps due to the preponderance of BEF men to the others, who thought that to be safe was to agree in all matters with the BEF men.

I met quite a lot of NCOs who had so far managed to evade going overseas. They were surprised to see me a sergeant so quickly – we used to tell them in the Mess that overseas meant either quick promotion or a quick death. When the beer was inside of us, the pent-up venom used to be let loose. The permanent staff would come under a barrage of fierce comment from the BEF NCOs. If it had not been for the RSM, who was a real good sort, much strife would have resulted.

At Xmas I was lucky to get leave and I spent my time home at Tidworth. Where would I be next Xmas, I wondered. After my leave I reported to the MO. He candidly asked if my wound and general health were all right. I gave a quick glance and was glad to see the last man preparing to leave; I was about the last to be seen. I told him that physically I was fit, but that I had the 'wind-up'. He did not know at first whether to laugh or be angry, but he said that after all, another three weeks would allow my arm to regain its full use, and by that time the 'wind up' will have to fend for itself.

Out in Bluetown that night I celebrated my three-week extension at my favourite pub. I told the landlady about my 'wind up' ruse to the MO She laughed and said 'That's the stuff to gie 'em". Bluetown was the name given to a section of Sheerness near the dockyard. It was very ancient and most of the houses were of wood, with a brick foundation of course.

The three weeks just flew along and the MO gave me my 'passport' for overseas. I never had the nerve to tap him again for a further extension – so you see that I really did have the 'wind up' after all.

The night before leaving Sheerness, I and others had a last 'bust up' in Bluetown. Reveille was at 4 am so we could not sleep much. We returned to the Mess about 10 pm. The landlord and his wife at the pub had seen to it that we had some lotion, etc. I had a bottle of whisky and cigars; the others had beer and port wine. These we got on the sly, no other customers saw the going of it.

In the Mess things got lively and we who were to go on the morrow were led away to our beds. Who could wonder at us carrying on like this? Perhaps it would be our last 'flare-up' on this earth. We knew what awaited us the other side of the Channel. No more regular meals, no more long nights in bed. It meant Goodbye to Sergeants' messes, pubs, 'pictures' or a seat in the 'pit'. No more taking one's clothes off without tearing one's skin to shreds. It meant that once again we would sleep rough and live rough. We would live in the earth amongst decay and filth, forever watching and listening for shells and bombs, awaiting the fateful moment when we should perhaps be wounded or killed.

At four we were roused. I was three parts dressed, so it didn't matter much. My head was throbbing, but one of the beer bottles helped to dispel it. A wash in cold water and a breakfast in the gymnasium and I was fairly fit for travel.

Back to Flanders

The Draft fall in is at 4.45 am. It is the last week of January and quite dark. Our teeth are chattering with the cold, so I take a sly pull at the whisky bottle resting in my haversack. We form up, the roll is called, all present! Someone is making a speech – can't see who it is very well in the darkness. I do manage to hear something about 'traditions, duty, honour', etc, etc.

The Draft number off, form fours and we are on our way to the station accompanied by the band which played that well-known march, 'Old Comrades'. If I'm right, I think the words which the troops have added are "Have you ever caught your fingers in a rat-trap", etc. In charge of us is an old dug-out officer whose job it is to conduct drafts across to France. I suppose these officers must hold the record for the number of Channel crossings they made during the war.

Once in the train, we try the whisky or beer, in fact anything in that line that we have managed to smuggle away. At Canterbury we have to change trains from the east station, I think, to the west station. I am a bit foggy as to the exact proceedings, it may have been east to west or perhaps vice versa. All I do know is that we marched through Canterbury just as dawn was breaking. Once safely in the second train I settle down to sleep until Folkestone is reached.

The Channel is green and with angry white topped waves a strong wind is blowing, so I know we will get a bouncing soon.

At last all drafts are aboard, sirens toot, megaphoned orders come from the bridge; the gangways are pulled away, hawsers are slipped off the bollards and the space between ship and quay rapidly widens.

We are packed rather tight on the after-deck, looking back at the cliffs now rapidly receding. Officers are grouped on the boat-deck, from a 2nd lieutenant to a staff general, also a few Belgian officers. One begins to heave his breakfast over the side and being on the weather side, we get the benefit of it as the wind blows it back across our deck. Needless to say, we rapidly shift our position. The crossing, though rough, is not unpleasant. The wind and salt air helped to clear our heads and in some cases, tummies as well.

Boulogne again! Down the gangways on to the quayside. Draft conductors and senior officers count and recount their respective flocks in case someone is missing, but no, we are all here, nobody has fallen off the boat en route.

By train to Etaples and into tents, line upon line of white dots on the sandy dunes, each border flanked by marquees and hutments. A huge military base in the course of erection. Every encampment is divided and subdivided into units, brigades and divisions, so there is no confusion.

Here is the famous "bull-ring", the name given by us to the training ground. Every Draft or new Regiment must be put 'through the mill' under the critical eyes and bellowing voices of the special instructors, who only keep their jobs, and incidentally save themselves from going up the line, by these methods. It doesn't matter a jot whether you're a VC, DCM or the son of a dustman or earl, or as a matter of fact, how much fighting you've experienced – you must go through the mill in the 'bull-ring'. Here trenches are stormed by numbers and the Boche are bayoneted by numbers also. Everything is as per rule so-and-so and death can only come to 'Fritz' by us learning the correct position on a sack stuffed with straw. What a farce it is, when all the drilling in the world goes by the board in the actual thing.

There is a sergeants' Mess in a hutment. The beer is good and a piano and gramophone help to liven up our leisure hours. I always remember one record, "The Optimist and the Pessimist" and, of course, we have "Colonel Bogey". He was everywhere! Our final, before leaving for the Front, is a short course of musketry. All we have to do is to fire 15 rounds rapid at about 25 yards range. Fifty men at a time fires, the musketry officer being perched up on a platform with a megaphone. He reminds me of a skipper on the ship's bridge.

After about eight days at Etaples we receive our orders to go up to the Front again. This time the familiar goods wagons are there to take us up. On each is the inscription "Dix Chevaux – 40 Hommes". We go by way of Boulogne and Calais, thence to Stomar. Once we leave the last-named place, we know that we really are back in the war. We are to join the Ninth Battalion of the 42nd Brigade and 14th Division, somewhere up at Ypres. This is a new army division which went to France during May 1915. They have already seen a good deal of fighting, like all those who experienced the Ypres salient.

The weather is raw and rainy and, as we approach Poperinghe and the train just crawls along, we cannot help but see alongside the railway line the ever expanding cemetery.

Row upon row of little wooden crosses and men digging more and more to receive those who die at the clearing-hospital in Poperinghe.

The train pulls up and we get out, not feeling any too 'buckish'. The roads are in a thick black slush, which has been churned and churned almost to a sticky paste.

"Where is our mob?" we enquire. "Up the line" is the reply. Whereabouts?" we repeat – "Het-Sas, near Boesinghe".

Oh well, we don't know where it is, what's the use of worrying? The only point we are concerned about is if it's quiet or if it's a lively place.

An officer from the battalion is here to meet us and guide us to the mysteries of Het-Sas. It is getting dark and we set off, leaving Ypres on our right. It is a long march and we are now 'fed up' completely. We pass through a village called Elverdinghe and on its borders are halted with the regimental transport who are camped there. Good news! We may not go into the Line. We learn that the whole division is to be rested, before going to Egypt? In any case the battalion is being relieved the next night and we shall only be required as a carrying party tonight sometime.

I think to myself, what a queer war this is! Here am I, back again after four months and it's not over yet. If anything, it has got decidedly busier. It is nothing but sheer madness, all this killing and maiming, day in and day out, week after week, month after month with no apparent result.

Ypres is being 'strafed' without intermission, I can distinguish the muffled roar of the explosions amidst the masonry. We get hot tea and a meal of sorts before going on fatigue. I am not included for the working party, for which I am more than thankful. About 1 am the men return – they describe the trenches to me, which is not flattering. They had to carry up rations and oddments for the REs, wire, timber, etc.

During the following day we have little to do except keep under cover. Aircraft are more plentiful and several times I see the bird-shaped German planes over our lines.

As soon as dusk arrives we follow the transport back again towards Poperinghe and it is early morning before billets are reached. We then are told off to companies and help get blankets, etc in readiness for the battalion's arrival. I am sent to "D" Coy and the billet is a group of farm buildings, isolated by several flat fields from the next group of farm buildings. This is typical of this part of N.E. France on the fringe of the Belgian frontier. The two nearest villages are Herzeele and Houdtkerke and at both of these I later patronise their estaminets!

The familiar faces of the 1st Battalion being 'somewhere else in France', I am some little time making myself familiar with the 9th Battalion and, more so, "D" Coy. However, there are a good many who I had met during my earlier years in the army and one or two from the 1st Battalion in France. It is not long before I am thoroughly initiated with the aid of 'vin blanc', etc and in a few days I am quite at home, if it is possible to use that term.

One night, returning to billets from a carouse at Herzeele, we indulge in an impromptu sports meeting. This takes place in the sodden meadows until we are wet through and exhausted. There are running and ditch jumping events, all this in the darkness and heavy boots and puttees on, too! It reminds me of a similar occasion during peacetime at Felixstowe, when we went into a field where horses were grazing and tried a bit of rough riding, the only outstanding event being that of a white horse, which bolted with Jock

Gilbert astride of it and was only stopped by AGA sentries. Jock was put into the clink for being drunk.

As regards our madness in the fields near Herzeele, it only goes to show what complete disregard we have for the war when we are anywhere back far enough to enjoy ourselves.

We are issued with "tin hats" – steel helmets, and fur jackets – the former to lessen the number of head wounds from shrapnel and the coats to make us look more hideous than we really are. More to carry about on our already overloaded persons. There is some dubiousness about the value of the 'tin hat', as it was a most unfortunate coincidence that one of the first to be killed, whilst wearing one, was the late colonel of the 3rd Battalion and who commanded the 9th Battalion at the time of his death, and that was Colonel Chaplin, beloved by all in peace and war. A hole was drilled by a bullet clean through the helmet. Naturally, it requires something stouter to resist a direct hit and the men, knowing that Col. Chaplin was one of the first to wear one, at once came to the conclusion of the non-effectiveness of them; nevertheless, the same helmets have saved countless lives during the course of the war.

Rumours are rife as to the destination of the Division: Egypt is the most persistent of them. All we do know, is that we are going south somewhere. If we pass Amiens we shall be lucky; troops who manage to avoid the Western Front are envied. In spite of the discomfort of heat, flies, fever, etc, it is considered preferable to mud and misery of the trenches in Flanders and to the perpetual bombardments, etc.

One clear, frosty morning we pack up and bid farewell to frontier villages and the Ypres Salient. A march of perhaps five kilometres and the usual goods train is awaiting us in a small village station. Away snorts the train and we settle down to a 'mystery ride'. We go by way of Dunkerque, Calais, Boulogne, Etaples, Abbeville and Amiens. It is about 11 pm and we have been all day cooped up in our wagons. There is a distinct nip in the air and it is freezing. Snow is lying where the wind had drifted it up into corners and against tufts of rank grass. We are grouped on the platform and permanent way, and it is a job to keep warm.

After some delay we move out onto the road, which is on a slight rise; from this point of vantage the never ending flash of the guns in the east can be seen. Are we going up there, or are we going back away from it? This question is vital, there's only three ways, parallel, towards, or away!

We march into Amiens, a long line of LGOC buses are drawn up; we scramble into them and become securely wedged until our destination is reached, which is a towny-village or a villagey-town , rejoicing in the name of St Ledger-d'Omar. It is quite 2 am and by the time we are unpacked from the buses and into our respective billets with a feed and hot tea, it is nearer 4 am – next day reveille is at 9 am and we hear we may stay for at least three weeks, during which time the programme will be composed of drill and field training! We hear that a great battle is being waged round Verdun, the issue of which still hangs in the balance. Anyhow, better where we are, doing drill and other silly antics, than anywhere in the Line!

A scale of parades is issued and specialist classes formed, i.e. Lewis-gunners, snipers, bombers, etc and we look like having a regular Aldershot time of it during the coming days, but fate once again steps in and abruptly cuts short our 'peace time' activities. It is the fourth day at St Ledger D'Omar when orders come to 'Roll all blankets in bundles of ten'. Of course, we know what that means! It does not take long to flit, all our worldly possessions we carry on our persons and we are soon ready. The inhabitants are sorry to lose us – we are perhaps the first British soldiers to be billeted on them, their own troops having always occupied this region. As we commence the march, so does snow begin to fall. This will not be pleasant if it continues!

We hear we are for Arras, which is quite fifty to sixty kilometres away from our starting point. The first day we march about 18 kilometres, or roughly some 12 miles, and are billeted in a small village for the night. The following day snow again begins to fall and the land quickly changes into an aspect of the 'frozen north'. From a gently falling snow, it soon resembles a blizzard. A sharp wind springs up and the flakes pile up on us and everything. Marching soon becomes difficult, our heavy boots slipping on the half-frozen surface of the roads. To make matters worse, our next stop is a much longer distance than yesterday's. We pass through Doullens in a regular blizzard and by late afternoon, after apparently wandering aimlessly about, over fields and through small woods, etc, we hear that we are lost! A kind-hearted CO suggests a cross-country route in preference to the snowbound roads. I think that it is a little like the 'Retreat from Moscow'. The snow lies quite thick everywhere and it is still coming down.

Being tired, or rather, overtired, we begin to straggle a good deal and many men fall out, too bodily weary to carry on. Darkness is rapidly approaching and still we plod on over the snow. When we have almost given up hope of reaching our night's billet, we trudge wearily into a long, sparsely-housed village, which is our resting place. The transport having been snow-bound, volunteers are asked to go with drag-ropes and help to get them along from a point some two or three kilometres away. We are absolutely done-up, but we know that so long as the transport remains snow-bound, there will be no rations or hot tea for us. Several of us, therefore, proceed once more to find them. This we do and our combined efforts release the limbers and all reach the village. Our billets are draughty barns. Nevertheless, we sleep from sheer fatigue, although we awake stiff and cold next morning.

Owing to the strenuous time we have had, we stay an extra night before setting out on our final lap towards Arras. The last day's march is different again. A watery sun casts its warmth over the whitened earth. Soon the snow on the roads begins to melt and by the time Simoncourt is reached, there is a thick slush which is constantly being churned up by the troops and animals. Simoncourt is to be our billeting place and the village is some eight kilometres from Arras. We are to relieve the French, who are required for the Verdun battle, which still rages furiously during the third week of February 1916.

Simoncourt is, at this period, all mud and dullness; we sleep in barns and sleep very cold, too! The only real warmth we have is in an overcrowded estaminet or round a brazier. One night our barn catches alight and we scarcely have time to salve our personal belongings before the timbered and thatch roof collapses. The owner, a dirty-looking old boy, does a war-dance, shaking his fist at us and yelling "Là-bas, Anglais!'. We have a good mind to pitch him on the fire, it would do him good.

A stay of four days in this desolate village and we are for the trenches. The whole battalion falls in about 5 pm and we march off along the highway that runs from Beaumetz straight to Arras. At the village of Agincourt, we split up into platoons and, led by guides, are taken to our positions. The sector is known as "H" and is nearly S.E. of Arras.

We cross the main railway lines at Agincourt that lead into Arras and follow a road to quite near the Front Line. It is extraordinarily quiet, not at all like Ypres or La-Bassée, only occasional spurts of machine gun fire or rifles and very few rocket lights are going up. At last we are settled, my Coy "D" is in support and the night passes without event.

The second and third day are the same. We get bold and sit on top of the trench, shoot rats, etc. One officer takes a gramophone into a sap near their line (the Germans) and plays records; it is the yarn that he had a German record of "The Watch on the Rhine" and played this, too!

Whether he did or didn't, the Germans had arrived at one definite conclusion and that was to put a stop to it once and for all. On the fourth day they start to systematically bombard our trenches with minnewerfers and 5.9 shells. He has the range nicely and creates havoc, blowing in two of our best dug-outs and several parts of the trenches. There are several casualties, including three killed in one dug-out.

To improve matters, our divisional artillery take over and from thence onwards things get lively. We do eight days in and eight out. Of those eight days in, four are in support and four front line.

Simoncourt and Bernaville are our chief billets and "H" our chief sector in the line. "H" sector is roughly a thousand to fifteen hundred yards of frontage; directly in front are the ruins of Beaurains, held by the Germans. Behind us the ground slopes gently down towards Arras. The Germans hold the pick of the ground and can look down from almost any point onto Arras and a good deal further. "G" sector is on our right, while "I", "J" and "K" and so on continue away to our left. Arras is the centre of a salient, not quite so pronounced as at Ypres.

When we are out of the line, there is not much rest! Men must be kept up to the mark, and that means many irritating and foolish parades. The first day is one of cleaning up ourselves and equipment, then follows an inspection of this or that, such as rifle and sword, gas masks, iron-rations, etc. Clothing and boots are renewed when possible and when new things do arrive, it is remarkable how scarcely anything reaches us rank and file, whereas the Coy QMs, CSMs and Battalion HQ are always 'spruced up'. I have frequently worn boots with the heels worn down quite flat and had to wait weeks for a new pair.

About the third spell from the line, we get a change from Simoncourt and are billeted in a village named Bernville. It is no different from the former, except that it is cleaner. The billets are the same barn-like outbuildings, and we sleep on straw which is perhaps better than nothing at all. From CSMs and upwards a bed of sorts is found, but all ranks beneath have to 'muck in' amongst the straw. To sleep in these barns is quite simple, I don't remember anyone complaining of insomnia, no matter how uncomfortable or hard the floor. On cold nights it is a masterpiece of man's ingenuity, to see how they rearrange and shuffle their clothing to sleep warm.

Myself, I first lay any sacks and my ground-sheet on top of the straw, placing a pack or valise with anything soft for a pillow. Boots and puttees come off, the puttees being wrapped loosely round both feet. Trousers are then laid on top of the ground-sheet. My tunic acts as a first covering, the one and only blanket comes next and on top of all, the overcoat. I snuggle well under and sleep quite sound all night.

Nothing very particular happened during the first weeks round Arras. The trenches were fairly quiet, that is, there was nothing exceptional, just the usual trench routine; sentries, working parties, standing to arms at dawn and dusk. Naturally, there were the unavoidable casualties from bomb shells and bullets.

I remember one quiet afternoon whilst patrolling the front line, there came a bullet from a German sniper that remains impressed on my memory more than any other, although millions came my way during my time at the Front. In one part of the trench, the ground dipped sharply and the German trench could be plainly seen – therefore, anyone passing along, more so if tall like myself, would make a good target. I was, no doubt, thinking of something else and quite forgot to duck my head at this spot. Realisation came to me by the vicious whip-like double crack as a bullet or bullets missed me. Naturally, if they hadn't I suppose I would have had R.I.P. over my grave, dated about 15-3-16.

The shock was so great at the time that I felt a perfect fool. I came all over with a clammy-sweat and shook as though I had just come out of a bath of ice cold water. Exactly how near that bullet was I don't know, but I suppose that it was just a mere fraction of space between it and instant death. Afterwards I was not ashamed to get well down when passing this spot. A notice was put up warning all comers to keep low! But one or two fell before the keen eye of the enemy's snipers.

In nearly all trenches, the latrines were a danger spot too. How many times did I have to curb the call of nature and run for it, gripping my trousers half down my legs at the same time. What a life this was, when one couldn't do this unavoidable action without the fear of death or mutilation! Many a poor devil was killed whilst on trench latrines. In trench photographs, latrines were unmistakeable – so I suppose that anything that looked like one was earmarked to be 'strafed' periodically in the hopes of catching some unfortunate man.

The next time out the Line we went into Arras to billet. This was quite a change from village barns! Our place was a "School for Young Ladies", which was proclaimed by an inscription in stone over the main entrance 'Ecole pour Jeunes Filles'. We slept in the classrooms amongst the relics of happier days and youth. Maps and atlases hung upon the walls. In our room was the British Isles, which was the centre of attraction, everyone pointing out his home town or village. When I showed them Tidworth as my home, they thought me a bit mad, I think!

One room was the art class – plaster models, sketch books, crayons, paint, charcoal and unfinished drawings. I could have made myself happy there, if there hadn't been a war.

We were in the main street that ended in the station approach, about 500 yards away. Daylight in Arras meant undercover; if one was out one must walk close in to the side of the houses. The place was under observation, so like all other places near the Line, it was to all appearances deserted by day and overcrowded after dark. The whole town was within easy range of bullets from the trenches and, at one point by Ronville, I don't suppose it was more than a mile to the enemy front trench. In spite of the close proximity of the fighting, many of the civil population were allowed to remain. If the proprietors of the various estaminets lived to enjoy the end of the war, they must have been very rich from the profits derived from the British troops.

The town on the whole had not suffered from annihilation like Ypres. The German gunners had concentrated on certain spots; the one time beautiful Hotel-de-Ville and the cathedral were a mass of rubble, as were the houses in their immediate vicinity.

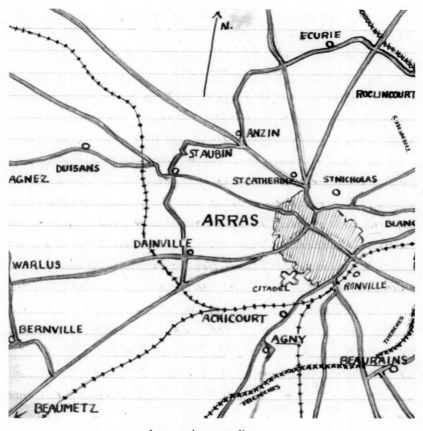

Arras and surrounding area

The railway station was also a wreck; some houses almost escaped scot-free, whilst others were entirely demolished. The percentage of the one-time inhabitants remaining was so small as to be almost negligible, about 1% only. There may have been a special motive to allow them to stay and it was, undoubtedly, for the express purpose of selling wine, beer, eggs, etc.

It was very queer to walk the streets of a town like Arras for the first time during daylight or darkness. Daylight exposed to the view the ghastly scars of war; darkness managed to cloak over a good deal from the vision.

The natural thing to expect amongst houses, buildings, roads, alleys, shops and all that goes to make a town was to see people going here and there, gossiping, bargaining, etc, to hear the gay laughter of children and to see them scampering about. Tradesmen's carts ought to be rumbling over the cobbles, pedlars shouting their wares, the shops and warehouses full of goods and merchandise of various sorts. Chimneys should be sending up smoke from stove and furnace; washing should be flapping in the wind. The postman delivering the mails; the gendarmes patrolling the streets; the shunting of goods trucks and shriek of engine whistles and all the sights and sounds of normal times. Yet it was a city of the dead, the inhabitants gone and everything left derelict.

Here are some shops, the plate glass fronts all smashed, exposing the interiors with smashed counters, broken show-cases and a jumble of plaster, wallpaper and splintered wood. Outside, the gilt lettering is all awry – some letters are missing and the electric arc lamps are broken, the wires hang down and sway in the breeze. The upper floors are the same, broken window panes, shrapnel scarred brickwork, roofs stripped bare.

Look at the railway station now! Great shell craters in the road outside, twisted and bent lamp standards. The station building with gaping holes, doors and windows blown out; smashed platforms, bent and broken rails. There is an engine, its funnel gone and the boiler peppered with shrapnel holes. Burnt out railway coaches, goods trucks lying on their side. One is reared up on end like some grotesque animal.

See this house, the whole front has been stripped bare, revealing the intimacies of one-time domestic happiness. A double bed is perched dizzily on the edge of the flooring. Pictures hang on the walls. There is a child's cot, tables, chairs, sideboards, carpets, curtains are all still intact.

Curtains hang limply from many a smashed window, they look so forlorn and dejected, as though bewailing the absence or the loss of their respective owners. Doors swing to and fro, shutters at all angles, while even cats and dogs have fled or are all killed. Huge piles of bricks and rubble are heaped up on each side of the roads to allow the free passage of transports, etc.

Arras was one great tragedy, as were other towns near the firing line. No person can fully understand it all unless they had to abandon their homes, or unless they went there as soldiers to help to defend the shambles that remained.

About this period we were getting a new type of soldier, the Derby men. The peculiar feature about it was the great disparity in ages – they were either too young or over 40. The man of 30 was rare – no line troops should have been sent into the fight under 21 years, on the other hand men of 40 were more reliable and level-headed, if not physically as nimble as their younger comrades. These men, dubbed 'Derbyites', were just as good as anyone else. No man individually was superior to the remainder, the only distinction was, after all, length of active service. Everyone was afraid. Anyone who boasted he wasn't was a liar! The only difference between us was that some could conceal their feelings, whilst most of us couldn't. I think it was somewhere about this time that the Military Service Act, or in other words, Conscription, came into force.

Officers did not remain with us long – a Platoon Commander or Company Officer was a very unlucky personage for the Germans earmarked officers in attacks, which was quite natural and he was a lucky man if he reigned six months in the same battalion. We noticed this, but after all there were barely twenty odd officers to a battalion and, naturally, casualties amongst them were more noticeable.

The majority of officers I came under were of the best, but a 'bad egg' is sure to be found at times. One such Captain came to us at Arras, a regular martinet, in or out the trenches. His name was Captain Dickenson or Jackson, it does not matter which. There commenced a time for us which was not any too pleasant. He had been a good many years out east, but I don't think he was a regular officer. The Company didn't object to his many years east, but did object to his manner and speech, as though he were still supervising native labour. We just made the best of it, that's all we could do. He and I did not get on together for some time and we had several rows: I am glad to think that prior to his death we were reconciled.

Happenings in and round Arras

One warm afternoon in the trenches, I was on duty. Things were quiet and one could almost imagine there was no such thing as war. From round a traverse appeared Captain 'Pukka'. We called him 'Pukka' as he frequently used this Indian expression. He looked rather grim as he told me to accompany him on a tour of the Company front. We had gone through perhaps five 'bays' (spaces between traverses) when he stopped and said to me, "Look!" pointing at the same time to a man on sentry. I instantly realised the reason for him bringing me and I involuntarily shouted the man's name. The man who, up to this instant, to all appearances was asleep although standing, at once responded to my call. This action on my part roused the ire of Capt. Pukka, who called me a 'blasted fool'. Not to be outdone, he placed the unfortunate man in arrest for 'sleeping on sentry'! He then turned to me, saying, "Sergeant, this man was asleep, d'you understand?" I said, "Asleep? And your evidence?"

We were due back in Arras again in a couple of days' time, and the poor chap was worrying as to his ultimate punishment. He was quite a nice lad and he thanked me for yelling his name and saving a bad situation from being worse. Capt. Pukka meanwhile made things nasty for me. We had three nights to do in the Line and on each one he sent me out on patrol. Perhaps he had a notion that my evidence would not be needed if I got accounted for whilst on patrol.

It doesn't take long to frame-up a court-martial at the Front and I was warned to attend as one of the principle witnesses. However, I had firmly made up my mind as to what I would say. My idea was that if a man was to be shot, it would be by the enemy and not like a bullock in front of a firing squad. I had had enough of the shooting of the poor fellow in the 1st Battalion.

With this resolve planted firmly in my head, I enter the Court Martial room in Arras. All eyes seem to be fixed on me, especially the accused man, and I could read the dumb appeal in his eyes. There were strange officers who comprised the court, Capt. Pukka was like a leashed tiger – he somehow knew that my presence has already shattered his carefully built plans.

I am questioned to some length:

"You were on trench duty from so-and-so hours to such a time?" – "Yes."

"You visited all the sentries at regular periods?" – "Yes"

"Did you pass the accused prior to Captain… coming to you?" – "Yes."

"Was he awake or otherwise?" - "Awake!"

This is something of a shock to the court and I see them kind of 'sit up and take notice'. The next question to me is a challenge:

"Are you positive?" and I reply, "Yes, sir".

"Now" said the spokesman, solemnly pointing his pen at me, "Did Capt.... come to you and ask you to accompany him at about so-and-so time?"

I reply, "Yes".

"When you both came to the accused man, was he asleep?"

"He was awake."

I know now that my word is more than vital and I am resolved to stick it out. "How do you know?" are the next words flung at me. Then I tell them that it is possible to be asleep in a sense and awake, too. The man was standing, admitted he had his head resting on his arms by the periscope, but when I called his name, he instantly responded. I tell them that I also had been the same – one part of the brain was wandering, whilst the other was alert the whole time.

The next question is to Capt. Pukka. He is asked if the accused responded immediately to his name being called and he admits that he did so.

At last it is over and I am outside again. The captain glares at me. I have put my foot in it proper in my efforts to prevent a firing squad. Gradually the news gets about and I am called a jolly good fellow, etc, but I am dubious about my future life under Capt. Pukka.

Two days after the F.G.C.M. the findings are read out on a Company parade. My heart nearly stops as I listen for the sentence. "The accused is found not guilty of being asleep at his post, but guilty of negligence in not obeying orders, i.e.

failing to be alert and watchful, etc. He is sentenced to twenty-one days' field punishment No.1."

Another life saved, I think, and that's that!

Once whilst in rest billets at Bernville, my Company had the obnoxious task of providing a firing squad to carry out the death sentence on another poor unfortunate man, or rather, boy – he was barely twenty. The information came at night from Battalion HQ. Sergeant Lanning was Orderly and told me the news. Six good men had been chosen, two stretcher bearers, a Major and Sergeant Lanning himself. Later on it was decided to include two extra men (in case any of the six would faint, etc). Lanning is in a stew and said he could not face the ordeal. He must have told HQ because he returned to me with the information that I was to go as well. I told him it was as bad for me as for him, I had already seen one death by shooting. After some argument he said he would go. I told him that he had nothing to do whatever, so long as the men shot straight, neither had anyone else anything to worry over. The only person who had the poor lad's death to account for was the C-in-C who signed the death warrant.

In some instances the death sentence may have been the only adequate punishment to suit the offence. I refer to those cases of men who were real criminals at heart, who never had any intention of soldiering, but who deserted at the first opportunity, who lived by robbery and violence, until combed out by the police. The so-called 'cowardice in the face of the enemy' was, in most instances, temporary loss of self control, which the best of men were subject to, during some period or other. Therefore, shooting was a most barbarous practice. Some of the staff who sanctioned these court-martials should have had a few weeks in the Line, then they themselves perhaps would know what the so-called 'cowardice' feeling was really like.

CHAPTER EIGHT

The next morning at 5 am the party set off for the scene of execution at Warlus, about three kilometres away. I did not go with them and was more than thankful! Sergeant Lanning returned a broken-spirited man. He was no further use as a trench soldier and was, eventually, sent away back as an instructor. The following is his narrative of the shooting.

I got all the men together and went to Major ....'s billet. His servant had prepared coffee, well stiffened with rum – biscuits were also given to us. The Major called me in and gave me a stiff whisky and soda to swallow. He himself, whilst explaining our duties, put back two or three tots. 'Well, Sergeant', he said 'We'd better be off but I'm damned if I put a bullet into the poor devil's carcase as I'm supposed to do – no, not for all the C of C's and King's regulations either'.

The poor Major was as upset as any of us, I can tell you. Anyway we set off towards Warlus just as dawn is breaking. Before reaching the village, two 'Red Caps' meet us and guide us away through waste ground to the spot chosen. The trees were fairly thick here and a slight clearing was the firing spot and at one end was a thickish tile covered wall. More officials now arrive, I saw a white tape laid on the ground – the men are told to lay their rifles on it. The Major comes to me and said 'Lanning, take the men back a little way'. We all go back as ordered and are joined by the Major and others. Our instructions are, that on a given signal they will go to the rifles on the tape, pick any one up and come straight to the present or firing position, with their left foot on the tape, and simultaneously push forward the safety-catches. Then, the Major who will be on our right, a little in advance, will hold a handkerchief up above him. When he lets fall his arm, all are to shoot.

Whilst waiting, we smoke and curse the war and everybody! We enlisted to kill the enemies of Britain, not shoot our own men in cold blood! If we refuse to do this, we know what will happen – more court-martials and punishments.

At last, the signal is given and we go to the firing point – nobody is talking, it is all signs – there was the man or boy or dummy to be killed. He was dumped up against the wall by two Red Caps who had carried him there! Christ, shall I ever forget those minutes or seconds – there were our chaps with levelled 'bondooks' and the Major as white as the handkerchief he held. Under the wall was the living target, tied by arms and legs to a chair, he was quite limp, just like a guy the kids rig up at home, his head lolled forward onto his chest and a white disc was pinned over his heart. The Major lets fall the handkerchief, six rifles crack sharply and the figure in the chair quivered and all but toppled over, chair and all! Red Caps and an MO go to him – he is quite dead – no need for a revolver to finish it.

Our stretcher men go across and he is laid on it and laid in a newly dug grave close by, cross and all ready. I tell I felt fair sick and so did us all. One of our chaps, who was in the firing squad, went off the deep end proper. He looked fair mad as he cursed God and man for permitting such things, we had a lively time until his temper had cooled. The Major stood by and gave us the tip not to interfere with the man. After all his raving, he finished up by crying like a kid.

One of the Red Caps came and gave us cigarettes, we then went to the Town Major's place and there was tea and rum. The lad who was shot belonged to our 8th Battalion in the 41ˢᵗ Brigade; third time he'd hopped off from the Line. Red Caps told us he was unconscious and knew nothing at all. He was well doped during the night – and a good job, too! Anyway, it's finished me, I'll go up the Line, but I don't care what happens to me, I shan't fire another shot in this blasted war and I hope old Jerry wins it, that's me!

That was the end of Sergeant Lanning's yarn and I could see the affair had broken him up. The news was scarcely a nine days' wonder, things happen so swiftly that it was soon forgotten. Major....... in charge of the firing party went on leave and never returned to our Battalion. All the men were excused the next spell in the Line.

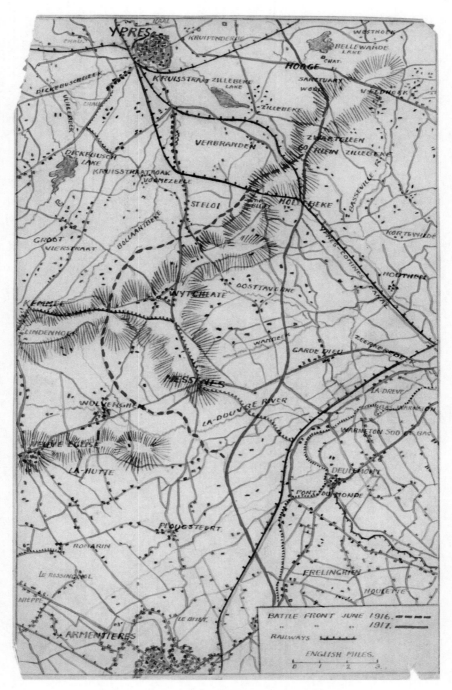

Map of the area between Ypres and Armentieres

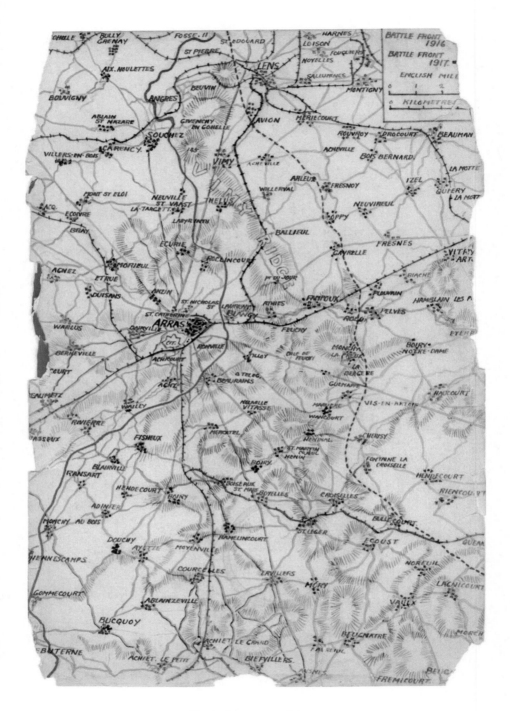

Battle front around Arras

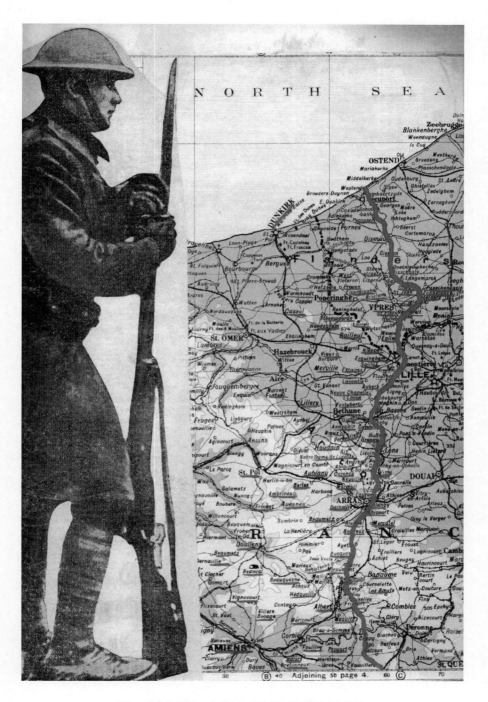

The dividing line between the opposing armies

What the average infantryman has to wear and carry

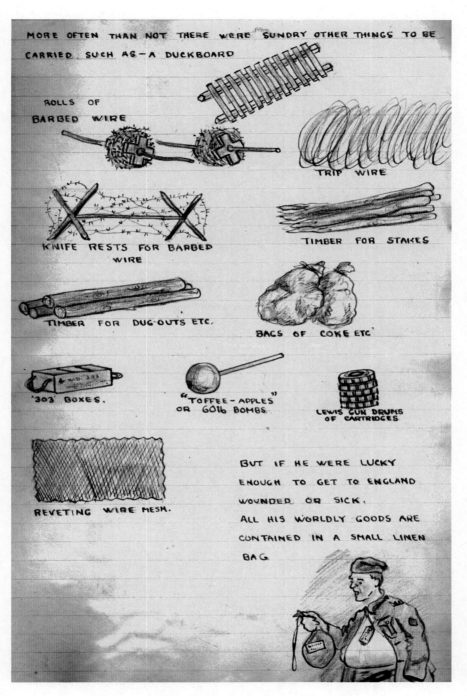

MORE OFTEN THAN NOT THERE WERE SUNDRY OTHER THINGS TO BE
CARRIED SUCH AS—A DUCKBOARD

ROLLS OF
BARBED WIRE

TRIP WIRE

KNIFE RESTS FOR BARBED
WIRE

TIMBER FOR STAKES

TIMBER FOR DUG-OUTS ETC.

BAGS OF COKE ETC.

'303' BOXES.

"TOFFEE-APPLES"
OR 60lb BOMBS.

LEWIS GUN DRUMS
OF CARTRIDGES.

REVETING WIRE MESH.

BUT IF HE WERE LUCKY
ENOUGH TO GET TO ENGLAND
WOUNDED OR SICK.
ALL HIS WORLDLY GOODS ARE
CONTAINED IN A SMALL LINEN
BAG.

Other items the poor infantryman has to carry

A singsong in an estaminet

caricatures of some typical German soldiers

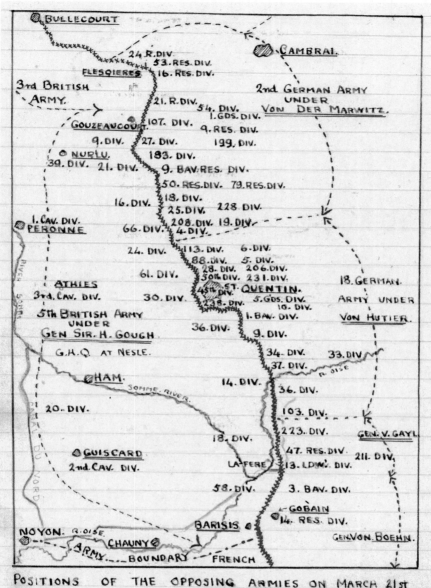

POSITIONS OF THE OPPOSING ARMIES ON MARCH 21st 1918. THE 5th ARMY UNDER GEN. SIR. H. GOUGH HELD A FRONT OF ROUGHLY 43 MILES, WITH ELEVEN DIV'S, AND FIVE IN RESERVE, OF WHICH THREE WERE CAVALRY DIVISIONS. THE GERMANS HAD CONCENTRATED NO FEWER THAN.

Positions of the opposing armies on 21.3.1918

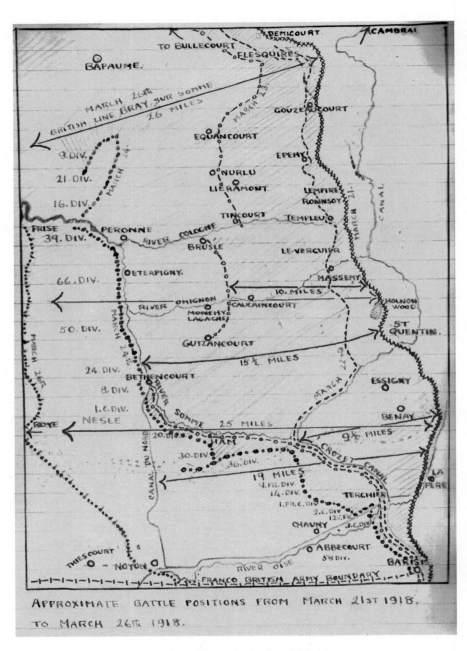

Battle positions, 21.3.18 to 26.3.18

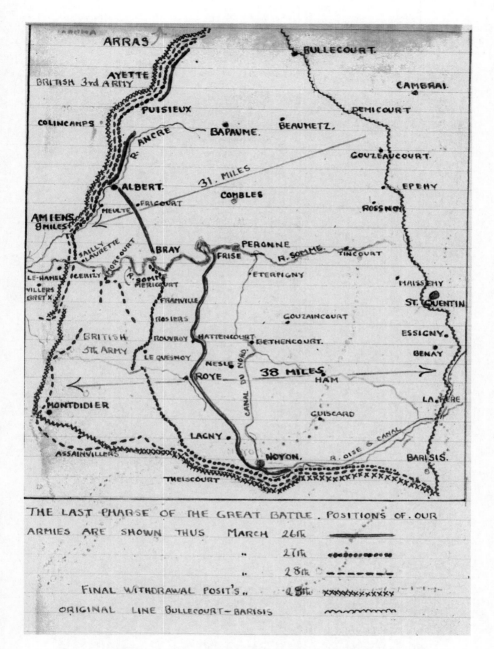

The last phase of the great battle, March 26-29 1918

Barrack Square, Rifle Depot, Winchester

Royal Victoria Hospital Pier

Maurice (3rd from left, back row) at the Red Cross Hospital camp
at rear of The RV Hospital

Maurice at RV Hospital (back row, first on left).
Photo taken outside Enquiry Office, 1919

Red White and Blue Committee. Entertaining wounded, Woolston,
March 26 1919 (Maurice is front, 3rd from right)

Maurice, Alice, Stephanie (1946)　　　Maurice in grounds of RV Hospital

Maurice when he joined the KRRs in 1906

Maxim Gun Staff. 1st KRR at Camp. Maurice peering out of tent.

Maurice and chum at camp.

Maurice's brother, Lance Cpl Alfred Graffet Neal

Maurice and other patients with some of the staff at
the RV Hospital (middle row, 5th from left)

Maurice at the Countess Cairns, Romsey (3rd row back, 6th from left)

Maurice and other patients with some of the staff at the RV Hospital
(middle row, 2nd from right)

Sgt Major Alfred Neal
(3rd Battalion KRR's) (1st on left)

Maurice (left, front row) with
Richardson, Cook and
Bayliss at Bethune

Serial No. **A 5647** *KRRC*   Army Form B. 2079.

NOTE—This Certificate is to be issued without any alterations in the manuscript.

Certificate of discharge of No. *7229*   Rank *Rifleman*

Name *Neal*   *Maurice Grailet*
         Surname.   Christian Names in full.

Unit* and Regiment or Corps from which discharged } **KINGS ROYAL RIFLE CORPS**

* The unit of the Regiment or Corps such as Field Co. R.E., H.T., or M.T., A.S.C., etc., is invariably to be stated.

Regiment or Corps to which first posted *KINGS ROYAL RIFLE CORPS*

Also previously served in .... *nil*

....

....

Only Regiments or Corps in which the soldier served since August 4th, 1914, are to be stated. If inapplicable this space is to be ruled through in ink and initialled.

Specialist Qualifications (Military) *3rd Class Educational Cert*

....

Medals, Clasps, Decorations and Mentions in dispatches { *1914 Star*   Wound Stripes* *nil*
British War Medal   To be inserted in words.
Victory Medal }

Has served Overseas on Active Service†   *HO 1906*

Enlisted at *Winchester* .... on *24 July 1906* 191...
*Each space is to be filled in and the word "nil" inserted where necessary.
†To be struck out in ink if not applicable.

He is discharged in consequence of *Termination First Period of Engagement Para 392 XX 7 Kings Regln*

....

after serving* *Thirteen* years* *3* days with the Colours, and
* *nil* years* *nil* days in the Army Reserve or Territorial Force† } Strike out whichever inapplicable.

*Each space is to be filled in and the word "nil" inserted where necessary; number of years to be written in words.
†Service with Territorial Force to be shown only in cases of soldiers serving on a T.F. attestation.

Date of discharge *2nd June 1920*

} Signature and Rank.

Churchward   *for Lt Col*

Officer i/c *Rifle* .... Records.

Winchester (Place).

Description of the above-named soldier when he left the Colours.

Year of Birth *1890*   Marks or Scars *Gun shot wound Right arm and Leg*

Height ....ft ....in.

Complexion *Fresh*

Eyes *Grey*   Hair *Brown*

(31617.) Wt. W1912/PP1133. 760m. 5/18. S. & C. (E3267.)   **P.T.O**

Maurice's Discharge Certificate

Army Form B. 2067.

NOTE.—The character given on this Certificate is based on holder's
conduct throughout his military career.

Character Certificate of No. 7229 Rank. Rifleman

Name heal Maurice Graffet

Surname   Christian Names in full.

Unit and
Regiment or Corps
from which
discharged } **KINGS ROYAL RIFLE CORPS.**

This is to certify that the ex-soldier named above has served with the
Colours for Thirteen years 314 days months, and his character

To be inserted in words.

during this period has been 'Very Good'

A smart clean sober, trustworthy + hardworking man

Eustace L facol } Signature
and
Rank.

Officer i/c Rifle Records.

Date of discharge 2nd June 1920 Winchester Place.

To safeguard the holder of this Certificate from impersonation it should
be noted that, in the event of any doubt arising as to the *bona fides* of
the bearer, reference should be made to the description, when he left
the Colours, of the soldier to whom this Certificate was given, which is
recorded on his Discharge Certificate (Army Form B. 2079, Serial
No. 126447.), and should be in his possession.

(A11310) Wt. W5166/RP2467. 150,000 7/10 Sch. 41. D. D. & L. [P.T.O.

WARNING.—If this Certificate is lost a duplicate cannot be issued. You should therefore
on no account part with it or forward it by post when applying for a situation,
but should use a copy attested by a responsible person for the purpose.

NOTE.—This Certificate is to be issued without any alteration in the manuscript.

Maurice's Character Certificate

Alice Theresa (née Gray)

View of RV Hospital and Red Cross complex at rear

Sgt Major Alfred Neal (3rd Battalion, KRRs)

14 Juillet 1919
DÉFILÉ DE LA VICTOIRE

Sir Douglas Haig

Sir Douglas Haig in Paris, 14th July 1919

The Battle of the Somme

July 1916

The summer of 1916 was fast approaching; buds and blossoms had fallen to give way for the young fruit to grow. Where nature was undisturbed by war, the fresh green of leaves smothered the trees and woods; young corn thrust itself up from the earth, profusely sprinkled with poppy, cornflowers, etc. Waste ground was thick with flowering weeds forming a carpet of many colours. Sunny days followed one another and it intensified the revulsion of feeling against everything connected with the war.

Under a clear blue sky, we would be sandwiched in between walls of earth with, perhaps, scarcely a breath of cool breeze to fan our clammy, hot faces, nothing whatever to do except wait and wait through the long daylight hours until the evening and darkness gave some measure of relief.

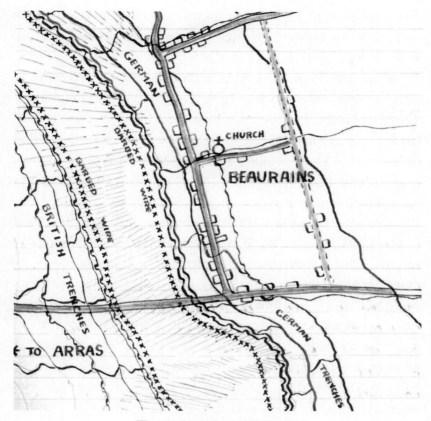

The trenches in front of Beaurains

Personally, I was always grateful for the hours of darkness, although it very often meant my prowling about in No-Man's-Land on patrol or 'listening post'. As a matter of fact I had become rather accustomed to it and treated the matter as though it was too trivial to be of importance. Capt. Pukka did not worry me much and must have regarded me as a sort of man immune from bullets or grenades on these nocturnal ramblings. He always expected a written account next day from me and was never disappointed in that direction. My confederates and I were soon past masters in lying on paper and lying in a convenient shell crater, neither of which came amiss to us.

When I was a novice in the art of wandering between the lines at night, I was too green and 'windy' to do anything other than carry out orders as far as possible. However, this method became dangerous and if I wished to be taken prisoner, killed or wounded, I was heading in the right direction! Therefore, caution and bluff were the main objects in my later belly-crawling adventures.

These night patrols were most eerie and nerve-tingling kind of affairs. One never knew what might happen to one at any minute. There were several hazards by which the 'coup de grâce' was liable to be dealt. In the first place you were between two fires, from the enemies trenches and from your own. Although instructions were given that a patrol was out, there was always a good chance of panic shooting at any time or that sentries, having forgotten what had been told to them, would begin to shoot until someone yelled out that it was their own men out in front. Then, perhaps, the German artillery would sprinkle No-Man's-Land with shrapnel, in the hope of catching someone – even our own gunners were quite liable to drop shells short, in which case the area would be between the front lines. German sentries and machine-gun bombers or minnewerfers were also to be reckoned with. Besides all these things to contend with, an enemy's patrol may run into you. This would mean a sudden severe tussle with grenades, bombs and revolvers and set both trenches into an uproar that would last until dawn.

As I have already mentioned, I knew the ground in front of our sector like a book, therefore when a young, newly-joined subaltern wanted to go and 'commit suicide' out on patrol, I decided to teach him a lesson. Capt. Pukka detailed myself and three men to go out, taking with us Lieut X for instruction. Just before dusk Lieut X came to me and explained to me where he was going and what he was going to do, which included capturing at least one 'Boche'! I let him have his say, then asked him if he had really become a member of the 'suicide club' (a term for any risky or foolish ideas). He didn't know what to make of me, but I explained to him why I had said it and arranged to meet him at 10 pm. In the meantime, I inform my three chums about the new officer. They laughed and we decided to teach him a lesson that night.

We arrange to split up when out in No-Man's-Land. Two men will creep away to our left, but keep us in view if possible. When I have gone as far as I think for safety, I have arranged to fling a bomb, at the same time pretending a party of Germans are in front. The two men on my left will then fling their bombs. This I know will cause a rumpus and frighten the lieutenant; my object in doing this is to prevent him from going any further and from getting himself and us killed or captured.

At 10 pm we all meet in the fire trench and I tell sentries to pass the word of our going out in front. We each carry four Mill's bombs and myself and the lieutenant, a revolver. Assuming a very solemn air, I tell the lieutenant to follow me and not to speak above a whisper. He has now lost some of his self confidence and tails on to me, meekly.

We go through our wire and make for a spot I know is fairly well protected from direct fire. I crawl on all fours, and the lieutenant and the man do likewise. During the journey, I frequently make signs to keep silent.

We lie quiet for some time. I do this purposely to let the

situation sink well in to the young lieutenant, who by this time is docile. Commencing to crawl forward again, I slip a hand into my jacket pocket and withdraw a bomb. Pulling the pin out, I manage to lob it well over in front of us, at the same instant whispering hoarsely to the lieutenant, "Germans!"

My bomb seems to make an extra noise and I pull the lieutenant, saying, "Quick, get into here!" We have scarcely settled into my pre-arranged safety hole when my other two men send about six of their bombs over into the void. I tell the lieutenant it is the Germans after us and that we must remain as we are. A scuffling noise behind and I see my two confederates rejoin us. We now all lie and await developments. They soon come. Stuttering machine guns and spasmodic rifle fire from the Germans. Then a deep 'Bomp' and a stream of sparks mark the line of flight of a German trench-mortar. It seems to be going straight up in the air! I suddenly realised that our bomb slinging has dropped us 'in the cart' and that the enemy are directing their mortars onto us!

The menacing rush of the missile is plainly distinguished in its headlong flight to earth. The lieutenant is the only one amongst us who is ignorant of our precarious position; he is new to all this – I rather envy him!

I shut my eyes, waiting for the end as I am quite certain that it will get us. It pitches behind, exploding with a mighty roar. "What's that?" asks the lieutenant as bits of earth and stones rain down. I tell him, at the same time casting my eyes skyward in time to see two more trails of sparks going up. By a miracle the mortars fall wide, while at the same time machine guns keep splaying bullets all around us, so I impress on the lieutenant to keep where we are until things have quietened down.

When this eventually happens, I send one man back to inform the occupants of our line that we are all safe and about to return. Before doing so, I have the opportunity of detailing a rough outline of a report, for the benefit of the lieutenant and myself. The Captain is pleased and hopes we have accounted for one or two Germans. The lieutenant says he is positive that a couple were killed. What beautiful liars we can be, when necessity occasions it!

There was to be a great offensive soon – on such a grand scale that in all probability, Germany permitting of course, the end of the war would arrive during 1916 and we would all be home for Xmas, or rather what remained of us. It was June, and we still drifted about from trenches to Arras and back again to trenches. The great question was, were we included in the initial attacks or not? Later we learned that we were not and would remain in the Arras sectors.

The days and weeks that followed were taken up with speculations and arguments on the coming offensive. Capt. Pukka was troublesome again. The eastern sun and life on the 'western front' combined were mainly responsible. To put things plain, he 'couldn't help it'. During 'Stand to Arms' at dawn and dusk, he reviled any man who was sensible enough to keep his head below the parapet of the trench. I knew of cases where he forced a man to show himself above the parapet and the poor fellow was 'dropped' by the keen eye of a German sniper.

About this time, I was taken queer in the line with a disease popularly known as 'trench fever'. I knew I had a temperature. Objects were distorted and sounds seemed far away. As I walked to the stretcher bearers' dug-out, I seemed to be floating and without legs. They took my temperature. It was 103°, so I was escorted back to the First Aid Post.

Here I was made a 'bed-patient' in name only. Our beds were stretchers laid on the stone floor of a house that was roofless; we were lucky enough to be protected by the ground floor ceiling, which was almost intact. Three days were allowed for the fever to abate. If by that time it still persisted, we would go further back, to a proper hospital. I anxiously hoped that my temperature would soar up on the third day, but I was disappointed – it dropped to 100° and on the fourth day it descended to normal, so I remained with the battalion, which was back to rest in Arras.

The Somme would be the scene of the British and French offensive and we heard tales of thousands of cannon being massed there to blast a way through the German defences. All along the British front from Ypres southwards, minor demonstrations would take place to distract the enemy. Practically all around Arras, poison-gas and bombardments would usher in July 1st 1916.

We again had the job of carrying up and installing gas cylinders in our sector, which took up three nights. At last all was ready and on June 28th we went into the line to wait for Zero Hour.

During the night of June 30th and the early hours of July 1st every man on the 'Western Front' anxiously waited for Zero Hour. This coming offensive affected all of us, whether we were actually in the early assaults or not, for we all knew that in time every fighting unit would have to bear its share sooner or later.

Many times during the night I looked at the wind vane to note the direction of the wind, but it swung back and forth in a slight breeze from the German lines. This would be of no use to us, the poison-gas would have to wait until the wind blew favourable for us.

Dawn of July 1st was just breaking, and away to the south

a deep throbbing and booming was continuous where thousands of our lads were assembled, waiting to attack. I think that life was very short for many of them – they would be dead before the sun has mounted the heavens.

The gas experts are with us now; it is their job to release the stuff. They are chemists and laboratory students specially incorporated into the RE for the work. By now the bombardment has intensified down south. From a distance it sounds ominous and terrible and we know that the carnage has commenced.

All day we wait for the wind to veer round, but it sticks in the same direction. We are told that we are to remain until the gas is released. This doesn't happen until the sixth day and I notice the vane points away from the enemy, signifying a wind blowing towards them.

We received our orders some days previously, so in a short space everyone is moving to his appointed position. The time selected for the gas to be released is about 11 am. As soon as it is seen that the wind is in our favour, things get busy. The gas experts arrive in force, telephones and runners are set going to various HQs with information and the hour of zero. Gunners stand by their batteries and we infantrymen remain cooped up in the trenches. Everyone except a few are to be withdrawn from the fire-trench back to supports. Those who remain are the gas experts and one or two Lewis gun teams and a couple of runners. I also have to stay and assist the RE experts, if possible.

The trench appears deserted now that our chaps have gone – I watch the REs fixing the nozzles onto the containers and cautiously poking the ends over the trench-top. Everybody is glancing at their watches every few seconds. At five minutes minus zero, we put on our gas masks. These are the hood-shaped ones and stifling. I undo my coat collar and top button and tuck the ends of the mask inside. The goggles soon become blurred with the heat of our breath - I daren't lift the mask to wipe them now! I stand near other figures, who now have no distinctive features to recognize them by – we all look identical and just as hideous as it is possible to be.

What use are we? We can do nothing, this is an RE show. So I stand still conserving my breath. Other hooded and goggle-eyed figures loom up to me, wag their heads and point vaguely towards the Germans. I realise that the gas is going over. How long we remain hooded I don't know, but I quite think I will suffocate if I don't soon get my head out of its prison.

At long last men cautiously raise their masks and sniff the air. I do the same, it is sickly and sweet, so we lower them for a little while and repeat the action. As no ill effect is felt, I pull my mask off and go along the trench. There is a deathly silence. Our artillery did not add horror upon horror to the unfortunate Boche – the gas no doubt caught them unprepared.

I see two REs dead and a third in the last throes of a torturing death. They had all lifted their masks too hastily and paid dearly for it.

When the trench is deemed fit for occupation again, our men come back. They tell me what they saw from the rear when the gas was released. It appears that the stuff was half way across No-Man's-Land before the enemy realised it. Our chaps heard the clanging of the alarm-gongs. Machine guns spluttered, but of what use are bullets against poison vapour? At one point three Germans died nobly. They hauled a machine gun on top of the trench by the road and although two men were without their masks, they hung on until overcome by the fumes. The third man continued to fire by himself and, fully exposed, waited to mow us down should we follow up the gas in an assault. It was a pity that he should die, but a man behind a machine gun is a great menace and could create havoc – so our own Lewis-gunners bowled him over. Their own artillery never put up an effective retaliation at all despite the urgent SOS signal sent up from their trenches. Our airmen reported that the gas was compact enough even as far as their battery positions, so that, in all probability, the gunners were asphyxiated too.

The day passes without event and as dusk comes on, the sickly sweet fumes of gas, which is hidden in the hollows and craters and grass, make themselves felt. It makes one want to drink and drink, whilst at the same time one's stomach is in revolt, trying to expel the noxious stuff. This combination of extreme thirst and the desire to be sick is not unlike the effect of chloroform.

At night we send out extra listening posts and stronger patrols. The men have to lie out on the gas-drenched ground. I visit them about 1 am. Three men are all but unconscious and I get them withdrawn to the trench. Other posts are in a similar plight. They are no use lying there slowly going off into unconsciousness! – I send them back, too.

Captain Pukka hears of this and he comes to me in a deserted bay of the fire trench. He at once explodes a string of foul words at me: 'Who the h…. am I?' 'What the b….y h…l did I mean by overriding his orders and withdrawing the men?' He calls me this, he calls me that. I am standing on the fire-step holding a very light pistol. It is charged. How I refrain from pressing the trigger, I don't know.

We have been in the line nine days and nights. Our nerves

are frayed with sleepless nights and I suppose the gas that still hangs about helps to upset our mental balance. My temper is up and nothing matters so long as I give vent to it. If he raved and cursed – so did I.

After carrying on in this insane manner until the want of breath makes me cease, the Captain abruptly sits down on the fire-step with his head in his hands. I stand like a fool waiting to be put under arrest. Instead of doing this, he fumbles in his tunic pocket and holds something towards me. I think it is his revolver, but it is his flask. "Drink", he says. I do so. He then pulls his cigarette case out and gives me one. I am dumbfounded! "Throw some lights over by their wire now and again, they may be up to tricks in revenge for this morning's gas", he says and abruptly leaves me.

The next day we are heavily trench mortared and sustain a few casualties besides the trench being blown in, in places. Good news - we are to be relieved that night by the DLIs. The day slowly wears through and evening is beginning to cast its shadow once again over the stricken land.

Just before Stand to Arms, the Germans open out with a heavy bombardment of our sector. It is so sudden that we are taken completely by surprise. Our front line, supports, communication trench, etc are heavily shelled. At the same time they trench-mortar our wire entanglements. Our reliefs must actually be on their way up, as we have everything ready in preparation to move. Everyone stands to arms. I get out reserve ammunition and bombs and hastily go along flinging a couple of bandoliers here and there to the men.

I can hear the enemy's batteries loosing off as fast as the guns can be served. They make a kind of double report, Br-r-romp! Br-r-romp! Br-r-romp! and the flashes are easily visible as it is almost dark – then follows the rushing scream of the missiles, followed by the bursts and the whine and drone of the splinters. Perhaps the Germans are coming over? If they do, what a reception for them! Our Lewis and machine guns are spraying bullets across No-Man's-Land whilst our gunners are already pumping shells into their trenches. Captain Pukka is going up and down the trench urging the men to bide their time and shoot to kill. He stands by me as I fire star-shells over to their barbed wire. We both strain our eyes trying to detect any movement. I send up light after light and as each one descends and bursts out its brilliance over the earth, I see only posts and tangled wire, a gashed and pitted ground. The descending light flings out the shadows further and further until it drops with a Thop! and dies out, leaving utter blackness.

Perhaps for the best part of an hour this goes on, until it finally subsides as any other rumpus is bound to do. It has been very severe and we were bound to sustain casualties, very hard luck, as we were on the point of being relieved after a trying period. The incoming battalion quite thought they were in for a 'show' and they were rushed up into support trenches. However, as I have mentioned, nothing came of it. The trench mortar did a good deal of damage to the trenches. Shrapnel inflicted the most casualties and the whole affair was a reprisal for our gassing them the previous day.

We go back to Arras for six days' rest. Capt. Pukka sends for me to go to his billet. When I get there he surprises me by giving me a 'dressing down', combined with advice and an apology concerning our midnight argument in the front line. He admits I am a good trench soldier, but too soft when dealing with men. He says an officer or NCO must not study the men too much. It is foolish for either of them. Discipline must dominate over everything, one must be relentless in all things, regardless of the men's feelings.

I listen respectfully to this harangue, at the same time formulating my own opinion as to the advisability of being 'relentless', etc. After informing me of the impending move of the division down to The Somme in the near future, he dismisses me. Closing the door after me, I make an expressive gesture of contempt with my fingers to the shut door of the Captain's room, which perhaps is fortunate. Dumb insolence is punishable as severely as spoken!

Somewhere about the 13th July, we once again occupy 'H' Sector. During our absence in Arras the Germans have been busy every day with trench mortars and heavies, so it is a very changed set of trenches we take over. The occupying regiment has undergone a rough time. The bombardment was so thorough that next day I have to crawl on all fours in places, the trench having been pummelled flat, whereas before, it was at least eight feet deep and fairly intact.

We are kept busy day and night digging and strengthening the battered places. Dug-outs have also been blown in and the whole place is a shambles. Duck-boards, timber, corrugated iron, sand-bags and equipment are heaped up indiscriminately. It is with a feeling of intense relief that the end of our six days approaches. 'H' Sector was a nice easy place once upon a time, but the projecting of poison gas and the general upheaval all along the British front since July 1st have heaped 'coals of fire' on our own heads. We always remarked on any special occasion that the enemy was 'strafed', that it was quite a good idea on the 'brass hats' part, but we poor b....y infantrymen always came in for the 'rebound'!

Back into Arras again before proceeding to the Somme.

Private houses are our billets and in a fresh part of the town, rummaging through the rooms, one realises the full poignancy and tragedy of this war. Nearly everything has been left behind just as the occupants had used them, there being no time to pack. I explored two or three houses and surmised they belonged to the Bourgeois class. The furniture is of good, solid wood – mahogany, rosewood, oak, etc, beautifully upholstered. Inlaid sideboards, cabinets, bureaus, etc. Several bits of furniture are of the horsehair variety, which I remembered as a kid; it used to stick in the seat of my pants and prickle. Books, photos, correspondence and intimate female clothing lie about. Little kiddies' play things have been left in the frantic rush to get away. We in England experienced nothing of this during the war!

Try and imagine a city resembling Arras – say Salisbury - with every man, woman and child gone, without cattle, sheep, pigs, horses, dogs, etc. Just a few cats who have stayed and live wild. The beautiful, tapering cathedral spire and the cathedral itself are a great shapeless heap of masonry. Fisherton Street and the railway station are the same and every other house in the town is damaged or reduced to ruins. If the situation had been the same in Salisbury as in Arras, the Germans would have been in trenches nearer than Harnham Hill and they would have dominated Salisbury for four years from every point of vantage in the low hills around the city. It is only by comparison with a town in England that one can get a true perspective of what the French endured.

There has been much said of the enemy and their methods in the occupied areas – of the brutalities and atrocities that were perpetrated; I know some of it is true and that some has been exaggerated and I also know that these particular species of war crimes are natural to a huge invading army. The only difference is that the Germans did all the invading in this war. Had the allies penetrated the enemy's land, excesses would have happened just the same, by British, French or Belgian. There was always present in us a strong undercurrent of revolt and passion waiting to be loosed, like a flood, on any occasion.

In the cellars of these houses we find about a dozen or so bottles of champagne. The chaps drink them like beer, and naturally rowdyism commences. They deck themselves up in women's garments, dancing wildly about, wantonly smashing ornaments and pictures, etc, and I am thankful that no women or girls are there. Had they been, it would have been an orgy, which would have disgraced the British khaki.

The remarkable thing is that they carry on undisturbed by anyone, showing that excesses are just as possible with us as the enemy. I do not imply that our officers would have condoned it, by any means. Nevertheless, human nature is the same the world over. Opportunity is the only fitting word to use. The average trench-going infantry soldier has little or no opportunity to indulge in 'women and wine'. The German infantry are the same. The majority of these crimes could be laid to the heels of the soldiery who never endured the trenches.

Off to the Somme

One warm afternoon about the last week of July, we set off from Arras on our long march to The Somme. The whole division was on the same errand, but of course, we split up and went devious ways to avoid congestion. Our division was made up of the 40th, 41st and 42nd Light Infantry Brigades and, with the addition of the necessary Corps troops, such as Divisional

Artillery and ammunition columns, RE, ASC supplies and the various HQ's, this comprised the 14th Division. Our Brigade was made up as follows – 9th King's Royal Rifles, Ox and Bucks Light Infantry – Shropshire LI – Cornwall LI.

The route chosen was one of some 60 kilometres and the way led roughly through Duisans, Sombrin, Bouquemaison, Beuval and Vignacourt. The weather was ideal, if a little too hot for marching; there is a vast difference between a long walk and a long march in wartime. We had our steel helmets and full equipment with rifle and 200 rounds of small arms ammunition, besides the various nick-nacks we hooked on in any convenient place on our persons. If we didn't carry anything we prized, we simply lost it for good and all. Our knife, fork and spoon always found sanctuary in our puttees. Tin mugs hooked on anywhere, canteen or mess tin on the back of the valise. Rations were thrown into a clean sandbag. On wet days rations always came up the trench in sandbags and, of course, on fine days as well. Wet days meant damp loaves and cheese, and any food not completely surrounded by tin became wet. The rough hairs from the sandbags were firmly mixed in with the perishable food; cheese and bread with whiskers!

Although every kilometre we marched fetched us nearer to an unknown fate, we made merry over it. Why shouldn't the men sing? It was glorious to be alive these warm sunny days. Of what use was it to worry? Anything might happen between now and us reaching the Somme. Even though we were to be flung into the inferno, some of us would have the luck to march out of it again!

We billeted in pleasant villages nestling among the trees.

Barns were available, but we shunned them for the open meadows and the sky for a roof. Bathing took place in any convenient stream, without any covering at all. In fact, we thoroughly enjoyed ourselves and gradually we became bronzed and fit, losing the pallor and nerve strain of the trenches.

Eventually we stayed at a small place named something or other Villers, I think it was Feinvillers. The Brigade was to undergo a short period of training in wood fighting; what useful purpose it served I fail to see. All the imitation of war antics and the practising of attacks was absolutely a waste of time and energy. The actual and the imitation were as distant as the poles are apart. In spite of all, we must obey the 'brass hats', so every day we went into a nearby wood and played at driving out an imaginary enemy.

A display was given of the new Stokes mortar gun. We watched from a hillside as the missiles were lobbed rapidly into a wood. It was all very impressive; the guns could loose off, on the average, ten shells a minute. There were four guns demonstrating, so that very soon the wood was all bangs and smoke. I think that Brer Rabbit and the little wild things were having a rough time.

The next item on the programme was for us to sham attack the wood, while dud Stokes gun shells were lobbed over in front of us. We did this, but with an ever watchful eye on the missiles that whirled over our heads. Some dropped into the bracken uncomfortably near. Should they happen to explode, there would be no Somme for some of us!

After about eight days of this foolishness, we were entrained and taken up to the back areas of the Somme. The train passed through Amiens and on to Corbie and Bray, where we detrained. There was ample evidence of 'something doing' in this district. We saw guns of all sizes in the advanced ordnance workshops undergoing repairs for minor injuries. I may add, with all due respect to the RAOC, it was the nearest I had ever seen them to the line and this was quite 10 kilometres or so.

From Bray-sur-Somme we marched to a village a little closer to the front and stayed as divisional reserve for a few days. All around there were troops. Acre upon acre of what was once long grass had been nibbled bare and trod flat by the feet of men and the countless hoofs of animals. Long lines of whinnying mules and horses picketed to the ground and row upon row of limbers and G.S. wagons marked the resting place of supplies and transport.

I had no conception of what the Somme was like, but judging from the never ceasing rumble by day and the gun flashes at night, it was going to be something bigger than I could imagine.

The weather was still sunny and hot and one afternoon we are given a demonstration of a new rifle-grenade. A young officer had been through a course specially at one of the numerous bombing schools and had just rejoined the battalion again. He was giving a lesson to each company in turn and ours was the first. Being hot, we paraded in shirt sleeves and the site chosen for the demonstration was a hillside already with the corn sheaved and stacked ready for gathering.

So that all could hear and see the better, we were grouped round in a half-circle. The officer was quite a decent chap and he expounded to some length the merits, the why and wherefore of this particular grenade. If he had continued much longer, we would have all been asleep, none of us being stood up, or as a matter of fact, interested in the business at all.

When he announced that he was ready to fire the grenade

we 'sat up and took notice'. It took some little time, whilst the officer very carefully detailed the method of loading, emphasising its destructive powers, etc. At last, he placed the grenade shaft down a rifle-barrel and pointing to some rooks on the corn-stacks about 80 yards away, asked the sergeant-major to fire at them. The SM, with a cigarette between his lips, knelt down with the butt of the rifle resting on the ground and tilting the rifle to the correct angle, pressed the trigger. The rooks took to wing, cawing loudly at the sudden explosion. A young sandy-haired kid next to me sagged forward onto his face, blood trickling from a hole near the temple. Another man was killed outright and a third died of wounds, whilst four were wounded. The grenade had burst prematurely!

The SM who fired escaped miraculously, also the demonstrating officer who stood quite close. Having no jackets, there were no field-dressings!

The two killed were buried next day, and we all attended the burial. The third man to die was buried at Corbie. So ended the rifle-grenade demonstration.

About the 12th August we again moved up a little closer to the line and stayed for one night at Meaulte, a kind of Clapham Junction for road traffic. The place was full of motor-lorries, staff cars and advanced HQs. A most undesirable spot for us infantry.

The next day we again set off, this time leaving the road and going over open downland, which reminded me of the Wiltshire Downs. The only thing that marred the resemblance was that the further we went, the reality that this was not the Wiltshire Downs was manifested everywhere. The earth was scarred with trenches and craters, rusty wire entanglements and the usual litter of empty tins that told of the recent habitation of the British Tommy. We passed a signboard which, recently erected, proclaimed the way 'To Fricourt'.

The thunder of the guns was quite loud and deeper booms, detached from the general noise, proclaimed the nearness of the heavier calibre guns. Coming to a gently sloping hillside, we were halted and later informed that we were to bivouac in the open until further orders. The spot on which we settled down was just behind our old front line of July 1st, the date of the big push, or rather its commencement. We were one side of a valley and as this place was now used as a resting and reserve area, the troops dubbed it 'Happy Valley'.

The view from our encampment was extensive, and as some thousands more troops were scattered about on adjacent hillsides, I marvelled why the enemy didn't put his long-range guns on to us. From our position on the hillside we obtained an unobstructed view towards the battle positions. At night time, it was a spectacle of terrific grandeur that was nigh impossible to describe. From away on the left and to our extreme right it was one unbroken line of vivid lightning from the guns. Battery after battery, field guns, howitzers and long range. Not guns by the dozen, but guns by the hundreds!

I wondered how it was possible for men to live up there amongst an inferno of explosions which never ceased. I was to go up there soon, in fact we all had to go; who of us would return unscathed? How many of us would remain up there for good?

We explored the old German line at Fricourt. The trenches were a good deal knocked about by our artillery and by the size of the craters, mines must have been exploded. We went down one or two dug-outs; they emitted a horrible stench and it was quite sixteen steps down. Holding my nostrils, I saw by our torches the long double row of wire netting beds, tables, chairs, stoves, rifle-racks, equipment pegs, in fact everything for comfort. Rather a contrast to our own dug-out!

Three dead Germans lay at the bottom of the steps; it was they that smelled. It was evident that someone had already explored here and taken anything of value away with them. We hurried up into fresh air again.

The second night in Fricourt, two hundred men were to go up the line to dig a communication trench, roughly 50 men per Company. We fell in at dusk with full fighting order, that is everything except our great-coats or valise. By sections we moved off and, gaining the road, were blended into the gathering darkness with the endless stream of troops, limbers and lorries. Going through Fricourt, we passed over temporary bridges of timber to span the network of trenches.

There was nothing left upright in Fricourt. To mark the site of the village, big boards announced "This was Fricourt". We passed on to Mametz, just another 'was once' of a place. Skirting Mametz wood, we went on to Montauban and drew picks and shovels. Guides now led us over the open and our objective was reached. The men were quickly strung out in a long line and commenced to dig. I had no idea of how far it was from our front line, but as bullets came swishing over our heads, I guessed it was not so very far off.

Rocket lights were constantly shooting up, coming from just over a low ridge to our front. When the lights were flaring, I could only make out the sharp outline of the ridge and a black mass of tree stumps. We stayed until 3 am, during which time the men had dug a good depth. Enemy shells were constantly coming over the whole time, seeking our batteries that were grouped all about us. Fortunately, the noise of our guns drowned the oncoming shriek of German shells. There was one battery directly behind us somewhere, not more than 60 yards, and there was no more nerve-shattering noise than our 18-pounders at close quarters. Every explosion and rush of the shell seemed to loosen our heads a little more away from our shoulders. To be behind a battery is bad enough, but in front is a hundred times worse.

As we were almost ready to return, a big shell managed to wound five men. These were our only casualties and very lucky, too! Marching back to Fricourt without further incident, we crawled into our bivouacs for a few hours rest.

We stayed two more days in 'Happy Valley', then received orders to move up a little further. Everything must have been thoroughly thought out months previously, because our progress from Arras had been gradual and no doubt to a pre-arranged time-table. Very gently, as it were, we found ourselves pushed nearer and nearer. Even in 'Happy Valley' we were on the fringe of the battle area. That night we would penetrate more deeply and perhaps the next day, or the day after, we should be the objective for German gunners!

There was much talk amongst us about what and where and why of the ultimate destiny of the Division. One thing was certain, and that is, a wood or woods of ill-repute awaited us. We heard of High Wood, Trones Wood, Delville Wood, etc, all of them scenes of bitter fighting these last couple of weeks. There was little to choose from as regards this, since the offensive commenced.

At dusk we once again took the road through Fricourt and Mametz. These journeys took a long time at night. We were but a few among many thousands who thronged the main roads to and from 'the Line'. Heavy shelling was going on all around by our guns and the enemy was dumping 'heavy stuff' round Mametz.

Barely two years ago, our army first came into action with guns outnumbered by the Germans by 10 to 1 or thereabouts. Tonight, August 17th 1916, we seem to have enough guns to blow Jerry into kingdom come. The whole earth appears to be belching out flame and steel, making an immense concerto of fury let loose. On the left of the road, on the right, in front, behind, nothing else but Bang! Bang! Boom! Boom! "Poor Fritz", we say, "What a time he's getting".

We reach Montauban again; it is nothing else than a crater-pitted road flanked by heaps of masonry and tree stumps. Striking across country we come upon a long trench (late German) – it has been christened 'Crucifix Alley' by our people. Here we are to stay as immediate support for the time being. We are in another valley of sorts, it has an evil reputation and is dubbed 'Death Valley'. A few acres of jagged tree stumps mark Bernafay and Trones Wood.

There is little chance to sleep, the gunners won't let us. A German shell or shells set fire to a big ammunition dump by Bernafay Wood. The glare lights up the countryside. We are fairly close and explosions take place by the thousand as grenades, S.A.A. and trench-mortar shells blow up.

All through the night we hear the cursing and shouting of drivers urging their teams on over the treacherous ground. There are pitfalls everywhere for the horses and mules as they strain and pull the laden limbers in the darkness. The batteries must be kept supplied with shells at all costs. Guns are hungry things, I have seen great heaps of brass cases behind each battery.

When daylight breaks, I see dead mules and horses dotted about – sometimes singly and two, three or even a complete team in a heap, all bellies and legs where a shell had caught them.

Near Trones Wood lies another heap of bodies. This time they are men, at least a couple of hundred from all regiments. Nearby lie stacks of rifles and equipment gathered up to be used again. Will my rifle and equipment be thrown there, too?

Delville Wood

On the night of the 20th August, we quit our temporary abode in 'Crucifix Alley' trench and go 'overland' towards the firing-line. I mention the term 'overland', because it is customary when going up to the Front to make use of any communication trench whenever possible. However, this method is not possible during a 'show' like The Somme. Trench fortifications are all anyhow and, in the present case, they were once German and, incidentally, much knocked about.

Stumbling along in single file, we gradually mount the rise towards Delville Wood. The one time village of Longueval lays sprawled out, a shattered heap; everything is a grotesque jumble of hideous objects that were once normal. One-time roads can scarcely be recognised, they are shell-pitted and dug across and flanked by trenches. Tree trunks lie at all angles and everywhere.

We follow those in front meekly, tripping up every few paces over things that seem to be put purposely in our way. There is a First Aid Post at the edge of the wood, stretcher-bearers crouch down in their 'cubby holes' wishing us 'Good Luck' and enquiring of us, "What mob mate?"

There are numerous shells exploding around and bullets have the nasty whip-like crack as they pass near. I suppose we have entered the wood now. Fallen trees are thick, whilst the stumps stick up out the earth in thousands.

We are not very optimistic of our future fate, as we stumble along through the wood. This is a charnel house! I had not, up to this moment, walked on and over so many corpses. They lie thick on every hand in every conceivable attitude, and it is nothing else but dust-grimed khaki figures. Fortunately, it is dark and we do not see all. The lights from flares show us quite sufficient.

Finally, we get into a trench that is very shallow and are led into another very rudimentary trench that is the front line. Four days and nights we must remain in this cramped position and then attack.

During the whole of this time we lead a very helpless existence. Here we are wedged in a trench, under continual shelling from the enemy. I don't think he is quite certain of our exact position, as this wood has been a tough nut to crack and positions have altered almost day by day. All we know is that the enemy is still occupying a portion and that on the 24th we are to drive him out, which to the layman seems rather simple.

The weather is unusually warm and the stench at times is overpowering. There are more dead heaped around than at first thought. They belong to all regiments. I notice several South Africans and our regiment, too. The 1st Battalion had already been here and our 2nd Battalion, I think. Very shortly some of us 9th Battalion will be keeping them company. It's a horrible feeling, this waiting to 'go over the top', more so when grim evidence of its folly is so visible.

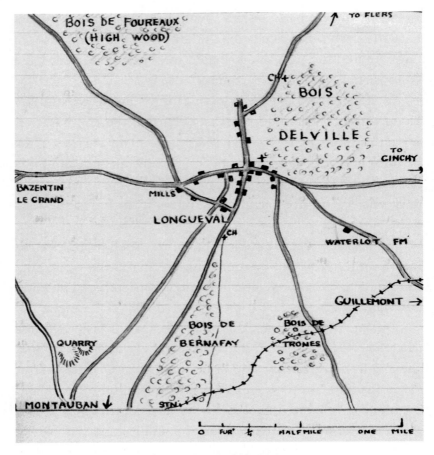

The woods around Longueval

I am sent out twice on patrol. The first night we are almost annihilated by machine guns and grenades. I wish I had been wounded on that occasion! I might have got back safely and sent 'down the line', thereby dodging the attack.

Captain Pukka asks me to go out, remarking that I am accustomed to it! He does not know how far away the enemy were, might only be fifty yards in places, or they may be a hundred and fifty. Anyway, we do not crawl far before the machine gun and hand grenades get us. Six of us go out. Three are killed outright, one wounded; I and the remaining unwounded man get back, helping the wounded chap along. He has caught it in the back somewhere.

The days drag through so slowly – hours do not count. Our lives are not systematic or regular by any means. We do not live by the clock at all. There are no beds or bedtime, there are no meal hours or sitting down to eat at a scheduled time. Very often there is nothing to eat whatever, this depends on the ration - limbers and luck – the food might get blown to smithereens before it's getting to us, in which case we're what is commonly known as 'unlucky'.

Our clothes remain on us for days or perhaps weeks, boots likewise. Here in this wood, named 'Delville', or christened by us as 'Devil's Wood', I am experiencing the full horror of this war more than I have previously done. Bluebottles and a myriad insects cluster round anything that was of the flesh. One can see them on the dead, on stumps of trees, even on the bare earth where, I suppose, blood has splashed.

There are no shelters or dug-outs in this trench, so we stand, sit or lie about in the stifling heat. The old obnoxious nasty taste in the mouth is intensified here. It is chiefly made up of thirst and fumes from explosions. There is a perpetual soot-like taste from the scorched earth made by shell bursts and the acrid smoke.

The day before our attacking, three of us sit, drinking tea that tastes like chloride-of-lime. There is a disinfectant put in the water, which coming up to us in petrol cans, gives off this unpleasant tang to the taste. As we sup the tea, Sgt. Bartlett remarks that it's all U.P. with us this time 'for what Fritz don't put paid to, our artillery will, by dropping their shells short or something.' He's an 'old sweat' from the South African war. Poor chap, he was killed the following evening.

We three are crouched down talking when I feel that my feet are on something pulpy and there was a strong odour about, too. Investigating further, I discover that a dead body lies under us. Earth barely covers it, but the successive trampings have gradually pressed it down flatter and flatter until it has merged in with the trench bottom.

From early dawn on the 24th August, we commence to count the hours to Zero, which is timed for 6 pm that evening. There is much shuffling about to be in our correct 'jumping off' places. No easy matter to move men in a narrow trench. During the morning, after much squeezing and blasphemy, the allotted places are found. Here everyone must stay until the signal lets us 'go over'.

The enemy shell us a good deal and their 'planes fly low over us repeatedly; one drops bombs but misses every time. Our 'planes are constantly overhead, too. There are some rare 'scraps' up above in the blue of the sky.

How the time drags! It is like a condemned man waiting to be executed. Many of us will be killed, that is a foregone conclusion. The question that forever remains unanswered is, Who?

At 6 pm the attack begins. From that fateful hour onwards, perhaps in only five or ten minutes, men will die like flies. It is a thing that cannot be avoided. Men are killed in the ordinary course of trench duty without any attacking or even appearing on the trench top. Therefore, when battalions and whole brigades carry out an assault, this is the opportunity for the defending force to let loose every death-dealing weapon onto them.

We know what to expect from shells, bombs and machine

guns, the latter being our greatest dread. We do not know this war in its general aspect; our ideas and lives are cramped and narrowed down to the few that are our comrades and to the earth we exist in. We infantrymen see and endure the worst possible side of this war. It is we who suffer perpetual bombardments, who are thinned out by bombs, machine guns, mortars, land mines, gas, etc, who live in open grave-like trenches, never knowing when we shall get killed or mutilated. How we envy the other men whose job keeps them behind the trenches. The artilleryman has some degree of latitude and his gun is like a living thing, to be served at all costs. During the height of a bombardment, this must serve as a distraction from brooding on one's personal safety.

The team drivers centre their energy on their mules and horses. The motor drivers are on their lorries, despatch riders on their messages, signallers on their instruments and wires, but we have nothing whatever to distract our minds. We just crouch down, staring at the earthen walls whilst a tornado of explosive whirls overhead.

The afternoon wears on, whilst orders are continually being passed along from man to man. "Captain so-and-so is wanted, pass it along someone". The message is mumbled or shouted from man to man.

"Stretcher bearers wanted by 'B' Coy".

"The CSM is wanted at once".

" 'A' Coy to move along to the left".

The above and similar messages are the only items that make some of us speak.

A young chap near me has been blubbering nearly all day; he will not be comforted by bullying or kindness, he just keeps on quietly crying. Captain Pukka gets it out of him, asks him what's the matter, etc. The poor chap replies that he is certain that he will be killed and the thoughts of his widowed mother mourning him had completely mastered him. The kindly encouragement from us, or from Captain Pukka, fail to rouse him. He persists to the moment of Zero that he is to die and is found later, shot through the head, on top of our own trench.

His forebodings came true. He was one of the first.

The gunners have been very active all day, but at 4 pm they begin to open out proper to prepare the way for our men to

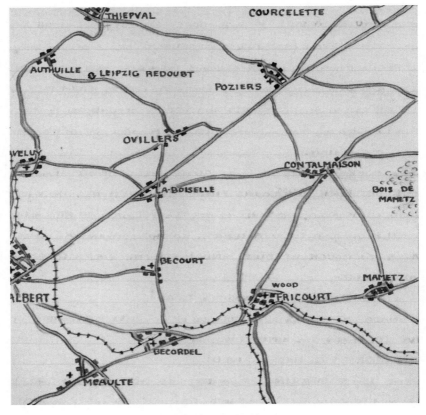

The Somme Battle Area

attack. When I say 'our men', I do not mean just my regiment alone, there is our division taking their share in it, too. Goodness only knows who else is in 'the show' – we are kept in ignorance of any general plan, our fate is that of the regiment we belong to. Outside this does not concern us at all.

The noise of this preliminary bombardment is quite loud enough. It will continue for one hour and forty minutes, then at twenty minutes to six, the fire will be doubled and trebled. At six o'clock the guns will 'lift' onto the German supports and batteries.

Acute nervousness is apparent in all of us. My own stomach seems to be revolving over and over. Wild thoughts rush to my head. Another hour and a half yet to live. Minutes go by, getting closer now, only an hour! The enemy are wide awake, too! Machine guns spray the top of the trench. Big 'woolly bear' shrapnel concertina out above us in thick black smoke, earth and stones shower down, the earth trembles.

Twenty minutes to six! With a mighty, ear-splitting crash, the guns begin the intensified bombardment and a deluge of steel roars down onto the German trenches. The endless concussions and explosions make our ear drums feel as though they will burst. The acrid smoke swirls and eddies around and orders have to be shouted and accompanied by a vigorous thump to attract attention.

Captain Pukka pushes his way along the Company, wishing the men 'Good Luck' and giving final instructions. He wishes me 'Good Luck' also, and this is the last I see of him alive. Although he was a terror to the Company at times, he was a thorough soldier and I, for one, was sorry that he was killed.

We fix bayonets, five minutes to go! The tornado of shells continues, is it possible that men will survive to train machine-guns onto us?

Six o'clock, Zero has arrived!

Everyone is scrambling upwards; some tumble backwards into the trench; others lie crouched forward on the parapet. Bullets ripped into them before they were barely clear of the trench. I wonder vaguely why the man next to me does not get a move on; his legs are sprawled out obstructing my getting clear and my rifle sling gets hooked in his equipment. All this is in a fraction of time, simple incidents seem to stamp themselves firmly in one's memory.

This actual going over is nothing but kaleidoscope of horror upon horror. One's nerves are strung up to such a pitch and one's brain so numbed by the totally abnormal happening taking place that it is impossible to describe truthfully any details. All I remember of that tragic advance is a blurred jumble of terrific explosions, great geysers of earth flung upwards, huge trees uprooted and the crack of the bullets.

Their wire has been smashed flat almost, there is a trench beyond it – we scramble over it. Self preservation is the chief and primary instinct in all humans and my first thoughts are to get down into somewhere, in fact anywhere out of shrapnel and bullets. Following along the parados, or back of the German trench, with several others, we come upon German machine gunners still doggedly scattering death across to our old line. Three of them surrender, but the fourth man persists in firing. There is only one thing to do and it is done quickly – so quickly that Mills bombs riddle the stubborn gunner and the men who cringe with uplifted arms.

I, in common with thousands more, must give tribute to the bravery and doggedness of the enemy's machine-gunners and bombers. These men are undoubtedly the backbone of the German infantry and their bravery cannot be disputed. A machine-gun team can practically decimate a whole battalion with accurate traversing fire.

Tumbling into the trench, we go warily along and meet others of our men. A communication trench is here. Going along this we come to the support trench. Germans dead, wounded and those who have surrendered are everywhere.

A Major of another unit instructs me and the first few men that are handy to consolidate a position and hold it in case of a counter-attack. Among us are some from other regiments; we always get mixed up on these affairs.

Evidence of the destructive fire of our guns is plainly seen on every hand. The earth has been churned to a pulp, and huge craters have almost obliterated the trench. Trees are flung here and there, pell-mell. Dug-outs are blown in and desolation is rampant.

There are about eight Germans cowering down in abject fear. One speaks broken English. He tells us of the awful fire of our artillery. "All day, all night, one week, two week!" he repeats, holding up his fingers to us. Another has shell-shock bad. He hides his face in his arms, blubbering and trembling violently.

There is plenty of 'Pilsner' in bottles to drink. We thought it was beer, but it is water.

Strange as it may seem, none of us take any notice of the German prisoners. We treat them in such an off-hand manner that they must wonder what sort of men we are. They evidently expected a bullying at the very least from us. Instead of this happening, we carry on with our job of consolidating the trench. It is not until this is finished that we take stock of our prisoners.

The one who understands English acts as an interpreter. He is told to "Hop it!" back across to our lines with the others, but they are too frightened to go, in case they are shot down by mistake. None of us can go with them, so they wait placidly watching us get ready to repel any counter-attack.

About 10 pm a Lewis gun and panniers are found lying by their dead one-time owners. This is a welcome addition to our little force. Two or three amongst us have an elementary idea of its working.

Shell splinters wound two of us and one German, all slight wounds. They are bound up and I pack the prisoners off to the rear, under the guidance and supervision of our two wounded; this clearance giving us much-needed room to move.

The dreadful night wears on to the accompaniment of breath-snatching explosions, the rushing shriek of shells, the yellowish flares of rocket lights and the spasmodic bursts of rifle fire. The Major comes again and impresses on me the importance of this position and to hold on at all costs. He takes my name etc, but I hear nothing more of it.

Two of us reconnoitre out in front and find there is no barbed wire. How far the enemy is I cannot make out, so I send a message asking for wire. This is brought up during the night by REs and others and is thrown out anyhow for the time being. The main purpose is for it to be an obstacle to the enemy should he attack.

I marvel at my being alive at all. It is a strange feeling, this reaction after a 'show'. Why is it that I am spared? We do not know yet any details of the success of this operation or who has been killed and otherwise accounted for.

Dawn begins to break and we watch for any sign of a counter-move by the Germans. The light increases and the first rays of the sun pierce upwards behind the clouds. Another hot day for us!

The enemy's gunners get busy, ranging onto his lost

trenches. It is heavy stuff, too, not the erratic firing of excited shooting during a bombardment, but the calculating and systematic lobbing over of shells with the main object of destruction. What a mercy it is that a fraction of an inch will throw a shell too far, or not far enough. If this slight movement didn't occur with the angle of the gun's muzzle, we would all have been wiped out long ago.

Later in the day, I go exploring along the trench to the left and the right. All along, our own men are mixed in with other regiments. Lots of dead Germans have been heaved up over the top until such time as they can be buried. There are numerous of our own dead, too. I recognise some of my Company and other Companies. These have been laid out in any convenient place under reasonable cover from further mutilation. It is hard to believe that these pitiable khaki clad figures were, a few hours previously, alive and our chums of trench and billet.

Oh well, I think, I am alive by a miracle, but my regimental number is inscribed on a bullet or shell yet to be fired.

This has been a day of heat and shelling. Many who came through the attack have been hit since. Our planes fly low to obtain contact and to know our exact forward position; this will be passed onto our gunners who, even now, may be dropping shells on us in error.

About 4 pm the message comes that my regiment, or rather what remains of it, will assemble at 'Crucifix Alley' trench, which we had left five days ago. NCOs or senior riflemen to round up all the men possible and make their way back independently to that point. No time having been stated, we hang on, or in army parlance 'sweated'. We successfully 'sweat' through another night waiting the order, during which the Germans heavily counter-attacked towards 'High Wood'.

The next day about 11 o'clock, the eagerly awaited order is sent for us to "Hop it!" Collecting up the few men round about, we set off in pairs, but before doing so I take all names in case any are hit on the journey. I also have a list of our dead, and a long list, too. We carry their pay-books and identity discs.

Being broad daylight the going back is very unhealthy. There is no communication trench, over the open is the only way. I marvel at first that we are not shot down, as the enemy must see us.

It is impossible to hurry; we have had but little to eat or drink for five days with scarcely any sleep. Vaguely, I see the still figures of our dead sprawled on the ground. We shall need plenty of new material to make good the losses!

As a matter of fact I do not care much if I am hit. I am past caring, physically and mentally; it has to come sooner or later, can't escape it forever!

Trudging along over the ghastly corpse-strewn earth, we seem to be totally oblivious of shell bursts or anything else, until we finally reach our rendezvous.

The Company cookers are up this far and we eagerly sup hot tea and eat bully-stew. Afterwards there follows the most poignant parade in a soldier's life, and it happens in this war all too frequent. I refer to the muster or 'roll-call' after an attack. My Company has lost all officers, six sergeants, three corporals, seven 'lance Jacks' and about seventy-odd men. The CSM, who did not go into the show, is almost overcome with emotion as he asks for name after name.

CHAPTER ELEVEN

A walk in the sun

We rest until dusk, then a sad remnant of a battalion marches back to 'Happy Valley' again. Nevertheless, we have not gone far before the old unquenchable spirit asserts itself and the men begin to whistle and sing, fling jokes and cheery 'Good Lucks' to those we pass. Reaching 'Happy Valley' we are again on the hillside, able to watch the cauldron which we had just left behind.

The following day we are paid out and I buy some tinned rabbit. We suffer for this; I and others keep vomiting and have a touch of colic. The MO gives us the inevitable pills and tells us it is slight potomine poisoning. How we cursed that 'canned bunny'.

Later on we go further back to Méaulte, staying two days, then into Albert.

There is an unusual honour awaiting us at Albert. We are to leave in the first train from the main station since 1914! The whole town is a shambles from one end to the other and I see the statue of the Virgin suspended perilously from the top of the battered steeple. When I mention the station, I only mean a station in name, for it is a replica of Arras or any other station near the fighting line. However, the French engineers and our own had packed up the permanent way to allow the passage of trains at a slow speed.

We pile ourselves into the goods trucks and the train slowly puffs out of Albert with the Union Jack and tricolour on the engine. Here is a slowly changing panorama for all to view. Albert with its demolished buildings and the tall church spire dominating them. The River Ancre flows placidly alongside the railway. Away to our front rise the low hills round Fricourt and Mametz, whilst in the distance is the ridge crowned by High Wood and Delville Wood, but veiled in smoke. Up in the sky are 'blimps'; the suspended observation baskets are mere dots. All spare ground that we pass and as far as we can see, are troops and transport. There are troops at rest, or waiting to go up the line. Bivouacs, hutments, tents, marquees, countless limbers and GS wagons, thousands of picketed horses and mules, whilst the roadsides are thick with parked motor lorries with a never-ceasing procession of transport in between.

Slowly the countryside changes from an armed camp into the unspoiled green of tree and meadow, of workers toiling in the fields, cattle and sheep peacefully grazing and villages untouched by high explosive. Through Corbie and Amiens and on to a small country town some 45 kilometres from Albert.

From the station, we march about 4 kilometres to a small village, the name I forget, I suppose it was a Saint something, or ended in 'court' or 'ville'. It is the 29th August and we are to stay at least 10 days.

On arrival I feel very hungry. Our transport has not come up yet, so I forage for grub in the village. It is a very small place and has not had British troops before, so the villagers were unprepared. There is a small shop and all I succeed in getting is a tin of 'petits pois' and half a loaf. Returning to our billet, I buy some fresh milk. Tipping the peas into the milk and dipping the bread in to soften it, I consume the lot, finishing up by eating apples, which are abundant. A short while after my tummy seems to be swelling and I have to lie down until this queer menu has digested somewhat.

During this so called 'rest', fresh drafts from the base join us. They are mostly in the 'raw' and do not seem to know much about soldiering, let alone warfare. Some have not been 'joined up' more than three months and can scarcely handle a rifle in ordinary drill.

One day we are being mucked about in a meadow by a newly-joined subaltern. "On the left, form this" or "On the right, form that". "Halt!" "Quick march!" "Mark time!" "Left, right, left, right!", etc. I am in one of my rebellious moods and hot anger is bubbling up at this playing at soldiers, when a few days ago we were mixed up in a death-trap of a wood on the Somme.

What I actually said or did on this parade I don't quite remember, but I am led off by the CSM and put on a sick report. The MO looks into the pupils of my eyes and makes me extend my arms forward with fingers extended. He looks for tremors, I suppose, although I feel perfectly normal. He tells me it's a bit of a 'brainstorm' and that my nerves are shaken up a bit, and asks me if I have been drinking much. I say no – but I had! He tells me to keep quiet, read books and not think of the war whilst in rest billets and I get 'excused all duties'. I am asked if I would care to go with a small fatigue party collecting fresh water in motor lorries round different villages. This is just to my liking, and we have a splendid six days touring around in circles.

Back to the Somme

September 1916

On September 9th our orders were to pack up and march to the little station we had so recently arrived at. There was some doubt about our ultimate destination, but I had gathered sufficient information to know that the Somme battle area would once more receive us into its bosom.

As the train wended its way, we got the reverse in our views now. Peacefulness was gradually giving place to military activity. From isolated figures in khaki and horizon blue, or occasional motors with officers, etc, the khaki grew into groups and the motors into convoys, with clouds of dust along the poplar-lined roads. Passing Amiens, we all knew where we should finish, except of course, the new joined drafts.

We detrained at Mericourt and marched up to Méaulte for one night. The next day we bivouacked in the open between Albert and Becordel. I was told that I would not take part in the coming attack, really good news indeed! It was the custom now to leave behind a few NCOs and men who were seniors or old members of the battalion. The object of this was to ensure that a small nucleus could help to make a battalion up again with new drafts. Our CSM didn't go up at Delville Wood, but he went this time and I remained a spectator, as it were.

On the 13th September the Brigade moved off again to a place between Mametz and Guillimont. At this spot everyone bivouacked in the open until orders came for them to move again nearer the Line.

There were strange and persistent tales of a weird iron monster that would make its debut on the 15th, a regular surprise packet for the Germans. In fact, we heard that there was more than one of them. The tale was that they would knock down trees or houses, jump ditches, climb anything, and were well armed. We had not the remotest idea of what they were like. All I could imagine was an armed steam tractor or a motor lorry surrounded by armour. When I did get a look at one during the night of 14th Sept, it was something so grotesque and malformed as to surprise me, never mind the Germans. It looked like a huge prehistoric monster as it rested by the roadside, well screened with broken tree foliage.

At daybreak on the 15th Sept the whole of the earth about us erupts in flames, smoke and the reverberation of hundreds of guns paving the way for our chaps and the 'tanks'. I am merely a looker-on in this 'show', but I am the better able to appreciate the tremendous happenings. The regimental transport is tucked away in a fold of the ground and must take its chance from the German shells which begin to drop about us; they are hoping to catch our batteries, which continue to fire quite unperturbed.

The whole ridge by Delville Wood – High Wood and to the right by the village of Ginchy is wreathed in drifting smoke. Looking through glasses, the long waves of little khaki figures can be seen moving up to the crest of the ridge. Explosions vomit up black smoke and earth amongst them. Big ugly black and yellow shrapnel opens out as by some magic above them, but it does not seem to make any difference. As fast as the little figures are swallowed up in the curtain of smoke, so another line follows, wave upon wave on about a 3,000 yards frontage.

Then we see the 'things'. There is no mistake, the lumbering ungainly objects are the 'tanks'. They seem to waddle along up to the crest of the ridge. They were evidently moved up quite near, early this morning. We see them dip their noses, like ships in a trough of the sea, disappear for a few seconds, then poke their snouts up straight and climb onto level ground.

I see two, but no more. What will the Jerries think of these iron monsters, eh? There is a bundle of little figures who alternately seem to scatter out and away from the tanks, then bunch in close to them. Gradually, the tanks and their attendants top the ridge and are merged into the smoke of the shells.

We continue to watch long after the assault is launched; it is something both dreadful and grand. We are anxious to know how our lads are faring, all those practically raw material of the citizen army that joined us a bare fortnight ago.

The big 6 in and 8 in Howitzers near us are belching up high into the air their huge projectiles. This is the first time I have ever seen a shell in flight. Howitzers have a very high angle of fire and the missile, therefore, a very high trajectory. On the other hand field pieces throw the shells at a very much lower angle and at a much greater velocity. It is impossible for the keenest sight to detect a field gun's shell in flight.

A 'Tank' in action, Sep 15ᵗʰ 1916

Howitzers are primarily useful to smash and demolish anything that is providing shelter for the enemy, such as trenches and all they harbour – enemy batteries, roadways, railways, buildings, etc. Trench mortars are nothing else than howitzers in miniature. It is interesting to watch the work of the guns and we bet with fags on seeing each shell in flight.

After some time has elapsed, it may have been two, three or more hours from the commencement of the attack, a procession is coming towards us – they are Germans, sixty or more. A motley crowd of poor devils, unshaven, hollow-eyed, gaunt, some with slight wounds, some bareheaded, others with the round forage caps or 'coal-scuttle' steel helmets. As they straggle by, we fling them 'fags'.

We Britishers are a strange people! By all the laws of humanity, we ought to vent our spite on this tatterdemalion crowd of Jerries, now that they are at our mercy. Instead of this we want to shake hands, or a feeling very much akin to it. We are genuinely sorry for them. Perhaps it is a reciprocal feeling of 'brothers in distress'. They are the 'cannon fodder' of the German army – we, likewise, are the same thing on our side. Being flung at each other under the iron hand of militarism and unable to choose any other course in this war is neither our fault nor theirs. The Germans who we really wished to see wiped off the map were artillerymen, machine-gunners, minnewerfer crews and snipers – all these were the bane of our lives, and the more of these that were killed, the better it was for our future existence.

The news that filters back to us about the attack is, as usual, of much variation. Progress had been made all along the line. The 'tanks' had put the fear of God into the Jerries and quite natural, too! The village of Ginchy had been captured and our chaps were pressing on beyond the village. As the day wears on, nothing definite is really known of how the operations had progressed.

German prisoners and our wounded keep filtering back in groups, the former to be guided to the cages and the latter to field dressing stations. Other groups are continually coming; they are stretcher parties with the badly wounded. Sometimes it requires four men to carry the stretcher over the trenched and cratered ground.

At night we are to go up to the Line with rations and water; this is a nasty task during a 'strafe'. However, everyone is willing enough to try and get food and water up to the 'boys' in the Line.

All the food is, for convenience, put into clean sand-bags and the water into petrol tins. Setting off about 8 pm, it takes two hours to reach a selected spot chosen for us to hand over the rations.

The Germans are shelling, rather heavily, all roads and likely means of communication to our front-line. It is a marvel nobody is hit. We hear news of how the battalion is faring. Our CO, Colonel Eric Benson, was killed. Capt. this or Capt. that also killed. Lieut. so-and-sos in profusion killed, missing or wounded! It is the usual tale of a regiment's sudden reduction in personnel and the obvious outcome of a daylight frontal attack.

Delville Wood 1916

Going back to our transport, we spend another day watching a skyline of shell-bursts, until the brigade is relieved. We move across to Montauban with Cookers boiling up to give tea and rum to the men. When they do begin to come back, it is by sections and platoons, or what is left! There is not much talking until all have satisfied themselves with the welcome hot tea, etc.

The new drafts bear themselves admirably, but they seem to have suffered the brunt of the casualties. They will persist in grouping up into bunches, making an easy target. They also begin to 'crowd' towards the 'tanks'. These things are the special target of hostile artillery and infantry and, therefore, a perfect death-trap to all near them.

Our Colonel, Eric Benson, went into action leading the Battalion the whole time, until he was killed. He displayed that wonderful courage and 'sang-froid' that made British officers the envy of all, and carried a cane as though out in the English countryside for a ramble. The casualties amounted to about 30% of the regiment.

I am unable to account for all that happened on that day as I did not take an active part, but I do know that the 'tanks' were an unqualified success and were, in some measure, instrumental in the capture of Ginchy and a good deal of enemy ground.

For the second time, we again leave 'Crucifix Alley' and Bernafay and go back to 'refit', staying one night in bell tents behind Fricourt, thence on to bivouacs near Albert, being held in divisional reserve for a couple of days.

Going still further back to a place near Dernancourt, we await orders, which may mean anything or anywhere from the Somme to Ypres at a moment's notice.

About the 20th Sept French mortar lorries, driven by both French and native French troops, are drawn up in a long line to transport us to another front. The ride is uncomfortable but pleasant; it doesn't particularly matter what inconvenience is suffered, so long as we are going in the right direction.

Reaching Bouquemaison, a stay of about two days is made and it is here that I meet my 'Waterloo'.

In this war, the most natural thing to do, whenever opportunity offers, is to enjoy oneself to the best of one's ability. This I never failed to do and to the best of my resources!

Big Shells Exploding

Naturally, the scope offered was very limited and five franc notes were scarce, too scarce indeed! There were no theatres or picture houses or any similar place to go for a few hours diversion. We infantry were never lucky enough to be billeted in a town possessing these things.

Invariably, and almost without exception, we found ourselves dumped in little villages or scattered farmsteads. The 'gay-life' was absolutely taboo! Women and wine were as far removed from our lives as the poles are apart.

Returning to these places from up the line was indeed a contrast. There was nothing to distract our minds, when it was most needed. All we could do was sit about in draughty barns or wander about aimlessly, with the trenches as the dominating terror to brood about. There was only one remedy, to try and forget, and that meant to get inside any house or village estaminet and get some 'booze'. I do not stand alone in this matter, I am sure!

The weather was beautiful and sunny, the Somme was finished with for us as far as we knew. We were going back up to Arras shortly and, moreover, any one of us may be killed in a few days' time, and we all possessed a few five franc notes. So, obviously, the only thing to do was to spend them and try to enjoy life for a few hours. This, some of us proceeded to do, which ended up rather differently than I imagined.

A skyline view on the Somme

On the day this happened, the 'High Command' has come to
the sudden decision to move us. Had this not happened, all
would have been well. I and two more sergeants discover a little
cottage where an obliging madame 'lushes' us up with eggs
and chips, named by the troops as 'oofs and bombardier fritz',
a bad corruption of the French 'oeufs et pommes de terre'.

It is our usual custom to order a meal of some kind first,
then follow this up by tactful manoeuvres until madame or
mademoiselle has sufficiently thawed down to bring us out
what we want. In this case it is good Malaga wine and vin

blanc. How many we consume, I forget, but we are nice and happy and that was all that matters.

One sergeant leaves us; he is the orderly 'buff stick' and cannot stay. I and the remaining sergeant continue to drink in blissful ignorance of the impending move of the regiment. We are brought back to realities by the sudden appearance at the door of a man who has been sent by the orderly sergeant that had recently left us. The man informs us that everyone is to parade in half an hour's time to move.

Turning this information over in our minds, we come to the conclusion that the war is still on and, moreover, that this sudden order can only mean a return to the Somme again. If this is the case, there's time to swallow another glass or two of wine, and this we do. Then, bidding a hiccoughy kind of farewell, we blunder out into the dazzling sunlight.

My pal makes his way to his billet and I to mine. Everybody seems to be getting ready – some have equipment on. Reaching the billet, the lads urge me to hurry – they have gathered together my rifle and other gear and willing hands harness me up. All being ready, we fall in and march out to the main road. Everything so far has gone off A1. Nobody has tumbled my condition except the men, and like the good fellows they are, they help to screen me as much as possible. I know full well that I have had one 'over the eight', but when one is in this unfortunate predicament, it is nothing short of a miracle if not discovered.

The fresh air and sunlight are the culminating point for me and this, coupled with the nervous strain of the Somme, 'knocks me over' as the saying is. The road seems to be dancing up and down, the houses and trees sway dizzily and I seem to see motor lorries and steel helmets all mixed up in a jumble.

First we go up the road, then down again, shuffling about

from one lorry to another. The men whisper hoarsely to me what to do: "Forward, Sarge" or "This way, Sarge", until, I suppose, I don't hear their good advice and wander off on my own.

This procedure calls down the wrath of the gods on my head. The adjutant and RSM have seen me! I am upbraided by them and I reply suitably, or rather, unsuitably, and am placed in arrest, put into a lorry with an escort, where I promptly sleep the whole journey.

We are taken to Bernville again. I desire nothing more than sleep, as my head is aching rather! The CSM comes to see me, calls me a b———y young fool and gives me advice for the morrow, and that is to plead guilty to being drunk.

The next day I awake a sober and wiser man to face the CO. This procedure is very formal and doesn't last long. The Battalion HQ is an ordinary house and the CO's 'office' is outside, consisting of a table and a couple of chairs.

A Major is acting in place of Colonel Benson who was killed. My offence is read out in the usual manner, "Whilst on active service, etc, etc". Acting on previous advice I plead 'guilty'. The Major then gives me a lengthy talking to and sound advice. Among other things, I learn that the Brigadier and his entire staff were in the village when we were being marshalled into the lorries and that the Brigadier Major saw me floundering about like a ship without a rudder, that it was a most unfortunate thing for me that the Brigadier Major had such keen vision and that there was nothing else for it at the time but to place me in arrest, that the late Company Officer, Captain Pukka, had submitted an excellent report about me. That had this affair not happened, I would in all probability had an offer of taking a commission! That I was an excellent NCO in the trenches and that I have the option of two courses:

revert to the rank and file, or in other words, 'dip three stripes', or, secondly, face a FGCM.

I have previously made up my mind about this and I give up my stripes there and then. I remember that, as I cut them off with a jack knife, I would have dearly liked to slit the Brigadier Major's gizzard, too!

They tell me that from now on, I shall be attached to HQ Company. 'Staff job', I think. Already!

At night, we are to go up the line and take over "F" and "G" sectors.

The other sergeant escaped scot free. He had to stay behind in Bouquemaison and follow later with baggage, lucky beggar!

German shells exploding near Thiepval

I suppose the effect of losing stripes on anyone is all according to a man's temperament. Some would take it to heart, whilst others would promptly forget it. Although in my case I never let the incident worry me to the extent of it being an obsession, I was sorry that I had lost them and more so in such simple circumstances. Everyone said I was unlucky that day and if it hadn't been for the hawkeyed 'brass-hat' I, no doubt, would have 'got away with it'.

However, as I have said, I was not one to grieve and I quickly adapted myself to the situation. One thing, there will be less weight to carry with three stripes less. The fat was in the fire and I must make the best of it.

As darkness settled down, the battalion fell in and marched towards the line. It seemed strange to me at first to 'number off' with the others and 'form-fours'. The thing I most missed was the company. But HQ were a decent lot, which compensated me a little.

A rifleman once again

Reaching 'Achicourt', the road leads away from our old familiar trenches in "H" sector. Bearing to the right, we pass into a communication trench that brings us to the semblance of a hamlet, with the undignified name of 'Agny', known to us hereafter as 'Agony'.

My job is Bath-Attendant! It's rather hard to believe, nevertheless it is so. Actually, baths within a stone's throw of the first line trench!

I am duly initiated into its mysteries by the man I relieve. He is not very thorough in detailing things. He seems in a desperate hurry to 'op it and in staccato bursts of talking, I glean a little knowledge. This is a sample of his speech:

"Ulloa mate, come to take this job over?"

"Been down the Somme yet? Rotten b———-y 'ole aint it?"

"There's some coal and coke, where's me b——— rifle?"

"Look out for smoke, or yer won't want any more baths".

"What division are yer? There's the steam gauge, got a fag?"

"Stoke up during darkness, but look out for sparks".

"War can't last much longer, where's me tin 'at gorn?"

"Well, so long mate, the mob's awaiting of me I expect'.

He vanishes out into the darkness, leaving me to solve the baths question on my own. I find the small boiler, which is of the geyser pattern. Also, a small stock of coal, but there is plenty of coke to use. As for water, there is a cistern handy and a hand pump connected up with a well. Everything is quite simple, all I have to do is keep the fire going and replenish the boiler and cistern. The REs had run off pipes along the ceiling and, attached at intervals, about half a dozen water can sprayers. Duck-boards serve as gratings to stand on and the ventilation caused by shells has been draped with sacking.

Supports moving up during the Somme Battle

This bath job is not at all bad. There is not much time lost before the first arrivals come in from the line. It is good to watch and hear them as they stand under the sprays, busily lathering themselves all over, joking and laughing as though the war were non existent, instead of the Germans being but a 1000 yards away.

I come in for a good deal of good natured chaff and I am still the 'sarge' when they address me.

When refuelling the fire, I keep dashing outside to see if any smoke is visible to Fritz, as I had been told that if shelling gets dangerous, to abandon the place, also anybody else if they were bathing.

Outside the door a trench runs along to the communication trench where there is a 'First-Aid' Post. This is very convenient, should we get 'bumped' at any time. An old wagon with one sound wheel lies just outside the door, it had once been part of a barricade in 1914.

There is ample opportunity for me to read, but it is difficult to get English books. Going round the HQ billets, I manage to get hold of various English papers and I learn more about the Somme and the war in general than I had done for some time.

There is no sentry duty for me or fatigues to do and I get all night off and can 'anchor down' if I choose. Some nights I go up to the Line and visit my old Company. Everyone is glad to see me on these occasions and I suffer a good deal of leg-pulling, such as, "Who's ever heard of a bath-attendant in the trenches?", etc.

The period spent at Agny was similar to most parts of the line during normal trench-duty periods. The time spent in the line was about six-days and the 'rest' period found us back at Dainville for a few days.

My 'baths' do a roaring trade and are patronized by all and sundry – officers included. Everything goes off A1 and Fritz does not injure us very much, although I am constantly on 'pins and needles' about the smoke. One day shells do fall uncomfortably close. There are quite a dozen men in various stages of nudity at the time and the first warning we get is the displacing of several tiles, accompanied by the angry roar of the explosions. The noise from the chaps talking, whistling, etc drowns the sound of the oncoming shells. About three minutes later we are again disturbed by two more explosions which shake the rickety building. This is followed by still more shells that seem to miss us by a mere hair's breadth.

Everyone makes a wild rush for their clothes. Some are stark naked and half lathered. Quickly, they slip boots on only and, to the sound of still further explosions, we rush out into the trench and dive into a dug-out for protection.

The shells now are pitching further over. We know what they are after, there is a battery of 18 pounders hidden. No doubt an enemy's spotter 'plane is up somewhere directing the fire. With what luck we don't know, but every few minutes the whole six 18 pounders would bark out their defiance, although the Germans seemed to be dropping their shells right on them.

After allowing a reasonable time to elapse, during which I get accused of drawing the enemy's fire with the smoke from my baths, we all go back to them again and the men carry on soaping themselves as though nothing had happened to disturb them.

I often go to the Company Cookers to yarn and, incidentally, scrounge anything that is to be had in the way of eating.

The front is fairly quiet here, but our old sectors to our left are much livelier. Staying in Agny for a few weeks, we go into Arras for a 'rest period'. I am sorry to lose my bath-attendant's job and I return to 'the boys' for duty.

The 'Baths' in Agny, SE of Arras

Our 'rest' is, in common with all other 'rests', a farce. The real place for a rest is the trenches, providing it is a quiet sector. As we are in Arras, there won't be any drill, unless we do it at night, or manoeuvre about the rooms by daytime. However, to keep us occupied during the next couple of weeks, a job has been found up at St Nicholas and Roclincourt. A communication trench is to be widened to allow the passage of a light railway track, such as those used by builders or road makers. The gauge is about a foot or 18 inches wide and the trolleys propelled by hand. The battalion is split up in various shifts for this purpose and the actual working time about six hours a day. Being November, we don't mind; the work it keeps us warm and it's a change from the usual routine. The place is roughly NE of Arras and new ground to us; it is not far from Vimy Ridge. Starting off about 8 am and getting back to billets about 3 pm is the usual time. The march occupies about forty-five minutes each way.

Winter is rapidly approaching again and there are some hard frosts at night, converting everything into frost-coated whiteness. Even rusty old barbed wire and supporting stakes

Infantry moving in the shelter of ruins

lose some of their grimness when 'Jack Frost' covers them. Our shovels and picks are stored at a 'dump', which is a shell of a one-time estaminet; a splintered board still bears those magic words over the door. Each of us takes a pick or shovel going up to work and flings it back again on the return.

In a very few days the trench is considerably widened. So far, the enemy's guns have not interrupted us, due no doubt to the misty and dull weather when the artilleryman gives the trenches a little rest. I do not mean that the guns cannot fire at all owing to mist. On the contrary, they could keep on blazing off if they so choose, by the map and onto any already ranged target. The only point of their doing so is that the result of such shooting cannot be seen.

One fine morning everyone is busy either talking or working. The Front is fairly quiet and the furthest thing from our minds is getting 'crumped' by shells. However, the appearance in the sky of various 'planes and the attendant balls of shrapnel from the 'Archies' ought to have given us some inkling that the 'planes may be out 'spotting' for the guns. We never take the war in the air very seriously, it is something apart and distinct from us, who are forever in the earth. Their job is up above, and how they do it is no concern of ours. We seldom look to see if the 'planes are ours or Jerry's. They all look the same high up in the sky and besides, if they are Jerry's we can't stop them from coming over.

The first warning we have is salvos of shrapnel from "whiz bangs" which, although close, inflict no material damage. Naturally we all down tools and flee for cover, which cannot be found. Later, we again make a start to work again, but not for long.

Once more the whistling shriek and simultaneous Bang! of

the "whiz bangs", then on top of this the menacing whine and drone of bigger stuff. This rapidly changes to a roar as the shells swoop down on us and explode with a shattering Crash! Over they come, roaring and shrieking to burst all about us.

The enemy has spotted us, either from above or from Vimy Ridge. It is everyone for himself! Casting aside my shovel, I and another chap bolt like scared rabbits. Others are wildly rushing to and fro seeking any sort of cover.

There seems to be none whatever to be had, so we two decide to get out on top. This, in a sense, will be safer than where we are. Scrambling up, we dash wildly across to what looks like another trench about 50 yds away. Reaching it without any harm, we literally fall into it and are thankful for small mercies. After recovering our wind, we smoke the inevitable 'fag' and watch the shelling, at the same time wondering as to the fate of our comrades. A big shell lands squarely onto the 'dump' where baulks of timber and stacks of rails, etc are. Amidst the black smoke we see the sections of rails, bent like snakes, go sailing up into the air.

When the bombardment subsides we go back to view the damage. The work of many days is ruined in as many minutes. The trench sides are blown in and there was, most fortunately, nobody killed, but five men are wounded. Our casualties would have been much heavier had we been actually holding the line, but as things were, we were able to abandon the place for the time being.

The following days are spent in 'shaping up' the damaged trench, but we never finish the job by a long way as we are due to leave Arras once more.

During 'off duty' times we manage to amuse ourselves somehow. First and foremost is bodily cleanliness, and I seldom met a fellow who was not constantly seeking for 'chats' or body-lice. These disgusting parasites are the natural outcome of overcrowding and lack of clean underclothes. We are as powerless to prevent them as to prevent the Germans from shelling us. The only obvious thing to do is to try one's utmost to keep them in check by constantly raiding their 'strongholds', which are situated chiefly in the seams of one's clothing, such as the fork of the trousers, under the armpits, the chest and collar. I have burnt a whole candle out going along all seams most diligently, besides cracking the stray members between my thumbnails, but in spite of this I was never at any time free from them.

Another item is mending our khaki. We are compelled to do this, because the stuff would expose parts of our anatomy which we would sooner keep under cover. As I have already mentioned, clothing is difficult to get and some of our khaki would be scorned by a ragman. Shirts were worn until almost threadbare and the repeated washings when in billets and the 'strafing' for lice has reduced their serviceable qualities to nil.

Some of us read, when there is anything to read. We play Pontoon or Nap and pitch coins called 'Up the Line'. There may be a mouth organ or two amongst us, this being the largest instrument we could find room for without losing them. Letter writing is another feature of billet life. Some can scribble off pages in a very short time, while others will sit meditating and pondering with the stub of an indelible pencil between their teeth. They usually get as far as "Dear so-and-so" and are then stuck for want of the literary gift to carry on further. In isolated cases some poor chaps are unable to read or write. One can imagine the task of reading a letter that perhaps contained bad news.

Arras: Ruins of the Hôtel de Ville and Cathedral, 1915

In Arras itself a certain percentage of estaminets remained open for the use of the troops. Specified times were allotted, generally two hours in daytime and two at night. These places were kept shuttered day and night and were packed to suffocation during opening hours. I did my share in them, like all the rest. It was, after all, the only real forgetfulness or distraction we had. During these two hours the chief object was to dispose of as much vin blanc etc as the funds allowed. The general plan for us was to pool our resources on an equal share-out basis – there never was any dispute on this matter.

If one had ten francs and another only two, or was even quite 'broke', it was just the same. The songs and choruses of any old ditty were let rip with the utmost of one's vocal powers. 'M'selle From Armentieres', 'One-Eyed Riley', 'Oh! Oh! I Don't Want To Die', 'Broken Doll', 'If You Want To Find The Sergeant' and a host of others.

"Red Caps" or military police were on duty in Arras. Their main job was the regulation of transport and the supervision of the military population, such as the rounding up of stragglers or any other unauthorised persons who wandered about. I don't think that the average English line regiments gave any trouble, but colonial troops were difficult to manage, once they got the notion to 'go wild' and when they did, discipline went by the board. They could never understand us saluting or addressing an officer as 'sir', or of putting up with the iron ring of discipline as we do.

Arras was simply an armed camp. It is amazing the number that seemed to swarm out of every nook and cranny after dark. During daylight the place was apparently deserted. If any movement took place it was almost unnoticeable, as everyone must creep along right under the houses and in single file.

Having finished our allotted work up at Roclincourt, the battalion went back to a village near Duisans for a few days and, whilst here, I was told off for another staff job and again found myself with H.Quarter Company.

The newest idea of the General Staff was active co-operation of infantry units with GHQ with regard to 'intelligence'. The idea is that each unit would train a few men for 'O' PIP work (observing). I don't know if I looked any more 'intelligent' than my comrades, but if this was the case, I didn't feel any more 'brainy' than the rest.

Battalion snipers were also formed at the same time and the two were merged into one under the supervision of an officer, who was known as 'Brains'. Three of us were picked for 'observers' and about a half-dozen for snipers and we underwent our initial training whilst at this village. The use of the Baring-Stroud Range Finder was taught us, also map reading in general. I managed to secure full points on map drawing, but my two chums were hopeless. I may add that a certain district having been given us to sketch at half an inch to a kilometre, I went into a nearby estaminet and copied it roughly from a map on the wall. With this in my pocket we traversed the route and on reaching billets, I rapidly copied from my sketch, adding a few details. My chums, having failed in the main subject, were relegated back to join the snipers, whilst two more were found to fill their places. The three of us being suitable, we were sent to a battery of artillery for five days' instruction.

The battery was an 18-pounder field gun outfit and they were in position near Ronville, a suburb of Arras. There were twelve of us altogether, three from each battalion in our brigade.

Our instructors were rather confusing as we seemed to be learning more of the intricate manipulation of an 18 pounder than of observing, which is what we were there for. However, the gunners were fine fellows, who never failed to impress on us the value of their support to us poor infantrymen!

The various OPIPs were revealed to us in all manner of queer places, amongst ruins and in earthworks. We learned all about trench-maps, the use of the protractor and the method of quickly ascertaining a desired spot on the map. Trench maps were issued for each separate sector of the Front from the North Sea to the Somme and were continually being revised.

A map of a sector was on a scale of at least 12" to the mile and was divided into about a dozen squares, all of which were numbered. These were again sub-divided into smaller squares, there being about 36 to equal one numbered or large square, so that all together a complete map consisted of 36 large squares and 1,296 smaller ones, these being numbered from 1 to 36 along the top and sides. The method of working one of these maps was very simple, but some fellows could not make 'top nor tail' of them.

The five days was most instructive, but I think that what interested me the most was the gunners and their battery. The delicate method of adjusting the time fuses of the shells was a source of wonder to me. Also, the ranging by the clock method. At night time each battery had a little lamp about 50 yards ahead of the guns. This was a kind of guide, and each of the six guns was able to range right or left of this light. Needless to mention, these lights were quite invisible from a few feet in front.

Having gained an elementary idea of all that was required for our future duties, we bid farewell to the gunners and rejoined our respective units. My battalion was at Dainville and two days afterwards we went once more to Agny or 'Agony'.

We of the 'brains' were with HQ, and therefore stayed in billets instead of going into the trenches. The OC, the Adjutant, the RSM, our own Officer and us three men all went to inspect the OPIPs on our own sector. There were originally two, but one had got rather badly 'crumped', so there was but one left for us to use. Taking it in turns, the short winter's day was split up between us.

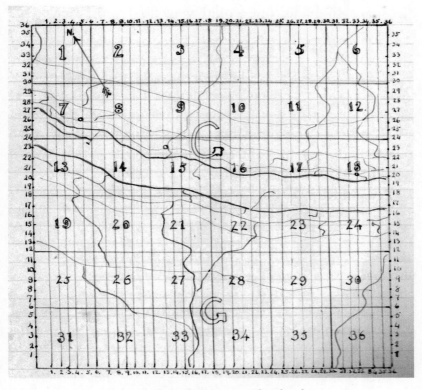

A typical trench map on a reduced scale

The place to be used was a partly-demolished house, situated about 700 yds behind our front line. The actual OP was up in the tiles and the means of reaching it was by ordinary ladders, in the absence of the staircase, which had been knocked down by a shell. Most windows had gone the same way, also doors, flooring and the greater part of the roof. The actual OP was cunningly concealed behind the few remaining tiles, undoubtedly the work of the REs. It was a box-like arrangement draped with dark cloths and paper. Just under the sloping roof was a flat table-like affair, whilst immediately on a line of a person seated, one tile was missing and through the space it made, one could view that most delectable landscape of No-Man's-Land and the wastes that encompassed it.

A trench map was spread out on the table – it was similar to the above and about two foot square. A telescope and field glasses were provided to 'spot the Boche', also a field telephone, a protractor and a compass to set the map true. To complete all, a watch, notebook and indelible pencil put the concluding items to the stock-in-trade of an observer.

Being novices at the work, we did not get much peace for the first few days. There was a constant procession from the CO down to inquisitive 'Tommies', who pleaded to "have a squint at the b——— Jerries". However, the newness ultimately wore off and we three could do our 'squinting' in peace. Being perched up in a fragile sort of box, at the top of a house that had lost most of its solidness and just a few tiles between you and stray bullets, was not a very enviable position!

Like all things in the war, one very soon adapts oneself to anything, so that when it came to staring out into No-Man's-Land for hours, with no one for company, I just tried to interest myself in the work, which rapidly became perfectly natural to me.

We had to be very careful that the sun's rays didn't reflect from the end of the telescope. If Fritz saw this he would at once wonder what a piece of glass was doing in the roof of a ruin and there would be but one answer to the query. A man's eye was behind that glass. Their artillery would be notified, also snipers and machine gunners and in a short time the offending glass, and the remains of the house with it, would disappear. Bearing this in mind, I would be most careful to prevent this from happening. The house faced almost due east, so the mornings were the most likely hours to be wary of King Sol.

All three of us were bent on one thing before all others, and that was to try and find out the approximate positions of the German trench mortar emplacements. These dreadful demoralizing things were the terror of all infantrymen, so it was up to us to do our best in this direction.

At the end of each day, our collective reports were handed in to the Adjutant. They were then re-edited by 'Brains', our Officer, and passed on to Brigade, then to Division and Corps HQ and the higher 'Brain'.

It was very strange to sit and watch a seemingly dead landscape. If one sat watching a stretch of desert or uninhabited land, it would not be out of place as it is a thing of nature, and that which is natural is not strange. On the other hand, before me was a land in which dwelled thousands in normal times, but now nothing was to be seen of them and in their stead thousands of field-grey and khaki-clad men were hidden in the earth.

The ground was fairly flat, but the Germans had the advantage of a slight rise, through which the railway from Arras to Albert ran diagonally across from our lines. Away to the left was 'H' sector and the ruins of Beaurains. A slight ridge ran from there across the front and culminated in a small hill and railway cutting which terminated my view on the extreme right. When darkness prevented us from carrying on, we went to our dug-outs in the village, talked of the day's events and compared our notes, writing up the reports to be handed in. Here is a typical specimen of a day's report:

Daily Report from Battalion O.P. 'G' Sector 21-11-1916

7.00 am	*Ground frost and mist. No visibility.*
8.30	*Mist lifting.*
9.00	*Visibility fair. 'G' 15. 13-23 new earth thrown up.*
9.45	*Trench-mortars from direction of 'G' 7. 5-26.*
11.15	*Movement of enemy seen at or near railway cutting Position 'G'18. 23-20. Probably working party carrying timber, etc.*
12.00	*Continuance of movement at 'G'18. 23-20. Gunners notified, who shell area for ten minutes.*
12.30 to 2.00 pm	*Nothing to report.*
2.20	*Trench-mortars active from direction of 'G'7. 5-26*
2.40	*Continuance of mortar fire. Notify gunners.*
3.15	*Artillery observer arrives who verifies position of mortars to be slightly behind 'G'7. 5-26 and approximately at 'G'7. 5-27.*
3.25	*Howitzer battery shell area around suspected trench-mortar emplacements. Firing continues for forty minutes.*
4.15	*No further trench mortaring occurs.*
4.30-4.45	*Light failing rapidly. No visibility.*

The above is a brief outline of an ordinary day's movements. Sometimes we had more to report, sometimes considerably less, in which case our method was to conjure up items to fill the report. One had to be careful in this matter, so as not to incriminate ourselves by a zealous officer probing into things to verify facts for himself!

The ruins used for an observation post

Very often it was so cold that we would descend to ground level to stamp our numbed feet and jump about briskly to get warm. Once or twice the enemy pitched shells perilously near to our rickety abode and very often bullets zipped into the tiles and woodwork. However, during the whole time at Agny none of us were hurt, which goes to prove that the whereabouts of our OPIP was not suspected.

Things were looking up in this war. The regiment had formed a concert party, also a drum and bugle band. The former possessed some really good talent, who later drifted into divisional and army concert parties. The band made a terrific noise, although it wasn't able to have the whole musical scale at its disposal. Still, the combination of the drums and 'snake charmers' or 'fiddlers' sounded ever so much better than buglers by themselves. The gentry who formed these items for our amusement did not go into the line.

Amongst the concert party, the two outstanding members were a man named Leeson and another named Hammersly. Leeson was an ideal 'low-brow' comic and a master in the art of mimicry. He could burlesque all the leading comic artists to perfection. Hammersly on the other hand was very much on the 'high-brow' side and possessed an inexhaustible supply of classical stuff.

At the functions held behind the line, many budding aspirants were allowed to make their debut, this being the cause of much amusement and rivalry between the respective companies to which the men belonged. If a turn was 'flat', it was not greeted in stony silence as is the custom in more peaceful days, but the poor chap was absolutely howled off the temporary stage. After one or two 'try-outs' the concert party was finally made up of about a half dozen or so.

These men were kept back out of harm's way so that amusement could be provided for us now and again. The O/C Regimental Signals had them under his care, he himself being very good at singing and on the piano. One of his favourite ditties was "Yak-A-Hula-Dicky-Dula". The other songs in vogue were "The Spaniard That Blighted My Life", "Can't Do My Bally Bottom Button Up" and "Sergeant Solomon Isaac Stein"; this latter chorus ended up with "He's the only Yiddisher Scotchman in the Irish Fusiliers". Then, of course, 'sketches' were arranged, with many sly digs at the various members of the battalion – the chief recipients of these were the Battalion Q. Master; 'Bombing Officer'; Company SMs and QMSs, Adjutant – in fact nearly all came in for it at some time or other. Such delectable songs as "One Eyed Riley", etc were strictly taboo.

On patrol in No Man's Land with the glare of a star shell overhead

The drum and bugle band would march proudly up and down the village street for our benefit. The only thing that rather spoiled this gallant display of martial music was the absence of several notes from the tunes. This was the fault of the instruments, not the men – a bugle trying to blow say, "Old Comrades" to the vigorous banging of drums would sound like nothing on earth. Nevertheless, they blared and thumped for all they were worth to soothe our shattered nerves.

What with the concert party and the band, things were looking up. I always remember one outstanding thing at each concert. There were the inevitable good-natured jokes about Fritz or Jerry and, at the conclusion, just as "God Save the King" was to be sung, a member of the party would step forward and give a little speech, ending by asking all present to think of "the lads that were absent". This short sentence always made a lump in my throat and I suppose everyone else, too, that had any fellow feeling.

One may think that all this business won't help much to end this conflict. As a matter of fact, it went a long way towards it. A good concert and a hearty laugh or two was the best nerve tonic the army possessed. Of course we had to be content with these rough and ready shows near the line. The real all star outfits were only to be seen many kilometres away, back where polished boots and shiny buttons abounded.

Everything now was progressing along smoothly; nothing out of the way happened. We went up to Agny and did a few days, hopping up and down the ladder of our OPIP. Then back for a few more days in rest-billets and so on right through November and December 1916. The weather was so dull and misty at times that no observing could be done at all.

Our officer then put us sniping at dawn and dusk and we

clicked for various little fatigues as well. The sniping was a farce at times, we simply used to wander along the battalion front and fire a few rounds at nothing in particular, then draw up a report about the number of Germans killed or hit. One man, I forget his name, was in the habit of killing half a dozen or so every day (on paper).

The officer, being dubious of this wonderful marksmanship, held an impromptu rifle meeting amongst us. The targets were bottles and jars, etc at about 75 yds range. Our wonderful marksman, who killed half a dozen a day (on paper), only hit the target twice in ten rounds! He found himself back with his Company.

On another occasion, during a period of rest at a place called Berloncourt, rifle shooting, range finding, etc was the principal item on our programme. One day, our officer being away, we were idling away the time and I was viewing the surrounding country through a pair of field glasses. I chanced to see two horsemen on a roadway quite 1,000 yds away. "Dekko" I said to a companion and handed him the glasses, at the same time pointing out what I wished him to see. He soon found them and, lowering the glasses, said "B———— Red-Caps"! I could not have done a worse thing than show him his pet enemies. He had a long standing grievance against all "Red-Caps"; I believe they ran him in whilst on leave once.

Picking up his rifle, he remarked that he was going to have a "pop at 'em", making good his threat by immediately firing a round. The horsemen continued placidly to walk their steeds, quite oblivious to the fact that a man was doing his best to shoot them.

Now the wind was blowing from them towards us, our bullets would have nothing else to pass over except stubble fields, etc. The temptation was very strong, so I determined to have a shot, too. Placing my shots at 950 yds, I aimed to frighten only. The bullet must have been very close, because both horses shied violently. My companion tried again, loosing off three rounds to my one. This proved too much for our 'Red-Cap' targets, I saw them lie low on their horses' necks and gallop to the shelter of a small covert.

Needless to mention, myself and chum quickly made ourselves scarce. A day or so later, orders were given that commanders must ensure that suitable ground is found when practice firing is going on, as complaints had been received of stray bullets imperilling the lives of 'Red-Caps' etc.

Of course, when firing we usually selected a bank or hillside. Our targets were home-made, supported on sticks. The "butt-marker" stood about twenty paces to the side and inspected the targets, at no little risk to himself.

Field gun in action

Once, a couple of cows persisted in wandering into the line of fire. As they would not be shooed away, we fired in front, behind or between them. All at once, a very irate lean, angular woman, all edges and no curves, came shambling across, shrieking curses at us and behaving like a demented person. Seeing our officer, she rushed at him and spat almost in his face uttering, no doubt, vile curses. The officer went white to the lips with temper and some of us hustled her a good deal, but she lay about her with a big stick and I got a crack on the knees from it. We finally drove her and her cows out of harm's way, but she never stopped her vile tongue the whole time. This type of French peasantry were happily few and far between, for their fanatical outbursts against us British did a great deal of harm to both the French people and us.

Another part of the Arras front was allotted to us, this to the left of "H" sector, and I think it was "I" sector and immediately in front of a suburb of Arras named Ronville. It was not a particularly attractive place. The approach was across the main railway lines by Arras station. Ronville itself was on a slight elevation which culminated by the trenches, the highest point being in enemy's hands, as usual.

We had three OPIPS to attend to, as we ourselves numbered but three. We should be well occupied, I thought! However, a solution was easily reached by the lack of trench maps, protractors, etc, so the chief thing to do was to select the best of the three. It was, perhaps, a trifle hard to discriminate on the favourable points of three smashed and dilapidated buildings, but we soon selected the most likely ruin as an OPIP. This decision was quickly arrived at, not by reason of its appearance from outside but because it was the only one that possessed a sound cellar. This was the most important item to think of beforehand – "Where do we go if Jerry strafes us?" Naturally, down into the cellar, whereas if there was no cellar the battalion would in all probability lose some of its 'brains'. The builders of those thousands of houses in the war zone little thought what a godsend the cellars would be in future years.

Observing in this sector was a good deal more exciting than at Agny. We were forced, on several occasions, to make a hurried descent into the cellar. One OPIP (disused) was entirely demolished; it was a lucky thing that we are not using it.

The trenches were also much livelier and there were several casualties from shell and trench mortar fire. Mines were counter-mined and even our own snipers sniped so that the war was not allowed to 'idle away' in this sector.

Ronville was in a complete wreck. All the upper end by the trenches was completely flattened. Downwards towards Arras the crazy shells of houses remained upright, but ready to collapse completely at any time.

Our OPIP was up behind the tiles of a row of houses, about six, parallel with the trenches. To approach them, one must follow a trench that led from the main street and which, unceremoniously, had pushed itself through the front of a house, out the back and across the gardens to the rear of our OPIP. Of the six tenements four scarcely exist now, but quite a dozen tiles or so remained to hide us in the attic of one. I don't know if former observers had met an untimely end, as we were told to be very careful and keep behind the steel plates as far as possible. These steel plates were the ordinary ones used in the trenches, with loophole and shutter for a rifle.

The weather was anything but ideal for observation, also it was very raw and cold and it seemed that it would be a hard winter. If we could not observe, other jobs were to be done during the day. One of them was burying. We dug one grave in a back garden to receive twenty-three of ours and other units. Originally there were twenty-two, but a premature burst from a gun not far from us killed a gunner, so they fetched him across too. At various times we buried ones or twos, as near together as possible. If a padre was handy, he would read a few prayers over them, but usually there was not anyone but ourselves to see the last of them. No choristers, no bands, gun-carriages, or firing squad. Not even a flag, or a blanket to wrap them in. They lay side by side in their drab, blood stained khaki.

Our battalion, like other units, was not up to full strength. This was the direct outcome of the Battle of the Somme, which was still proceeding in a desultory fashion in a waste of mud and water. Regiments, brigades and divisions had all had their full share of its horrors and the drain on new material to make good the losses must have been severe. It was this shortage of men that drew us 'HQ' men into the arms of the REs for fatigues.

One night we are to take 'toffee apples' up to the TMB men. The toffee-apples are the bombs used by our mortars. They weigh 60lbs each and derive their name from the resemblance they bear to the toffee-apples sold in sweet shops for a halfpenny, during happier days. The top, or explosive part, is the size of a football. This is mounted on a thick, steel rod, about three feet six inches long. To fire the mortar, the rod is placed full length down the gun's bore, the ball resting on top. On the gun being fired, the ball and rod go sailing over to Fritz to explode with great violence. In many instances the rod is sent whizzing back by the explosion back onto our trenches, and woe betide if anyone is in its way. The TMB men are drawn from the RGA and it is their invariable habit to fire a few rounds and bolt to earth in a convenient dug-out. Incidentally, when Fritz retaliates, we get it in the neck!

It's a typical December night, black as pitch and raining, as we assemble to go up to the line. In addition to carrying a toffee apple each, we have equipment and rifle and a waterproof cape or a ground sheet over our shoulders. Arriving at the dump, we each pick up a toffee apple and go off in a long line, meekly following a guide. Tripping, slipping and floundering, we follow our invisible guide. We halt frequently, go up one trench, down another and back again. Over the open, through craters with water knee deep. We seem to have travelled along half the western front and got no nearer to our objective. How we curse that 'guide'! He is but human and only keeping up the reputation of all guides in this war, that is, thoroughly losing himself and us.

It is no joke with a 60lb weight, not including the oddments, to be lost on a dark, wet night. Every step seems to add an additional pound onto us. It takes us about three hours to reach the appointed place, which is a bare 600 yds away from entering the trench.

During our wanderings, about eight men become detached and not knowing what to do with a mascot like a toffee apple, they dump them into a convenient shell hole and wait our return.

We also go out wiring. This is not an enviable job either. We take up knife, board and rolled barbed wire. The night is cold with the moon on the wane. After we have been working for half an hour or so, a machine gun whips its bullets right into us. It is ghastly, all stomachs and legs. Fritz knew where to aim. The poor chaps groan with pain and they are got into the trench, only to die later. We have to continue on working and again the machine gun rips at us, but we lie flat as possible. Then whiz-bangs burst on top, sending the splinters buzzing wickedly all round. This is too much, it is no use, we cannot continue further, so we get into the trench.

The O/C is furious with Jerry and with the casualties we have suffered. He gets busy with the TMBs and our supporting artillery and next morning at daylight we are compensated in some measure by seeing Jerry's line almost blotted out by smoke from explosions.

I and a mate went up to our OPIP to watch the fun. I know that I was highly elated to know Jerry was being punished. We lost one or two good lads out wiring the previous night. I suppose some of our 'toffee apples' went over, too. I'm glad I took mine up.

Altogether, we give Fritz something to get on with. Rifle-grenades, 60lb bombs, the 'flying pig' (a torpedo-shaped mortar bomb), Stokes bombs, 8 inch and 4.2 inch howitzers, besides field batteries. Altogether, a well assorted mixture of explosive.

Now Jerry is not one to accept gifts like this without returning the compliment as soon as possible. In fact, he was so quick with his return that we shot pell-mell down the ladder for cover and dare not move until the affair had abated.

Of course, I do not mean that all this display of high explosive was due entirely to the loss of a few men whilst out wiring. On the contrary, there were several reasons, the chief of which was to destroy his defences which had shown great activity of late. In all probability he had "sniffed the wind" as to a coming offensive on our part.

A chilly Christmas

At Xmas 1916 we were back at Dainville for a few days 'rest', so we were able to have our Xmas in comparative quietness in billets. Dainville failed to offer us anything in the matter of amusement or gaiety of any kind for Xmas. The only outstanding event was the payment of an extra ten francs and a dinner that even boasted a portion of goose. The puddings were sent out ready for warming up, so we really couldn't grumble.

The disappointing part was that we ate the dinner in all manner of places, out of our mess tins. Some were out in the open, others in barns; concentrated somewhere handy to the Company Cookers. The weather was bright but cold, making it impossible to enjoy one's food. It is something like having to eat a nice dinner in the garden, or in a field. Anyway, we wolfed it in quick time and made for an estaminet, or anywhere where there was likely to be a fire. We had a concert, but the barn was not big enough to house us all, which was a pity.

The village was a straggling one and had escaped being damaged very much. It was near the FBG de Amiens and three kilometres from Arras. Quite near were our big howitzers, which disturbed the peace of Yuletide. Jerry sent his long range shells over now and again, in an effort to locate them. There was a single line railway near; it came from Arras via Achicourt and went towards Duisans. In a deep cutting nearby, a huge gun now and again crawled up on its carriage mounting, fired a few rounds, then crawled away out of range again. We crawled into any old dug-out or trench when Jerry was 'searching' for it.

We drank white and red wine, 'blanc and rouge' and anything in the wet line, so that all suffered later from slight headaches and hoarseness through yelling "M'selle from Armentieres", etc over and over again.

I was sent to a divisional, or really an area, OPIP to look round. It was dug out on the side of a hill behind Achicourt and the view was wonderful. I could see the whole panorama of war from Vimy Ridge on the extreme left to Bullecourt on the right. Arras looked like the ruins of Troy or somewhere I had seen pictures of. One side of the cathedral reared itself up like a sentinel, above the rubble heap that surrounded it. The houses had no semblance of order; they just appeared to be piled in heaps one against the other anyhow.

The whole countryside was strangely still; there was no movement to be seen anywhere. Miles and miles of waste and wreckage. Roads streaked out from Arras in various directions, but nothing living trod them. Jagged stumps marked the place of the once-stately poplars that lined them. Scattered heaps of bricks and masonry, intermixed with rafters, marked the places of villages.

As I stood looking at this man-made wilderness, I began to wonder if it could possibly be true. Behind me was life, but here in front was surely death and desolation. Far away across the German lines was life, too! But this lane of barbed wire and trenches, between the two zones, stretched from the North Sea to the Swiss frontier. It was hard to believe. And all the way were countless watchful eyes facing each other, waiting, always watching and waiting. And behind them were thousands of cannon with bared muzzles, continually hurtling steel across at each other, every yard of ground under the keen eyes of gunners.

As I looked through the telescope, I could see the long sinuous streaks of piled earth that were the trenches, miles of them. 'No Man's Land' was difficult to discern at this distance, it was swallowed up in the maze of earthworks. The NCO in charge then invited me to look through the telescope. He fixed it on to a desired spot first and I took a peep. I was amazed to see figures moving about. I asked him what the location was and he told me it was about a mile or so behind Jerry's line and the figures were Germans, but quite hidden from an ordinary 'OPIP'. Other points were shown to me and I was surprised to see soldiers moving in the open at several points, behind both lines.

I made two visits to this OPIP, then moved into the line at Agny again on Dec. 28th, where I had a much closer view of the trenches from our old point of vantage.

New Year's Eve was a memorable one, marred by the death of three men by a mortar a couple of hours before the end of the old year. I saw all three lying side by side by the First Aid Post where they had been brought before burial. As far as possible everyone killed in the line is buried, if the body can be got at.

Our regiment did a very daring thing on this night and that was the bringing up of the band, or rather the drums and bugles. At about a quarter to twelve, the buglers let rip a rattling bugle-march and the drums joined in. Everyone expected a deluge of shells over, but as nothing happened, the gallant band carried on. When it was over, a faint cheer came from across the German trenches.

Just before twelve, the buglers blew the 'Last Post' to speed the departing year, and this evoked another cheer from Jerry. On the first stroke of the New Year (1917) the Reveille was blown, followed by a brisk march with the drums as an accompaniment. Instead of a good "whiz-banging" from our neighbours, they too began to sing and cheer, until both sides gradually quietened down. Our Lewis gunners kept on firing in the well-known style of "Pom, tiddley-om-pom, pom, pom!" But with the omission of the "pom-pom" at the end. This was furnished by Jerry or vice versa. It was rather amusing to hear this done and required a most delicate touch of the trigger finger to get the desired effect. I may say that this "pom-tiddly-om-pom, pom-pom!" business was prevalent up and down the whole line.

1916 had gone, and with no regrets whatever from us who manned the trenches. The outstanding event had been the Battle of the Somme, and we had no desire to take part in a repetition of it during the year that had just been ushered in, in such strange circumstances.

January was bleak and cold and we were fluctuating around the Arras sectors the whole time. Sometimes we billeted in Arras itself, once or twice in the French cavalry barracks and also in houses. In one house we were allotted the upstairs rooms that faced the railway. Bullets came over and went "thwack!" against the bricks or tiles. One fellow was wounded in the thigh whilst de-lousing himself. He was highly delighted, as we had heard nasty rumours of another 'affair' to happen shortly.

Whilst in the trenches in "H" sector, I had occasion to go in the front line with our officer to "spot the ground" in front. Turning round a traverse, we saw a man lying on the ground, groaning. His arm was shattered. Two other men were attending to him. After enquiring we should have passed on, but the officer went to look at a periscope. He said, "What's this?" I looked and saw a rifle, firmly held down at its muzzle and butt by sandbags. It was quite obvious what had happened. The poor chap with the shattered arm had shot himself, by first placing his rifle in position and securing it with the weight of the bags. No doubt his intention was to remove all evidence after he had shot himself, but he was so badly hit and in such great pain that he could not do it. My officer did not want to have anything to do with it and it was a good thing a platoon officer turned up at that moment and that we continued on our way, thereby escaping by a hair's breadth the unthankful task of giving evidence. The man's forearm was badly singed and burnt, showing that he must have placed it almost against the muzzle.

He was placed in arrest and sent back to hospital. Later he faced a FGCM on a charge of an S.I. wound and was sentenced to two years' imprisonment. I don't know whether he actually did this sentence as he finally had his arm amputated just below the elbow, so I suppose he was discharged from the service without pension, etc.

The Advanced Dressing Station

These early days of the New Year hung on us heavily. There was something brewing in the air and we all knew in a sense what it was going to be. Men returning from home off leave, or coming out with new drafts, told us a little of the outside news.

We heard of the rationing system for everyone and of the destruction of our shipping by the ruthless U Boat campaign. We also got specific information about the air-raids in "Blighty". All this didn't cheer us up much. There was more than sufficient to put up with out there as it was, without the knowledge of the bad way things were getting to in England.

The war had been on now for nearly two and a half years and we fully realized that here in France, the Germans were a long way off from being beaten. The Somme offensive had proved it last year. There, the Germans had ultimately worn us down to a standstill, without conceding very much ground, the capture of which, in lives and money, was enormous. However, it was not for us to criticise the general staff, even though they committed unpardonable blunders.

All around Arras there were unmistakable signs on every hand of a coming offensive. The gradual influx of troops and, more especially the artillery, was a sure portend of coming trouble. For some weeks nothing definite was really known by us lower ranks, but as I have already remarked, we knew full well what was to happen.

During these early weeks, we took turn and turn about with trench duty and billets and we could not shake off the Arras front at all. Once, we went a few kilometres back to 'rest' in a half-baked sort of village. Here the new box respirators were issued and we did the 'alarm' drill time and again. At another place, a few kilometres distant, was a practice gas chamber. Batches of us marched there and had to pass through the gas-filled chamber to test the new respirators. The things turned a presentable human face into a perfect nightmare when worn. The ugly ones and the good looking were all standardized by every detail as regards appearance, but once the "Box Respirator Mark I", or whatever it was, was fixed over our 'dials', we were completely standardized all over.

In the village, there were only about two estaminets worth mentioning, but a canteen had been provided and we had a fair-sized place for the concert party to entertain. My billet was a small cottage; there was only one civil occupant, a deaf old man of near ninety. We called him "Peter the Hermit", because he was something of a recluse and hid himself most of the time. I don't believe he had washed himself for years, the dirt was grimed thick on him. The only time we fully realized his presence was at night, when he coughed and hawked like a wheezy motor. Other village people, when asked about him, would put their fingers to their heads significantly, so we guessed the old boy was a crank or simple.

One of my chums got into trouble here. We had been out during the evening to the estaminet and had 'a few'. Sometime during the night he got up in a semi-stupor and was attracted by the face of a sergeant, who was peacefully dreaming of home or somewhere. My chum promptly urinated on the said sergeant's face, who promptly woke up spluttering and cursing. All might have been well if these two had not had differences of opinion previously. The upshot was seven days' No.1 field punishment and the knowledge from the CO that he was a 'filthy beast' into the bargain.

Field punishment was a very degrading thing, to say the least of it. Of course, it all depended on the unity whether it was carried out strictly or otherwise. I had seen the poor devils undergoing this form of punishment tied to posts, trees or the regulation limber wheels in all kinds of weather. Truly not a very edifying spectacle for anyone to see, let alone the French people. In many cases it was done close up to the line, within easy range of field guns!

I shall not dwell on this particular subject, because of its beastliness and the inhuman method of a great nation in the treatment of its soldiers, who were unfortunate enough to break the rules contained in the Army Act. However, Commanding Officers ought to be excused a little. They had to inflict punishment to suit the offence committed. They did not draw up the forms of punishment, but they had to punish to maintain a strict code of discipline, especially in this war. I don't suppose, for an instant, that they agreed in any way with the Army Council or the Army Act in the administration of active service punishment.

Preparations for another offensive were actively going on during February and March 1917 and we had our share and more of it. During our trench duty periods, we were mainly at Ronville and to its left. We never went to Agny or to 'H' sector. Away back at Dainville, Bernville, Simoncourt, etc, huge ammunition dumps were being made, light railways were being laid and piles of stones were accumulating all along the route to Arras.

Troops were packing into all the villages and in the open, too. Batteries were taking up positions where no guns had been before. Nissen huts appeared in all manner of places to accommodate the ever-growing military population.

Whilst in the trenches, our powers for observing grew less. The enemy was suspicious and let fly at everything that hurt his eyes. Our only O.PIP was dangerous and I expected to go to kingdom-come in pieces at any minute, whilst perched aloft.

We were to look for any signs of extra defensive work going on in Jerry's trenches. Strange as it may seem, there was little or no evidence of his making any preparations at all. From our O.PIP I could view his communication trench for some distance and, at one point, we had a view of the road running through the village of Tilloy. At these two points, we noticed that the enemy had large working parties all day and every day. The queer feature about this was that when they appeared to be carrying things, it was not towards us, but away! There was a good reason for this, which we found out later on.

I was beginning to get rather 'windy', but I tried not to

show it, if possible. This was the most important point in this matter. Some plainly gave themselves away, whilst others appear quite normal. In many instances the latter were actually more 'windy' than those of their comrades who outwardly displayed it.

Who could wonder at us being 'windy'? As a matter of fact, who can truly say they are not so, after a couple of months 'in the line'? The ordinary human was never made to withstand such a long succession of brain-numbing horrors without suffering in some way for it, whether at the time, or in years after. The physical discomforts were alone sufficient to put up with and our bodies would respond, in most cases, to build up strength and recover the lost vitality. On the other hand, the mental terrors were deeply rooted in us, perhaps for all time.

Big German howitzers firing at night

The approaching offensive seemed to hang over us like a nightmare. I already had the premonition that it would spell 'finis' to my war service. I did not actually make up my mind that I would be killed, but in some way, something seemed to warn me that I would be accounted for in some way or other.

The true cause of this was not hard to seek. Every day since August 1914 men were being killed and maimed up and down the whole front. Every time we went into the line, we came away minus a few men. Every time a 'show' took place, we emerged a mere remnant, nothing better than a nucleus from which a new regiment was formed. Every time one of our chaps was killed, I either knew him by sight, or had spoken with him at some time or other. Therefore we got the grim idea into our heads that our turn was bound to come.

The whole of the Arras front, for several miles, was livening up from the new guns that were ranging onto the German positions. Behind the myriad of field guns were great monsters that ranged from 6 inch up to 12 inch howitzers. They squatted in their position pits like immense toads, their thick muzzles at a sharp angle, ready to vomit their huge projectiles.

The end of March found us back in a 'rest' area, preparatory to taking part in the coming 'show'. Here we were kept busy, doing sham attacks on cultivated ground. Tapes were laid to represent the trenches and the whole brigade carried out an imaginary assault in perfect order. Everyone kept in touch with everyone else. The 'mopping up' parties did their task with the utmost sang-froid which, after all, was quite possible with nothing more fearsome than tapes to confront, and the respective COs were quite satisfied with it all. The chief thing was to please the Brigadier General, etc, but the Battalion Commanders must have smiled to themselves when they knew what an utterly futile thing it all was, this practice, compared to the actual business.

The rather startling news came to us that Jerry had retired from his trenches. This was done to straighten the salient caused by the ground lost on the Somme. The actual withdrawal was from a point east of Arras down to the River Ancre and the narrowest point of his retirement was by Arras. This manoeuvre, coming shortly after the terms of peace offered by the central powers, gave rise to a good deal of argument and speculation. Was Germany after all, worn out and beaten? Had the Somme taught them a lesson? And was she fearful of our coming offensive? We all thought 'Yes' was an answer to these queries, but we were to be sadly deluded by happenings to come.

The retirement of 'Fritz' had, in a manner of speaking, upset the plans of our GHQ to no small degree and a good deal of the original plan of attack had to be altered to fit the new situation that had arisen. This meant the pushing forward of hundreds of guns to new positions, also the moving up of the whole of the assaulting troops to fresh 'jumping off' places.

On the 29th March or thereabouts, we found ourselves once again in front of Arras. The attack would take place on the 9th April, so we had 10 days in which to prepare. The Germans on our particular front had not given up much ground. They had gone back about two kilometres; they held a commanding ridge and were known to be strongly entrenched. Our people had gone to much trouble and labour for weeks on end, in preparing chalk quarries (which were underground) for the reception and concentration of troops. These underground quarries were really wonderful and they extended for goodness knows how far. In places the roof was as much as 20 to 30 feet high and the meeting of several tunnels made a space as large as a small church. Our engineers had installed electric lights, which gave the whiteness a romantic touch. A light railway had been run its whole length and thousands of troops had rested, knowing that the biggest shells could do no harm to them.

Giving a drink to a wounded man

The enemy's trenches, which were assigned to us in the attack, were known as 'the harp', by reason of the shape, as revealed on aerial photographs. In reality it was a system of fortified earthworks forming a very strong redoubt. We had to occupy these at all costs, so the GHQ said, as it was a most important position. In the meantime, preparations were going on day and night for the 9th of April. Field guns and 4.2" howitzers were dragged up during darkness to within a few hundred yards of our first line, practically point blank range.

The chief point of the operations was the capture of Vimy Ridge, which extended for eight miles from a point near Givenchy and Souchez down to Gavrelle and Point-du-Jour. The offensive would also take place across the valley of the River Scarpe and the smaller River Cojeul, which is the area allotted to the Division, whilst further south our troops would go forward - or attempt to go forward. The French would also make an attack round the Chemin-des-Dames on the Aisne.

Altogether it promised to be a very big affair and conducted on lessons derived from the Somme. The 'creeping barrage' following an intense bombardment would be the procedure. The barrage, or curtain fire, was first introduced during the Somme battle. This was the means of us infantry getting a few more casualties, because it was a bit risky following behind a line of exploding missiles at about 50 yards. It only required the attacking infantry to go a little too far, or quickly, or the shells to drop a little short, to create havoc. Nevertheless, the barrage was a very good idea, which made 'Fritz' keep low to the very last minute.

We went into our old line trenches for a couple of days. It was strange to us, although we were more than acquainted with them. Once we had to keep our heads down, or our ears and eyes on the alert night and day, but now we could get on the top with impunity and survey the ground that had held us prisoners for so long a time. Troops and still more troops kept massing as the days went by. Thousands were in Arras itself, thousands in every disused trench and billet, thousands down the deep chalk quarries. Working parties were toiling hard, digging new trenches, building up roads that had not known the tread of hoof or the rattle of cart wheel for over two years. Bridges had to be made across every disused trench or large crater, to allow the passage of heavy transport.

RE miners had the work of months to no purpose. All the prepared mines were useless on our front and it was too late now to commence all over again. The air was thick with our 'planes, who were kept busy keeping off German 'planes which repeatedly flew over to watch our movements. Duels in the air were a daily happening and we scarcely took notice of them, unless they were flying low. One day a formation of our slower machines was attacked by a fast German machine. In spite of it being three to one, the German shot one down, which crashed by Beaurains. He then attacked a second one and we saw it catch alight and in a very short time it plunged to earth, a blazing mass. The third machine just managed to escape by the intervention of three more of our fast planes. During the Somme battle I had witnessed the headlong crash to earth of several machines, both ours and German, also the destroying of observation balloons and the pendulum-like descent to earth by parachutes.

As we could not do our usual duties during an attack, we were told that we should be utilized as runners and for this would be with our various companies. I was asked to accept a stripe again, but I declined, at the same time saying that, should I come back safely out of the coming 'show', I would consider it, because I really did not have much hopes of surviving it.

CHAPTER FIFTEEN

The Battle of Arras
April 9 1917

Heavy bombardment on a first-line trench

For three nights previous to April 9th, all hands were put to dig trenches for the 'jumping off' positions. The REs, as per usual, did the marking out and we did the digging.

The enemy had 'smelt a rat' and he traversed the ground with machine guns repeatedly, at the same time illuminating the darkness with a succession of star shells. Shrapnel was also exploded amongst us, but in spite of this, the trench must be dug at all costs. Daylight had revealed to the German airmen the newly-forming trench and his heavy guns got to work to demolish it. A narrow trench wants some hitting at a range of say 6,000 yards. It is not like an ordinary trench with bays and traverses, or with fire-steps, dug-outs, etc. This was just a temporary trench, where one could crouch during the bombardment. It was useless for protection and its purpose was simply for concealment and to make the distance to be covered less.

The shelling of it by big guns rather helped us, because every shell made another crater, either on it, or handy to it, so it was much quicker for us to link up crater to crater. The advanced trench was at last finished and we sustained a few casualties, but luckily not so many as expected in the circumstances. A man working near me was decapitated by a shell; it was some time before his head was found in the darkness and confusion. It was put in a sandbag and taken back to be buried with the body. The gunners of both sides were warming up and for miles around Arras, the skyline was stabbed at night with the continuous explosions.

Our little gang was broken up to rejoin their companies, but I was to keep with our officer during the 'show'. He told me all about it and what was expected of us. My orders were to keep with him wherever he went and to run any messages, etc.

Just as darkness begins to settle on the evening of April 8th, the battalion forms up by Ronville to move up into the temporary trenches. I follow my officer obediently here, there and everywhere, with messages for O/C 'A' Coy or 'B' Coy, or to O/C Battalion Bombers or Lewis-gunners. Going back and forth as I do among the different companies, I cannot help but take notice of these lines of men on the eve of battle. It is getting too dark to note their features, but their eyes appear to glare beneath their steel helmets. Little glowing red dots are here and there where they smoke before moving off. Many of them will not live to see tomorrow's sunset. They know it and I know it. We are all terribly strung up, for our fate is yet undecided. Like the Somme, some will come back for certain, but whom? If we are not condemned to die, we certainly feel like it.

Every man is in 'battle order', that is full equipment minus valise or overcoat. Iron rations consist of tea and sugar, tin of 'bully' and a few biscuits. Then, of course, any oddments in the food line that we can add or find room for. Nearly all have an extra 50 rounds of .303 in a bandolier, making 300 rounds. On top of this is a thing called an apron, which some have to carry. In this apron device are Mills bombs and rifle grenades. Three or four sandbags are also poked on somewhere and a shovel is thrust down between the haversack, which is on the back also. A waterproof or groundsheet with perhaps a few bits of dry box-wood are also carried, the wood in case we get a chance of brewing some tea, without which the 'Tommy' could never have existed for long. We are well loaded for these affairs; the unfortunate part of it is that it is with equipment instead of food. If by any chance we have to stay up in the 'strafe' for a number of days and rations cannot be brought up to us, then we shall be as famished as a starved wolf and still have the same weight to drag about on our persons.

Behind us and, what appears to be in Achicourt, is a great glare, accompanied by the roar of explosions. We learn that it is an ammunition column going up in pieces; lorry upon lorry loaded with heavy howitzer shells. The village market square, which hitherto had not suffered much, is now a splintered rubble heap. The Germans know that a great deal of road traffic came this route towards dusk and they, therefore, bided their time until the eve of our attacking. The result is now vividly proclaiming itself by the red glare and columns of smoke belching up to the evening sky.

The order to move is given and the long lines of men move away into the darkness, over old trenches, through networks of old rusty barbed wire, past a maze of shell craters and pot-holes, until our destination is reached. Everyone is to keep quiet and no firing unless necessary. It is about 8 pm and we are to remain until 6 am. Ten hours to crouch and ponder on what tomorrow will bring. Bank Holiday, too! Was there ever such a Bank Holiday before, I wonder?

The night is cold and raw and driving sleet sweeps down onto us, making our limbs ache with its coldness. My officer sends me on several messages, which occupies my mind a little and keeps me warmer than standing in the trench. It is none too safe either, as Jerry is nervous and constantly sending across shrapnel and machine gun bullets.

Among the general noise can be distinguished the much deeper rumbling of our 12 inch shells. We called them motor-buses because of the rattle and roaring whilst in flight. When they explode, it is just as if a gasometer has fallen onto the earth from a great height. The whole night through is nothing else but bangs, roars and explosions, of which the Germans contribute a goodly share.

CHAPTER FIFTEEN

According to circumstances, time plays us many tricks. Minutes may drag like hours, or hours fly like minutes, but on an occasion like this, when a definite zero hour is known, the time hangs on one something dreadful. Once I enquired the time from my officer and when he replied twenty minutes to five, I could do nothing else afterwards than mentally deduct the minutes approaching zero hour.

Just as dawn begins to show itself in the east and the outlines of men and objects take definite shape from the general blackness, the whole of our concentrated mass of guns behind us belches out in a great shattering roar of sound. Never before have I heard anything so terrific, not even on the Somme. Thousands of projectiles are roaring and shrieking

In the assembly trench before an attack

through the air at once, accompanied by the bark and deep reverberations of the guns and the ear-splitting bursting of their shells. Thousands of guns firing madly and each with its own special target.

Shells on their wire entanglements and fire-trench. Shells on their support reserve and communication trenches. Shells on all roadways behind his line – shells onto his batteries, in fact shells onto anything that is likely to assist them. Although it is still cold and with sleet and snow, we have no time to worry about physical discomforts. Bombardments like these will either kill you or drive you mad if they last any time. At times it seems that the earth is being split in two and that the sky is rent and torn to shreds. There is flame and smoke above and all about us. So stunning is the shock of noise that we all tremble as with ague , but we fumble with trembling fingers for a 'fag'; it may be our last!

Enemy shells are now dropping round us. We do not 'duck' for we cannot hear their approach in the uproar. They are on top of us practically before we realize it. They burst with a vivid sheet of flame and the debris rains down onto us. Men are hit, but they go unheeded. The air is thick with the acrid smoke and with the fumes from gas shells. Our eyes smart and little rivulets run down the men's faces, and such faces, too! As grey as the dawn, with lips that are blue. Some that are mere lads with tragic eyes and mask-like faces.

It is not far off zero hour, bayonets are fixed, they glimmer coldly in the early light. The bombardment has increased in intensity and the ground rocks and quivers as with earth tremors. Orders are being mouthed from one to another, such as "B" Coy half left - "C" Coy straight on", "Lewis gunners to keep up with companies", etc. My officer yells to me to follow him and I trail him down the trench, squeezing past the crouching men. Suddenly, there is a scrambling up the trench side, whistles are blowing, men are yelling and shouting. "This way!", "Come on lads", etc. My officer climbs out, saying to me, "Now we're for it, Neal!" I follow him and we walk forward into the maze of smoke and shell bursts.

Ahead of us I see the half stooping outlines of our lads. Some are dropping, and I am expecting to get popped off at any second. Bullets are cracking like thousands of giant whips. The earth suddenly opens in front, behind, and all about and up go geysers of black smoke and soil. Sometimes other things are mixed up with them; it is impossible to determine what really is happening. Outlines of men are by you, then in a second they are gone. "Through that gap, through that gap!" I look for the gap and the owner of the voice. It is my officer. He is pointing the direction with his revolver. The gap is just to our left, I make a dive for it, our men are bunching up by it and I fail to notice why they do until I am up to them. A great many have been knocked out by machine guns which are trained onto this point and their bodies are already obstructing the way through the wire. Turning to look for the officer, I am flung with great force to the ground by a shell explosion. It is some seconds before I realize that I am still alive and only severely shaken. Just as I am about to rise, another explosion occurs but a few feet away and a body is violently pitched across my legs; I stare at the horrible mangled mess and quickly withdraw my legs from its weight and grope for my rifle and steel helmet. Grabbing up the first I see handy, I follow on behind a group of Lewis gunners, at the same time searching for my officer, but I cannot see him anywhere.

I am up to the corpse-blocked gap in their wire again. Men are picking their way through and I follow them. The machine guns in front are silent, but the deep hollow detonations that are taking place are bombs.

No doubt the shell that blew me over with its concussion has saved my life, for the moment. The gap in the wire was a death-trap and nearly all those who attempted to pass through it were accounted for by the enemy's machine gunners. By the time I have got on the move again, the nest of machine guns has been silenced.

I am actually in the German line without knowing it. In places it has been pummelled out of all semblance by our gunners. Many Germans are here, both alive and dead. Passing them, we go forward over the cratered ground towards the unmistakable noise of a hand grenade tussle. Passing dug-out openings, I get the odour of the stale air from them, mixed with explosive. Meeting an officer of ours, we are led by him over the top again to a point of vantage, near the hand grenading. He motions us into any convenient crater and goes forward to explore further, with fatal results. We see him pitch forward onto his head. More of our chaps now come along and we all go forward again, to be greeted by a machine-gun and bombs. It is too late for the enemy, as we are right on top of them. Mills bombs are great little things for killing at close quarters. The handful of Germans who have been causing so much trouble are quickly despatched. A Lewis-gun corporal and a man shoots everyone. including the wounded and the few who gave themselves up as prisoners. This sounds rather drastic, nevertheless it is quite true and nothing unusual in this kind of war.

The Battle HQ are now with us and I report the loss of my

officer. I am told to try and find him, if possible, and report if a casualty. Going over the same route, I search for a figure with trench boots and Burberry. Reaching the original German fire trench, I look for the fatal gap in the entanglements and instantly recognize it by a heap of bodies. Going over to these, I find my late officer lying face downwards amongst the others. A part of his 'Burberry' is hooked on a barb and there is a long rent in it. I have no need to examine him closely, because there is a large hole in the back of his skull; blood is congealing from a hole in the back and the side of the neck, so the poor fellow has had at least three bullets through him.

There are two of my late chums not far from each other, both shot through the head. Some of the dead are tangled up in the wire, half suspended by it, their poor bodies sagging limply until they can be lifted off.

Getting back to report, I am again blown down by shell concussion. This time it bursts behind me and although instinct is making me duck my body the shell completed the movement for me and I am sent sprawling face down. The feeling is as though one's whole inside has been lifted clean out of one's body.

Picking myself up, I am able to finish the journey in 'peace'. On reaching our lads again, I am rather dazed and an officer gives me a swig from his flask, which puts me right again. Things are happening in front which require our attention. The ground slopes away gently, then upwards again, and on the ridge of it is the Germans' new position.

In the intervening space of perhaps six furlongs are numerous groups of the enemy. At first we fire at random into any of the groups, but later we see that some have their arms raised and are ambling along over the shell-stricken ground towards us, whilst at the same time, other groups are retiring to their new line. It is unfortunate that so many of the enemy were shot whilst endeavouring to reach our lines. There are already a good many Germans with us, wounded and sound, and the addition of all these coming over to surrender will make a goodly batch.

By this time the German gunners have our range and we get well bumped. This is the cause of more confusion. The prisoners are terror stricken and want to bolt and one cannot blame them! They can see their own men surrendering in large numbers, so the guns are trained onto them too, which is the Germans' method of wishing farewell.

We stand on top and hurry them up. They are trickling through our lines, by us, and on both sides. There is no time to dally and they scramble across their old trenches and disappear behind us.

Tanks now waddle across in ungainly fashion. One is disabled, its endless chain tread is broken by a shell and it is curved into a letter 'S' shape. Smoke is pouring out of it and it is now the target for 5.9s from Jerry. Another tank is vainly struggling to go forward, but its endless tread cannot grip the wet, sticky ground and it is just like a huge monster of Jules Verne's ideas. This tank is not far from the disabled one and it is also a target for Jerry's guns.

Having accomplished that which we set out to do (the capture of 'The Harp' redoubt) we may now rest on our laurels, as it were, while the offensive will be pressed by other units.

Already Labour Corps men, Pioneer Battalions and REs have come up through the barrage and are working and dying, at the same time endeavouring to bridge across trenches and craters for the passage of guns, etc. A crowd of them are trying

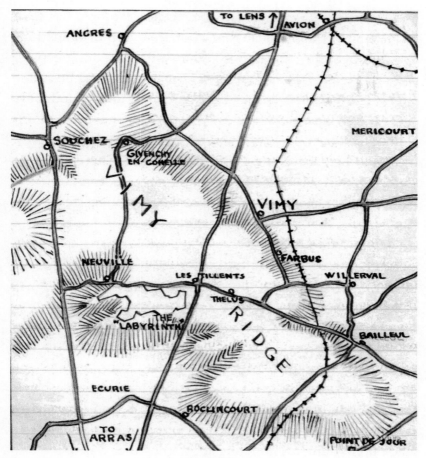

Vimy Ridge

to get the bogged tank to move and a salvo of 5.9s drop in amongst them, doing terrible damage. We go out to them and get the wounded into an old German dug-out. By a strange coincidence the tank got a grip almost at the same time as a few helpers were pitched into eternity and it lumbered off towards the German line, where in all probability it met its 'Waterloo'. The other tank has been abandoned to its fate, but I don't think it was hit again.

Our orders are to 'clean up' the recently captured trenches. By 'clean up', I don't mean that we are to sweep it, or anything like that peaceful occupation. What we are to do is explore them thoroughly, comb out any Germans that may be still in hiding down their deep dug-outs, attend to any wounded we come across and get rid of any dead, also to collect up any material left over by Jerry in his flight.

About half a dozen get together and go off to explore. In the original fire trench are quite a number of dead Germans. We purposely avoid them, as I had already suggested to my companions that we may find some grub in a dug-out. This suddenly reminds them all that they are hungry like myself. Coming to a dug-out entrance, we descend down the steps into its blackness, at the same time shouting down to Jerry to come out, but there is no answer. Getting lower down, the way is obstructed by the bodies of three dead Germans. After a good deal of exertion on our part, they are hauled up into daylight. Going down again we grope about in the dim light, until a man rakes out two issue candles from his haversack. Sticking them upright into their own wax, we can see what we are about. The dug-out possesses sixteen rabbit-wired beds, made up in bunk fashion, one above the other. There are also two tables, a few chairs, equipment pegs, rifle stands, shelves, etc. Blankets and even one or two feather pillows are there, all of which were probably taken from villages and farms.

I am fortunate to find some black bread and some saveloys, also three eggs uncooked and butter in a tin, which tastes like lard. Someone else also discovers some bread and a canteen of coffee and it is quickly wolfed after being shared.

The aroma of the dug-out being somewhat stale, we make up the stairs again into the open until we come across another entrance and repeating the same formula as previously, we descend to explore.

This dug-out was evidently used by officers. The fittings are more elaborate and the gas curtains are arranged so as to work instantly, on the pattern of ordinary roller blinds. Once inside, candles are lit and everyone makes a dash for loot, regardless of any of the enemy who may have been in hiding, or of booby traps which may have been set for our benefit. I am lucky to pounce on a fine pair of field glasses in the case and I sling the strap over my shoulder to make it secure from any of my chums 'winning' it from me. One or two find revolvers and automatics, also a folding camera and case. We are lucky to get a little more eatables, mainly sausage and French bread (very chaffy), cold coffee and a bottle or two of vin blanc.

I am just about to leave, having suddenly remembered about the 'booby traps', when I see a leather wallet, or rather a despatch case, lying on the floor. Picking it up, I go up into daylight to examine it. Fortunately, there is also a strap with which I am able to hook the case onto my person, until such time when I intended to examine its contents.

Events have been happening whilst we have been down the dug-outs. The battle line is now in front of us about a mile away towards Henappes and Wancourt. Fresh attacking waves of our infantry have passed through us and are now mixed up in the haze of smoke ahead. I am now a sort of 'spare file' since losing my officer, so I am able to attach myself to any group I take a fancy to. Going along the trench, I find a few of my old Company and remain with them. The fighting has become more spectacular – cavalry are going into action for perhaps the only occasion since 1914 except, of course, on the Somme on September 15 1916.

The main street at Ronville

18 pounders and light howitzers are up to us and even in front. They are firing from positions quite devoid of cover. My blood tingles as I see the horses straining at the traces, foam-flecked and nostrils a-quiver, the guns and limbers bumping and swaying over the uneven ground. Such noble creatures, and as sensitive to danger as we humans.

Getting out my German glasses, I am able to get the best view of battle action since being in France. Our cavalry are through on the left front and I see the mounted figures trotting towards a dip in the ground, where they are lost to view. Our infantry have gone to earth over by the next ridge. They must

229

have been held up by wire entanglements; a big belt of it can be seen almost on the top of the ridge. Shells are exploding all along the skyline, so that a clear view is impossible. Besides, my chums all want to 'dekko' through the glasses, too.

Everyone is in high spirits as we really think that, at long last, the Germans are on the run and that the war will be over soon. One chap (his name is James), is so certain of it that he produces various photographs of his mother, sisters, etc and his 'best girl' who, as he explains to me, is waiting for him, so as they should be wed on his return.

Poor chap, he is blown to pieces not five minutes after. After we have recovered from the shock of the explosion, we suddenly miss him. The cheap postcard photos he treasured so much are lying scattered about, like the remains of poor James. We could not help noticing that all are unsoiled, except the one of his 'best girl', which is soaked in blood. The untimely end of James is soon forgotten in the whirl of brain-numbing happenings that succeed each other with swift regularity.

Later on, the news comes that the village of Wancourt has been taken by our troops, but further progress is impossible for the failing light and the depth of ground already taken. Everything connected with an advancing force must keep up with them. Transport and supplies of every grade have treble work thrust on them, with a considerable increase of personal danger, much to the annoyance of QMs, QMSs, ASC, etc.

On our left front, across the River Scarpe, great progress has been made and cavalry has penetrated into the village of Monchy-le-Preux. The use of mounted troops is a bold gesture on the GHQ's part, which has proved abortive, as it was bound to do from the beginning. Horses cannot jump clean over barbed-wire entanglements as thick as forest undergrowth,

A trench scene

neither can they leap across trenches which are perhaps ten feet wide from parapet to parados. Besides these obstacles, which are on every hand, they will receive the special attention of machine guns, grenades and artillery.

We are not surprised when we see little groups of horsemen straggling back. Lame horses and riderless horses are mixed in with mounted men. They come across through the smoke, bobbing up and down over the numberless shell craters, stumbling over trip wire and pot holes. They converge by a temporary bridge thrown across nearby. We go up to them to get any news and to lead the riderless horses over.

Troopers tell us that it was a wash-out. The wire was 50 feet deep and they were forced to tumble off their mounts and take cover in craters, whilst other troopers led the terrified animals back. Dozens of the poor beasts and their riders were piled up in heaps, riddled with bullets. Looking at and stroking the trembling horses, our chaps feel more pity for them than for ourselves. The days of spectacular cavalry charges are gone. The awe-inspiring sight of thousands of horses thundering over the ground, with the glint of lance and sword and the hoarse cheer from their riders, is not for this war. Half a dozen machine gunners could practically wipe them out in five minutes.

Having a few minutes leisure, I proceed to delve into the despatch case I found in the dug-out. This proves to be a collection of excellent photos and correspondence in type and writing in German. The photos are about 6 inches by 8 inches and depict aerial views of the Arras front, also ordinary views taken from points of vantage in their lines. The correspondence being unintelligible to me, I decide to hand them over to our HQ. As regards the photos, I select six for myself and replace the remainder with the papers. The six photos I keep are three aerial and three ordinary, and I fondly hope that one day they will accompany me home as souvenirs. Photos are lighter to carry than nose-caps, etc. I often wondered at the patience and doggedness of some fellows, who lumber themselves up with 'old iron' in the form of nose-caps from shells, or splinters of shrapnel, etc. This useless extra burden they hump about on their person from place to place, for weeks sometimes, in the hope that one day they will repose in a place of honour on the 'sideboard' or somewhere. If these collectors survive for any length of time without "Blighty" materializing, they either lose their valise or fling the souvenirs away in disgust.

Taking the case, I hand it to the Adjutant, who thanks me for it, saying that it may prove interesting when time permits its examination.

Snow and sleet again begin to fall and night comes with a touch of mid-winter weather. We huddle up together for warmth. Dug-outs are forbidden because we may be called upon any moment and it would be difficult to find us if we stowed ourselves away in dark corners. Besides, the dug-outs smell horribly of sweat and death, so I am quite satisfied to flop down on the earth and sleep. It is so cold that we have to waken frequently and stamp about to restore circulation.

Tanks in action, April 1917

The Germans have by this time recovered from the shock of the morning's happenings and are resisting stubbornly everywhere. All around, the semi-circle of skyline is lit up by heavy gunfire.

For two more days we remained in the same position, during which snow and sleet fell heavily, covering all the recent fighting area in a white mantle. This was succeeded by a thaw, which converted the snow into a slippery, boggy slush, much to everyone's disgust and inconvenience.

On or about the 12th April, we were relieved and made our way back towards Arras. Some of us had augmented our stock-in-trade of lethal weapons by the addition of German revolvers, etc. I was carrying a German sniper's telescopic sights from his rifle, in addition to binoculars and photographs. The late owner of the telescopic sights lay dead in their first line trench. He had, like all their first line troops, stuck to his job until the last, whilst all about him was the evidence of his recent activities in the shape of hundreds of empty cartridge cases.

Some of the lads dragged a minnewerfer gun back with them. It was an exact replica of a small howitzer and was the cause of much violent cursing by the scratch drag rope team of our fellows, until it was parked and labelled with other war trophies. I heard that it ultimately found its resting place in the Rifle Depot at Winchester.

The village we were billeted in was a quagmire, relieved by a collection of scattered barns and cottages. Our beds were of wire netting suspended in two tiers along the barn's side. As only one blanket was issued to us, it was a masterpiece of ingenuity to see the way a man would rearrange his whole clothing and, with the aid of one solitary (and lousy) blanket, wrap himself up and lie warm. Our pillows were valises and our quilt an overcoat. Should our bed be the floor, some warmth was derived because we lay packed together tightly.

The usual procedure of things took place whilst in billets. First a census of all those present and correct and of those who were absent through death or wounds, or missing or sick. Then followed inspections of rifle and sword, gas-masks, emergency rations, etc. Perhaps, if we were lucky, a bath and a clean shirt and, above all, at least one pay-day. This would enable us to have a few drinks and buy a little extra grub from some money-grabbing old woman at twice its usual price.

Burying the dead

Drafts from the base joined us and we are soon ready for 'up the line' again. A move in this direction was made about the 18th April, when we went forward to a place more handy to the fighting.

By this time I had an obsession that my number was up and that I should be accounted for in some manner. Thank goodness the weather had altered and all trace of the slush and mud had disappeared. The sun had worked wonders in a few days and all nature was responding to it. Fruit trees in blossom and the young buds of the poplars, etc, were shooting out in various shades of green. This was the third spring for me in France.

From now onwards we kept in the open and when night came we lay on the ground in the lee of a wall or anywhere to get shelter, as it was still cold.

NCOs were getting short, especially those with any experience, and again I was told that I must take promotion. However, this was deferred until we had been in the 'cauldron' again. I was also thanked for the photos and documents I handed over, the latter being of some importance, being the late property of a German divisional intelligence officer, also I was told that my name would be, or had been, forwarded through the proper channels, etc, but of this I heard no more.

A couple of days later we arrive by our old first line trenches in a strange part, some few kilometres SE of Arras, and on the night of the 21st April we march parallel with the old fighting line until we meet the road to Beaurains. This is the road that spelt DEATH past a certain point, for two and half years. Now brother Boche has retired voluntarily and received a further push back, so that now we can pass along it with confidence.

It doesn't seem much of a matter for excitement; nevertheless, we who knew this roadway have some cause to be excited. For this is the road that passed clean through both lines, as so many other roads do all along the Front. How many nights have we patrolled on our tummies along the stretch that lay between the trenches? How many times were we compelled to bury our noses in the earth to avoid detection? Nothing living has trod its pave for over two years, until now.

As we plod along, the old ration dump is reached and passed. Here it was that limbers crept up at night and, under the supervision of Coy QMs, the rations, letters, etc, were duly handed over to the waiting men. Sometimes the Regimental QM would come this far. I say sometimes, because these gentlemen preferred to remain in the region of the transport lines. In many instances, if they did come up with the rations, it was to bring up special despatches, officers' letters and, more often than not, a bottle or two of something with a 'kick in it'. Naturally, all QMs are not the same. Personally, I know of some who see rations up to the trenches on every possible occasion, whilst others will only risk it under the pressure of higher officers. Anyhow, most battalion commanders fully appreciate the value of a good QM, who is able to make things so much more comfortable for all concerned in the rest areas.

This time the familiar dump is behind us. On the left of the road, the communication trench twists and winds almost parallel. We pass over our old first and second lines and now see the black pits that are the bays of the fire trench. As we look down, it seems well nigh impossible to imagine ourselves living in it through the four seasons. Under the road, a tunnel links up the fire trench. It was a favourite refuge for myself and many others, during a 'strafe' or in wet weather.

CHAPTER TWENTY EIGHT

The road to the trenches

Now we are actually passing our wire entanglements and the one time dreaded No-Man's-Land is around us. I smile to myself when I recall the nights I spent crawling over its surface, when every crater seemed to be a bottomless pit and every little mound a mountain. Even if we had got only half way across on these affairs, our trenches seemed to us to be miles behind instead of a bare fifty to a hundred yards, and one had the impression of being entirely cut off and isolated from mankind.

It hasn't taken us long this time, for already the posts and barbed wire of the Germans loom up. Now we pass over their old first line trench, where they had to live and endure the identical life that we did! There is not a particle of difference between the ground that flanks either side of No-Man's-Land – same battered defences and rusty entanglements, same collection of refuse and clutter of tin cans, the same piles of pummelled masonry and stumps of trees. Passing through the village of Beaurains, which is only there by its name as it is flat with the earth, we go across the open land, crisscrossed by trenches and wire, until we reach a long wide trench hard by several batteries. This is to be our temporary halting place for a day or so.

We are now somewhere between Wancourt and Gemappes, but to us it is just the same as the Somme or anywhere else. The whole countryside is a waste of land, frequently relieved by columns of black smoke and earth spurting up. The sky is forever being dotted with white woolly bursts of shrapnel, which mark the position of airmen, both British and Boche. All around, in every fold of the ground, and in the open too, are battery upon battery, their guns continually firing the whole time.

Along the roads from Arras are motor-lorries and an unending procession of ammunition-limbers and supplies, also field ambulances, all for some particular battery or unit, and marshalled along by traffic police.

The night passes uneventfully and next day we go to bury some dead. There are about 50 in the party detailed for this job. The burial ground is in an old churchyard, bits of the old iron railing still remained, but there is no sign of the church, unless a stalagmite heap of masonry is all that remains of it.

The position of the burial spot is decidedly unhealthy. We find ourselves perched up on a bluff of land and exposed to the open ground in front. A sunken road cuts through by one part of the cemetery and the part facing the enemy's lines slopes abruptly down like a steep railway embankment.

There are quite sixty bodies to be interred, so the sooner we get it done, the better for us all. I notice men of all regiments amongst them and about a dozen officers, five of which are artillery. The bodies have already been overhauled for identity discs and pay-books. The only thing required of us is to put them as near together as possible in one common grave. Someone has laid a tape into a rough square to mark the limit of our digging. Stripping off our equipment, we commence to work and in a short space of time, we have each dug down sufficiently to protect us a little if shells come over – and they do!

We have laid about twenty bodies in when the first one comes. It is what we called a 'woolly bear', because of its reddish-black smoke. Sometimes they name them 'concertinas' by the manner of their burst. They are really heavy shrapnel and they open out exactly like a concertina, about thirty or forty feet in the air.

We never take much notice of that one, but when big percussion stuff suddenly swoops down perilously near, to send the earth and splinters all about, we simply flop face down on top of the corpses for protection. The whole time we never have anyone hit, until there remain but half a dozen bodies to put in.

I am just about to climb out, to help carry one, when a big shell explodes behind me, just missing the bodies. Some of our chaps are there. Two are killed and five wounded.

This is the climax, to lose two of our own men! The wounded are attended to and taken to a First Aid Post, whilst the dead are buried alongside those they themselves so recently helped to bury.

Reaching our regiment again, we hear we are for the Line tonight, also that we are to leave our valises and overcoats behind. This means business again! And I think that it means goodbye to my photos, etc.

About 8 pm the regiment parades and, led by guides, we move off by companies. Our way takes us over the hill, which leads to the cemetery where we have buried the dead this morning. Passing through the valley that once sheltered the village of Wancourt, the way now is up the opposite slope of the valley, which is resounding with gunfire.

A single line railway passing through a cutting brings us to high ground leading to the firing line. Numerous dead, British and Germans, strew the ground all about. Star shells and Very lights are illuminating the semi-darkness of moonlight and bullets swish past us by the thousands.

We are walking on top. It is quickest but more dangerous and, in any case, there are no communication trenches, so there is no option whatever. Finally, the front trench is reached. It is nothing else but shell craters linked up hurriedly, with trip wire out in front.

A couple of hours after, I and others have to go forward and occupy a large shell crater. The night is very noisy and, when the guns work up into a drum-fire, with the accompaniment of machine guns and dozens of star shells, we know it is either a scare or a local attack taking place. We are ignorant of how far the enemy is away, but he cannot be far, because his star-lights pitch clean over us and they will only carry about a hundred yards.

During the early morning, shelling becomes heavy. Shrapnel bursts almost at ground level and we have to keep as low as possible in our hole. Despite this precaution, one man is decapitated. We do not know of this until the shelling ceased and his body is lying crumpled up.

Shells come from all directions and we are not safe from ours behind even. It is a matter left to providence, this night gunnery, and we infantry are its puppets.

Just as dawn creeps up, we go back to the main line of defence and we spend four hellish days and nights. We are shelled constantly and men are being buried alive and knocked senseless, or even killed by concussion. There seems no time for anything but to drag comrades out of piles of earth and debris. As fast as this is done, others are killed and maimed and we do our best to dress the wounds, but it is hopeless to cope with it all.

My turn comes to be buried. Three of us are trying to brew a canteen of tea during a lull. Crouching on the trench bottom, we split a piece of box-wood up into strips as thin as matches with our jack-knifes. This is to get plenty of flame with the minimum of smoke. I am helping the fire by constantly blowing at the wood and we are on the point of being rewarded for our trouble when there is a mighty whistling shriek of a descending projectile, with the almost simultaneous explosion.

A terrific weight suddenly presses me down from all sides, accompanied by complete darkness. Being in a crouching position when blowing the fire, I have to remain so, but it helps to save my life as their remains a certain amount of air space beneath my body. Several times I feel the ground rock with the shock of explosions. How long I remain in this position I don't know, but I think what a queer end to such a hectic life.

Extra pressure coming from the side rouses me up and I heave with all my might. This must have some effect, as someone gets a grip of my arm and with the united efforts of those outside and myself, I am dragged out into the air again. One of my chums gets clean away, but the other one, named Slowman, was buried deeper than I was. He is almost dead when rescued.

I am somewhat shaken up and have the feeling that soon I will get clouted and put out of action altogether.

That night we go out in front digging a sap. It is fortunate that shell craters are in places so thick that their lips touch. This is excellent cover and, besides, the craters are quickly linked up, one to the other.

"Lest We Forget"

We stay out until 1 am or thereabouts and a few fellows are hit by machine gun bullets. Shelling continues intermittently all the while, so that it is impossible to rest or sleep, even though the chance occurs. It is possible to sleep during the uproar of the trenches, providing one has the knowledge that danger is not threatened every second to one's personal safety. On the other hand, if shelling is directed onto your own little patch of ground and its immediate vicinity, the knowledge of this alone will keep one continually 'on edge'.

Personally, I myself have slept quite sound during a most awful din, but before doing so, I knew that the shelling was directed elsewhere.

The next day I am moved with others, along to our left. Our trenches are on a hill and from our new position a view is obtained down its slope, across a valley, where flowed a river (Scarpe or Gogeul). Other hills flank the valley on its opposite side. We are not in an enviable position, being somewhat exposed to the enemy. Enfilade fire comes from across the valley and "whizz-bangs" are frequent, so we have a lively time.

The day wears through slowly, until thick mists lie like a ghostly blanket all along the valley. The air reeks with the sickly smell from gas-shells and the night is a long nightmare for us. We have to keep a sharp watch and a Vickers gun team reinforce our post. Frequently, we all blaze away in a semi-panic, down the slope of the valley, at what we imagine to be the enemy. Red and green distress rockets shoot up, to be succeeded in a minute or so by rapid rifle and machine gun fire, the dull detonations of grenades and the pounding of artillery. The night is all flashes and explosions, the excited yells of overstrung humans and the stench of decay and gas.

One poor chap goes mad. He gibbers and sobs, or else laughs wildly. We restrain him from rushing out into No-Man's-Land on several occasions and it is not till daylight that he is taken off our hands by some stretcher bearers.

The last day in the line is quieter and again we conjure with oily water and little strips of wood to make tea, the first warm drink for three days.

On top of the trench is a dead German. He is partly covered with soil, but one arm is half raised with the index finger extended, as though admonishing someone. Every time we push his arm down or bend the finger downwards, they slowly rise again to their original position. This arm, that seems to rebuke us, gets on our nerves for no apparent reason. At first we laugh, but it is uncanny to watch the way the arm slowly raises itself every time. Suddenly one chap jumps up, saying "For Christ's sake Fritz, are you dead or still alive?" He grabs hold of the corpse and gives it a shake. The loose soil gives way and down rolls the body almost on top of us. We gaze at it stupidly, until some wag says "Fancy having an argument with a dead Jerry", at which we all laugh, regaining our composure. This little incident is proof to the state of our nerves.

On the 29th April we are relieved again and go back to reserve trenches by Wancourt. Although batteries are grouped all around us, this fails to disturb our sleep, which is one of complete physical and mental exhaustion.

Mails are distributed and I have a parcel from home; amongst other items it contains a cake and café-au-lait in tinned form. This was familiarly known to us as 'coffee-hooray'. At this time, bread was scarce and it was common to share a 1lb loaf between four and very common to have six or even eight men to share. In the event of this happening, some agreement is arrived at whereby the loaf goes to one particular set of chums, and the next time a loaf arrives, another 'band of hope' splits it between them.

I am ravenously hungry and we have no bread, so I share the cake and open the tin of café which we spread on it like jam. Our principle of devouring this impromptu meal is far from conforming with the rules of digestion, or best manners, and I suffer with a bad attack of sickness afterwards. However, our tummies cannot agree with dainties. We are more accustomed to cold 'bully', hard biscuits, petrol-tainted water, bits of cheese interwoven with hairs off sandbags and the usual clay and earth as a flavouring to everything.

The second day in reserve we go again on a working party with the REs. We are to help at a big dump to load and unload lorries. Arriving at the dump, we set to work. Considerable shelling is going on by both sides, but nothing threatens us so far. After some four hours' work, we put our equipment on and start back again.

We have just topped a rise when we are heavily shelled with gas shells. These come over with the usual rush and shriek and

Shells exploding over a tank

explode immediately on impact, to be followed by a cloud of green-yellow vapour which scarcely rises up over the height of a man. A slight breeze blows the fumes onto us and everyone fumbles madly to adjust a mask on their faces. I had a little difficulty in getting mine to ackle, so I jam an oily rag out of my haversack over my nose and mouth, but not before I have inhaled a little of it. The gas-shells continue to drop everywhere round us, so I do a smart sprint to get out of the zone, continuing to press the oily rag to my mouth. I feel as though I should burst for want of breath and, at last, in desperation I take the rag away and involuntarily draw a breath of air and gas into me. I immediately adjust my mask and join some of our lads, who have all scattered.

The officer in charge of us comes along and gets us into some sort of order again and, with signs, directs us until the danger area is passed. We have to support and half carry about half a dozen who had failed to adjust their masks, or cover up in any form. Three were left behind by some batteries to be attended to. My throat and chest ache and burned as though an inward fire is consuming them. On reaching our rest trench, I just flop out and gasp for breath. The craving for water is intense, but this is forbidden by the MO. My throat gradually gets better, but some are sent back to the hospitals.

About this time, two events of great importance had taken place. Russia had collapsed and the Czar had abdicated. This would mean the release from the Eastern Front of hundreds of thousands of Germans, who would be transferred to the French and British Fronts.

To somewhat counterbalance this disaster to the Allies, the United States had entered the conflict against the Central Powers and although it would take months for them to have an efficient fighting force in France, we who had been at the Front for any length of time fully realized that their help would be badly needed.

The second day, counter battery firing was exceptionally severe and our guns were undergoing a warm time of it. Owing to the close proximity of several batteries, we came in for a good deal of the shelling, too.

Ammunition supply columns were, at this time, coming right up to their respective batteries during daylight. This is nothing remarkable during a 'strafe', but usually this is done at night-time in ordinary trench-times.

About a hundred yards from us, four limbers and their teams were involved in a terrible mix-up. Some big shells, aimed at their battery, fell among them. We saw the poor terrified horses plunge and rear madly with fear. The few drivers were incapable of pacifying them. One team bolted, dragging the near-side wheel horse, which was hit with them. Another team were all hit except one animal, and to hear the screams of the poor brutes was terrible. We could see that something was amiss with the drivers as only one or two could be seen, vainly rushing about from one team to the other. An officer of ours was by us, watching. He was quite young and recently out at the Front. He was trembling with emotion and told us he had seen some sickening sights in a short while, but the horses capped the lot. He told us he had a lot to do with horses in civil life, wanted a commission in some mounted branch, but had to accept the infantry. He suggested we had better do something and we thought so too! I told the officer that all we wanted was our jack-knifes and a couple of revolvers. Our party consisted of the officer, a Lewis gun corporal and four or five of us men.

Shells were coming over in salvos every few minutes and we quickly got across the intervening space to the animals. The corporal and I went to the team, where only one horse remained alive. The sight was sickening, it was all legs and gashed bellies, a great heap of mutilated horse flesh. The poor beast that stood quivering had not escaped either, blood was oozing down its rump from a large gash. There was only one thing to do and it was done quickly with the corporal's revolver. He could not do it himself, but handed the weapon to me. I must confess I closed my eyes as I pressed the trigger and sent the poor beast to the "happy pastures". The truth is, I could not bear the pitiful look in its eyes.

The officer, with the help of RFA drivers and our chaps, released three unwounded horses from another team, shot two more that were badly maimed and got away three wounded drivers.

The team that bolted were entangled in some wire, so we all went to them. It was a difficult job to release them from it, but with the aid of wire cutters and a multitude of 'Whoas' and 'Good Boys' etc, the five horses were set free from the barbs and their dead comrade.

Artillery officers and others put in an appearance and we were very highly praised for what we had done. The O/C of the particular artillery brigade afterwards came and personally thanked us and said we should be mentioned in divisional orders, but I never stayed long to hear the result.

Farewell to the front line

On the morning of May 3rd 1917, I was sent for by the Company Officer. I wondered what would be the latest news for me. Would it be to accept promotion again? Or did he want a fresh servant?

When I saw him by his dug-out, he told me that orders had come through that two men per Company were to be sent 'down the line' for a rest. The only qualifications being length of time out in France and the backing of the necessary officers, etc.

I and another old trench soldier are the two lucky ones to be selected and the skipper hoped we'd make the best of it and look after ourselves. He added that, pending further instructions, we must wait with our Company. This prospect of a rest umpteen kilometres back from the line made us more cheerful than a small fortune could have done. The Regiment was to go into the line tomorrow night, May 4th, so we should dodge it all right.

Every hour of the day, we eagerly waited for the order to come for us to pack ourselves off to transport lines, but nothing happened. About 6 pm the 'skipper' sent for us again. He very much regretted, but men were short in the Company and a large working party was required that night to go up to the Line. His instructions were that we must go with them and, as soon as we returned, we could go back to transport lines and the RQM'r would see to us.

My chum remarked to me that something always happened when one was 'sweating on the top line' for something. He hinted that perhaps we would go down the line for a rest on a stretcher, or have a long 'rest' from a bullet or shell. I somehow agreed with him, because the feeling that I would get knocked out had returned with redoubled force.

The sector of the line we are to go to is very 'hot' and every yard of approach is likewise. The coming of darkness sees us preparing to set off. As I fumble in the darkness with my equipment, gas-mask, rifle, etc, I see visions of the base, with its expeditionary force canteens, YMCA concert parties and comfortable bed, etc and think to myself, not for me now, or ever!

There are about 50 of us as we form up and march off towards the skyline of leaping lights and stabbing flame. The guns are pounding away hard and the sound of concentrated rifle-fire can be heard plainly. All the way to the dump are batteries, field-guns, howitzers, both light and heavy, and all firing.

The usual congestion of night time is apparent everywhere. Long lines of 'tin-hatted' figures loom up carrying shovels. As fast as they pass, another crowd appears, everyone bent on some special mission. The traffic in both directions is ceaseless – limbers, lorries, ambulances, GS wagons. The only language is commands – "Keep to the right!" – "Mind the wire!" – "Look out! Large hole!" If it isn't orders, it's cursing from one and all.

Leaving the road, our guide goes across a hillside which descends into a valley by Wancourt. As soon as we top the rise, we see below us a great expanse of ground which is like the crater of a volcano. The whole area of the valley is a rapid succession of bursting shells, a great wall of flame on its far edge, and the continual explosions were once a small arms dump (grenades, .303, etc). Our way lies right through this pleasant place and I say to myself, It's goodbye 'rest'. However, we have already begun the descent into it, so we stumble on mutely, knowing some of us are 'for it'. Going in a bit of a semi-circle, we gradually approach the burning dump. What with our own guns blazing away and the hurricane of shells from the enemy, we scarcely know the why or wherefore of anything, owing to the din.

Some 50 yards from the dump we halt and, whilst doing so, a shell lands near and puts out of action four of our fellows. In fact, shells are dropping all about indiscriminately and it is just pure luck in not getting hit.

We now file up a narrow roadway and one by one, two petrol tins of water, tied together, are placed across our shoulders. We now turn about and follow the man in front. Out we go and slowly we dawdle along until all are loaded up.

The dump fire has by this time expended most of its energy and small arms, but in places, flames leap up anew, or ammunition explodes like thousands of crackers. Where the flames have ceased, a bed of blood red embers remained.

All of us are getting very 'windy'. Shells continue to swoop down and explode. We scarcely know who to follow or where to go to escape the tornado of steel.

The glow from the fire and the flashes from the explosions throw an unearthly light onto everything and everybody. To carry two petrol tins full of water, besides rifle, ammunition and equipment, is no mean feat in ordinary times during darkness, but to trample on a red hot bed of ashes and be incessantly shelled into the bargain, not knowing when one will be 'knocked-out', is about the limit. Blindly we stumble forward and when we bunch up unexpectedly, the cans clash one against the other as we press up to one another. Now we're off again and have scarcely got going properly when there is a blinding flash simultaneously with a deafening noise of explosion. A dull burning pain shoots through my right groin and I drop to the ground – I am hit!

I am fearful of moving; the dread of a stomach wound was always uppermost in my mind. How many had I seen slowly die with their entrails perforated, or gashed and protruding. My first thoughts are to wonder how long will it be before unconsciousness sets in, as I feel certain that I have a stomach wound.

There is much excitement all about. I gaze stupidly at the petrol cans that fell with me, at my rifle that also came to earth, at other rifles and petrol cans, steel helmets and khaki-clad figures that lie with them. Cautiously, I put my hand down to where the wound is and I withdraw it, wet and sticky.

Shells still burst in venomous fury and I have resigned myself to ultimately being killed before I could be got away.

Presently, helpers come amongst us and I attract their attention. They help me up to my feet and it surprises me to know that things are not too serious. Two of our own stretcher bearers assist me back to the road and in the protection afforded by old gun-pits, a first field dressing is applied. They find another wound in my right thigh, which nipped a piece of flesh out about the size of a half-crown.

The explosion

The stretcher bearers are good pals but cannot stay with me. They are busy attending to more than myself, and the water etc must be taken up that night, even though another 50 men have to be sent for. After they have gone, I lie quite indifferent to what may happen to me.

Later, the Lieut i/c of our working party appears in company with the senior stretcher bearer. It is the same Lieutenant who helped us with the horses. He flashes his torch on me, exclaiming "Hulloa, you've stopped one, eh?" They enter me down as a casualty and tell me that they cannot help me as they must push on with what is left of the working party, at once. The lieutenant tells me that so far eighteen men have been killed and wounded and that there will be precious little water to arrive up the trenches at the rate it's going on. Bidding me good luck and telling me that I must manage somehow until collecting parties find me, they are quickly swallowed up in the darkness.

Oh well, what's the use of worrying, so I get a fag out and take a swig of water. Two gunners come by. "What's up mate?" they ask. I tell them. "Shouldn't stay 'ere if I were you", they say. I tell them that if they help me onto my pins and give me two shovels that are lying near, I may be able to walk. This they do. When they see that I manage to shuffle along fairly well, they point the way to safety and urge me to stop the first limber or wagon that appears.

When I was hit, I became quite oblivious to the danger of the shelling, but I again realise that danger a hundredfold and am determined to get away at all costs. My whole right side is getting more painful than ever with every step and I am becoming a little weak from loss of blood. To stop would mean to remain until I am found, so I keep on and on. How far, or how long I travel in this fashion, I don't know.

Somehow I wander off the road and find myself in a land entirely deserted. It is a wilderness of craters, old trenches and rusty barbed wire and also of things that lie rotting. Realizing that I have 'took the wrong turning' as it were, I flop to earth and getting out my water bottle, drain it dry, as thirst from wounds is intense. Taking another 'cig', I smoke and examine myself. Placing my hand inside, I grope gently to feel if any of my 'innards' are protruding, or if a vital part of my anatomy is missing. Being reassured on this point, I take stock of my surroundings.

The only thing for me to do now is to find the road again. The whole of the skyline on one side is lit up with the guns and Very lights. I am out of danger from falling shells, which is the main thing, and an overpowering desire for sleep comes over me. This I dare not do; I may never wake. Well, with a bit of luck I shall really be going back for a rest in spite of the promise of that morning. I wonder how my chum, who was to accompany me, has fared.

The valley by Wancourt still flickers and flares with barrage of shells and I am more than thankful that the two artillerymen persuaded me to 'op it from there. Deciding to make a move towards the road again, I receive a nasty shock, with the knowledge that I cannot rise. There is only one way and that is to crawl. This I commence to do to the best of my powers, but it is much harder than I imagine and I take frequent rests. After some little distance I am exhausted and give it up, deciding to lie where I am until daylight, or until someone sees me.

Just as I am giving up all hopes of ever getting nearer to 'Blighty', I hear voices and some men appear out of the darkness. Shouting to them, they come across to me and at once carry me (armchair fashion with hands crossed) to the road, which I feel certain I would never have reached otherwise. The men belonged to the RE Signals and one stays by me until a horse-drawn ambulance appears. We shout for it to stop and I am helped into the already crowded vehicle. However, room is found on the rear step and with the help of the safety strap behind me and the willing arms of those inside, we jog along towards a field dressing station. A wagon load of battered humanity, but with the good humour of the "British Tommy", which always finds vent in the most adverse circumstances.

We pull in to a canvas hospital at the village of Tilloy. This village originally lay about two kilometres within the German line for over two years and therefore is now but a rubble heap.

I am carried into the marquee. My steel helmet is dumped onto an ever growing heap and a woollen comforter is given to me to wear. The tent is full up with casualties. Stretchers are covering all available space, whilst the walking cases sit about on boxes, forms or on the ground.

We fresh arrivals are attended to as quick as possible. My turn comes to furnish all particulars of regiment, brigade, division, etc. Following this, NCO medicals give a new dressing to our wounds and I get a first sight of myself. My trouser is slit from thigh to puttees and congealed blood covers the cloth and skin of my thigh. The left knee is torn also and my right hand is cut with the thumb-nail almost wrenched off. This I never felt anything of previously.

The next thing is inoculation against tetanus. I am then labelled and put on an empty stretcher. Hot cocoa and thick slabs of bread and jam are given to us to occupy the time until we are moved.

We smoke and talk of our respective experiences and of our probable destiny and duration away from the fighting, whilst all the while the throb and thunder of battle is heard quite plainly. There are numerous groans and whimpers from those who are badly knocked about. Intermingling with them is the cheery talk of those who are lightly wounded. Drowsiness again comes over me and I have gone off into a doze in spite of the pain.

That other part of the brain that never seems to rest gives me the first warning of danger and I am awake instantly to hear the high-pitched whistling shrieks of descending shells.

Everyone else is on the alert too. There is no mistaking that sound for us. We hear them thud into the earth and masonry near at hand. There is absolutely no protection whatever and shrapnel will tear the marquee to ribbons and us with it; we all know this full well. Every few minutes a salvo comes shrieking over and every time this happens, we get more 'windy'.

The shelling stops for half an hour or so, but commences again. There is an explosion very near. The rending of wood and iron can be heard and we are all cowering down in fear. Perhaps after all, this is to be the end, when we are so close to safety.

The Medicals now gather the walking cases together and they are led outside. We wonder what is happening. Presently, the stretcher cases are taken outside, but those that are too serious are left behind. Anybody who could manage to crawl along with the help of one or two orderlies is told to go.

My turn comes and I go rather painfully into the darkness. The throb of running motors is heard and motor lorries are waiting. These have been hastily requisitioned on returning from the line empty, having been used for taking up shells, etc.

We pile up into these, both officers and men and I get by the tailboard. No sooner are we loaded than we are off, bumping and jolting over the uneven road. The last sight of the Line comes to me as the lorry ascends a hill towards Arras. Then the crown of the land gradually rises behind us, blotting out the horizon of flame and shells and the flashes from the guns forever.

Final view of battlefield from lorry tailboard

World War I - a brief diary of events

1914

June 28th	Assassination of the Archduke Ferdinand of Austria and his wife at Sarajevo, Bosnia
July 28th	Austria declares war on Serbia
August 1st	Russia and Germany commence hostilities
August 3rd	Germany at war with France
August 4th	Great Britain declares war with Germany
Aug 12th	Great Britain declared war with Austria
Aug 13th	German armies overwhelm Belgium
Aug 16th	British Expeditionary Force lands in France
Aug 22nd	Charleroi and Namur seized by Germans
Aug 24th	Battle of Mons
Aug 25th	Louvain, Belgium destroyed
Aug 26th	Retreat from Mons
Sept 4th	Retreat ends. Battle of Marne
Sept 11th	Battle of Aisne
Sept 16th	Trench warfare becomes general
Oct 10th	Fall of Antwerp
Oct 20th	1st Battle before Ypres commences
Nov 5th	War with Turkey

Nov 21st	First Ypres Battle subsides
Dec 18th	Heavy fighting at La Bassée
Feb 5th	Renewed fighting round La Bassée

1915

March 10th	Battle of Neuve-Chappelle
April 25th	Landing at Gallipoli by British
May 9th-18th	Battle of Festubert
May 23rd	Italy enters the War against Germany
May	Second Battle Ypres and first use of poison gas
August 6th	Suvla Bay, Dardanelles
Sept 25th	Battle of Loos
Oct 11th	Belgrade captured by Germans
Oct 13th	Nurse Cavell shot by Germans

1916

Jan 9th	Evacuation of Gallipoli
Feb 20th	Great Battle at Verdun launched
April 29th	Surrender of Kut to the Turks
May 3rd	Second Battle at Verdun commences
May 25th	Military Service Act comes into force
June 5th	Lord Kitchener drowned with HMS Hampshire
June 30th	Second Verdun Battle ends
July 1st	Commencement of Somme Battle
Nov 10th	Somme Battle succeeded by Ancre, Beaumont-Hamel

1917

March 17th	Bapaume taken
April 9th	Battle of Arras and Vimy Ridge
April	Revolution in Russia. Czar abdicates
April 16th	French offensive on the Aisne
May 11th	Bullecourt captured
April 5th	USA enters war against Germany
June 7th	Capture of Messines Ridge
July 16th	Assassination of Czar of Russia
July 31st	Third Battle at Ypres
Sept 4th	First Night Air-Raid on London
Nov 20th	Capture of Cambrai by British
Dec 9th	Jerusalem captured by British
Dec	Collapse of Passchendaele Battle

1918

March 21st	Great German offensive begins; attack launched by 40 Divisions (frontage 50 miles)
March 23rd	British thrust back eight miles
March 24th	British lose all Somme battleground (15 miles); Fall of Peronne, Bapaume, Nesle, Chauny, Noyon
March 26th	Loss of Chaulnes and Roye. Old line from Albert to Bray lost
March 27th	Albert lost. Montdidier captured
March 28th	Germans reach Hamel, 10 miles from Amiens

March 30th	Germans surprise world with huge gun that throws shells into Paris, about 52 miles
April 4th	Germans claim 90,000 prisoners: 1,300 guns
April 9th	British driven back between Armentiers and La Bassée
April 10th	Armentiers evacuated by the British and seven miles of ground lost
April 14th	Gen. Foch appointed Generalissimo of Allies
July 18th	Brilliant counter stroke by Gen. Foch
July 23rd	Forced retreat of Germans on the Marne
July 27th	Enemy's retirement becomes general
Nov 9th	British capture Maubauge. Sheldt crossed. Revolution in Germany
Nov 11th	British enter Mons. Armistice signed.

The price of victory

The Royal Navy lost 22,258 killed or drowned and the Merchant Service 14,700 killed or drowned, while the Army wounded amounted to over 2,000,000. The total British killed or died of wounds or sickness amounted to 1,104,890.

TALLY OF THE LOST

	Officers	Men	Missing
Western Front	34,659	620,000	230,000
Italian Front	91	1,020	753
Dardanelles	1,787	31,837	7,600
Salonika	289	7,430	2,830
Mesopotamia	2,356	30,768	15,900
Egypt & Palestine	1,098	15,830	4,120
East Africa	381	8,724	1,019
Other Areas	133	690	1,000

There are over 600 war cemeteries in France and Belgium, with numbers of graves ranging from ten or twenty up to 15,000 or more.

British widows amounted to over 165,000
Amputation of one or more limbs 40,000
Blinded 2,300
Insane 6,800
Epileptics 3,420
Tuberculosis 45,000

A few facts and figures

Hostilities opened on August 4th 1914 and ceased on November 11th 1918. The war lasted 1,561 days.

The British first came into action at Mons and recaptured it on the last day of fighting. The conflict ended with the downfall of the thrones of Germany, Austria, Hungary and Russia.

The total strength of Army at Home and Overseas, on the Outbreak of War, was 256,141 of all Arms.

The firing line strength available was about 131,000 Officers and men.

At the end of the War there were 8,000,000 including The Dominions, Indian Army, Garrisons abroad and those just called up under the 'Conscription' Act.

Our soldiers fought on three continents and in every climate, From Artic to Equatorial heat.

Practically two-thirds were continuously in France.

Victualling was required for approximately 2,700,000 during the height of the Army's strength in France.

There were 46,800 motor vehicles on the Western Front, also 500,000 horses and mules.

Roads to be kept in repair behind the lines, 4,500 miles. 340 miles of broad gauge railway were laid, and 1,420 miles of narrow gauge.

The British flying strength on August 4th 1914 was four squadrons, 166 Aeroplanes 45 Seaplanes 7 non-rigid Airships, 285 Officers 1,853 Men

The British Expeditionary Force

The original British Expeditionary Force consisted of six Divisions and a Cavalry Division, with a total strength of roughly 160,000 men, 60,000 horses, 490 guns and 7,000 vehicles. That portion of it that landed in France first numbered about 100,000 men (1st, 2nd, 3rd, 5th Divisions) and 15 Cavalry Regiments. The remaining two Divisions were landed later.

Of the 490 cannon belonging to the BEF, only 24 were of "medium" type, the remainder being 18 pounders and light howitzers. There were no "heavy" guns whatever.

During the Battle of the Aisne, a further supply of 16 six-inch howitzers of inferior pattern arrived.

There were only two machine guns to a Battalion, or roughly 142 throughout the original B.E. Force.

At the time of the Armistice, the British possessed close on 6,500 guns and howitzers, of which 2,500 were medium and heavy calibre.

There were also 50,000 machine guns.

The Western Front always had an evil reputation and it never deserved it more than during the winter 1914-15.

The British, after the desperate first Battle of Ypres, had to face the most atrocious weather, with long periods of continuous rain, wind, snow and frost. The trenches, which were of a very rudimentary design, were waterlogged; men stood waist deep in places. Communications between the first line trenches and the rear were as bad as they could be and the sufferings endured were almost, if not quite, without parallel. Every man was new to the work, while thousands had recently returned from the tropics, and some 23,000 men were invalided during the winter with trench foot and frostbite.

The retreat from the Mons–Condé line to Dammartine, which was 15 miles from Paris, covered 170 miles and took place between August 23rd and September 5th 1914. By September 12th the Germans had been pushed back 60 miles to the River Aisne.

On October 4th 1914, the British were moved up into Flanders to act as left flank between the French and Belgians. On October 12th the first great struggle at Ypres began, ceasing about November 17th 1914. The whole world agreed that the stand put up by our troops against terrific odds was the greatest in history.

By December 1914 the original BEF had ceased to exist. It is estimated that quite 75 per cent of its personnel were casualties. Nevertheless, regiments, brigades and divisions were rapidly reinforced by reserves, while new armies were being formed at home.

The Germans never succeeded in capturing Ypres, but they were only 43 miles from Calais.

The early British line extended from the region of Armentières down to La Bassée, roughly 14 miles, but British, French and Belgians shared from Armentières to the Belgian coast.

During 1916 the British held about ninety miles of front, from NE of Ypres down to the River Somme. A further extension took place in 1917-18 when the line reached the

River Oise, or about 140 miles. This distance is about equal to that of Southampton to Nottingham.

Following on the winter of 1914-15, came the Battle of Neuve-Chapelle on March 10th, Festubert, May 9th-21st and the second Battle of Ypres and the first use of poison gas by the Germans. Stalemate followed until the Battle of Loos, Sept 25th 1915, in which our casualties amounted to about 40,000.

Trench warfare continued up to July 1st 1916, which was the commencement of the Somme offensive. This gigantic effort on Britain's part lasted four months and we suffered some 400,000 casualties. The latter stages of the battle were fought round Beaumont-Hamel and River Ancre and lasted almost to Xmas 1916.

The year 1917 made great demands on the British. Our casualties for the year were no fewer than 795,390 in killed, died of wounds and sickness, missing, etc.

The enemy also commenced his ruthless submarine campaign on February 2nd 1917 and our Merchant Fleet was being sent to the bottom twice as fast as we could build new ships.

During April 1917, nearly a million tons of shipping was lost, equal to about 180 ships averaging 6,000 tons each.

The first Russian Revolution took place early in 1917. To counteract this disaster, the Allies began a vigorous offensive, which opened out by the British on April 9th and was known as the Battle of Vimy-Ridge and Arras. It lasted over six weeks and ended with a brilliant victory.

June 7th 1917 saw the capture by our armies of a supposed impregnable position, Messines-Ridge. The next great struggle during 1917 opened on July 31st and was known as the Battle of Passchendaele. The weather was vile and the fighting was waged in a sea of mud and slime, which continued for weeks on end. This cost us about 255,000 casualties.

During November we attacked again near Cambrai. Four hundred tanks were used for this purpose. The Germans followed up this rapid victory of the British with a vigorous counter offensive, regaining practically all the lost ground and ordinary trench warfare continued from thence onwards.

On March 21st 1918 the Germans began their gigantic attack, which was to force a decision and end the War, as they fondly hoped. Under cover of thick mist and a terrific bombardment, they attacked, the British Fifth Army under General Gough. Their object was to drive a wedge between the British and French, and they all but succeeded.

For this, they massed 40 Divisions of "storm troops", or roughly 450,000 men, with the support of nearly 6,000 guns, against fourteen British Divisions and three Cavalry Divisions, sadly under strength – in all about 145,000 men.
Sheer weight of projectiles and men drove our troops from their positions back eight miles the first days.

On the 24th the whole of the old Somme battle area was lost and fifteen miles of ground gained by the Germans. On March 27th the Germans had reached Montdidier, only eight miles from Amiens.

To make good our enormous losses, 300,000 men were rushed across the Channel within a fortnight. General Foch was given supreme command of the allies on the Western Front on April 14th 1918.

The Germans bombarded Paris with a huge gun at the range of about 55 miles. This first took place on Sunday 30th March, killing 75 and wounding 90 worshippers in a church.

US troops were brigaded with British and French on April 1st. On the 4th April, 20 German Divisions attacked towards Amiens and advanced three miles. By this date the Allies had lost 90,000 men and 1,300 guns.

April 8th: a great bombardment opened on our lines from Arras to Armentiers. Our troops are driven back on a ten mile front between La Bassée and Armentiers.

April 10th 1918: The battle spreads northwards to Messines. Armentiers is evacuated.

April 11th : We lose Merville, Bailleul, Estairs, Lestrem, etc. Depth of German advance is 7 miles.

April 12th 1918: Germans capture Neuve-Eglise and claim the capture of 21,000 men and 230 guns in this area.

April 16th 1918: Further withdrawal of our line near Passchendaele.

April 19th 1918: We regain lost ground at Festubert and Givenchy.

Between May 15th and June 1st base hospitals were bombed from the air on seven occasions, killing 248 and wounding 693 men.

By April 26th 1918 the plan of the German High Command of destroying the British armies had failed. The situation was critical in the extreme. Our troops, exhausted by continual fighting, had their backs to the wall and everything depended on them holding on until fresh reinforcements arrived.

There was a pause of a month, which gave time for the new troops to arrive, but on May 27th an attack was launched between Soissons and Rheims, held by British and French, and the enemy reached Château-Thierry. It was here that US troops came into action as independent brigades and divisions.

The first great counterstroke by the Allies began on July 18th 1918. 30,000 prisoners and 500 guns were taken and the enemy was driven across the Marne.

The Allied offensive was now pressed on all fronts, particularly in the Amiens district. During the first days, a further 33,000 prisoners and 700 guns fell to the British. The enemy was driven back right across the thrice-stricken Somme battlefront.

On Sept 2nd the 'Wotan Line' was stormed and won, and our troops swept forward to the famous "Hindenburg Line", supported by 4,500 guns. By Sept 27th this was accomplished and the Canal du Nord was crossed.

Up in Flanders the Allies pressed forward. New ground was won every day. By Oct 17th Ostend was captured and the Belgian coast lost irrevocably by the Germans.

The last great battles opened on Oct 23rd in the Selle district. This continued till the fighting at Valenciennes on Nov 1st. Mons was reached on Nov 10th and an armistice signed on Nov 11th.

Our losses during these operations were heavier than any other ally and the territory recovered, greater than that of any other ally.

Wit, humour and verse from the Front

Oh, to be in Flanders, now that winter's here!
Lift up your heads, Oh ye people, and be ye lifted up, ye everlasting grousers,
and so will ye help in what is yet to do.
When this blooming war is over, how happy I shall be,
When we get our civvy clothes on, no more soldiering for me!

THE MENIN ROAD

There are many roads in Flanders where horses slide and fall,
There are roads of mud and pavé, that lead nowhere at all,
They are roads that finish at our trench, the Germans hold the rest,
But of all the roads in Flanders, there is one I know the best.
It's a great road, a straight road, a road that runs between
Two rows of broken poplars, that were young and strong and green.
You can trace it from old Poperinghe, through Vlameringhe and Wipers
(It's a focus for Hun whiz-bangs and a paradise for snipers)
Pass the solid ramparts and the muddy moat you're then in,
The road I want to sing about - the road that leads to Menin.
It's a great road, a straight road, a road that runs between
Two rows of broken poplars, that were young and strong and green.
It's a road that's cursed by smokers, for you dare not show a light,
It's a road that's shunned by daytime and it's dangerous by night,
But at dusk the silent troops come up and limbers bring their loads
Of ammunition to the guns that guard the salient's roads.

It's a great road, a straight road, a road that runs between

Two rows of broken poplars that were young and strong and green.

And for hours and days together, I have listened to the sound

Of German shrapnel overhead, while I was underground

In a damp and cheerless cellar, continually trying

To dress the wounded warriors, while comforting the dying

On that muddy road, that bloody road, that road that runs between

Two rows of broken poplars that were young and strong and green.

R.M.O.

The above was written by a Regimental Medical Officer in a First Aid Post on the Menin Road.

Little stacks of sandbags,

Little lumps of clay

Make our blooming trenches,

In which we live all day.

Merry little Whiz-bang,

Jolly little Crump,

Make our trench a picture,

Wiggle, Woggle, Wump!

VERSE BY AN INFANTRY BRIGADIER

In my dug-out (where the plans are laid)

I sing this song to my brigade.

You chaps who in a scrap have been,

Will "compris" fully what I mean.

Just lately in the stunts you've struck,

273

You haven't had the best of luck.
You've had the kicks without the pence
And always struck a stiffish fence.
You've had the mud; you've had the wet;
You've had the shells as well. And yet
You never grouse, but just hold on
When all except your pluck has gone.
We know the cheery way you curse.
When things are getting worse and worse,
Yet if I ask for further work,
There's not a damned one of you would shirk.
The higher staff quite understand,
But know the old division, and
They know all they have but to ask,
And you will carry out the task.
So, I have pledged my knightly word,
To stick it out, or get "the bird".
And though I pledge it with remorse,
I pledge it hopefully, because
I know the stuff of which you're made,
I know the old "umpteenth" brigade.
I know you'll always play the game,
(Although it is a b.......y shame),
And so in tempest and in rain,
In shells, and shells, and shells again,
Just understand (it's nothing new ?)
How proud I am of all of you.

If the Hun lets loose some gas - never mind.
If the Hun attacks in mass - never mind.

If your dug-out's blown to bits,
Or the C.O's throwing fits,
Or a shell your rum jar hits - never mind.
If your trench is mud knee high - never mind.
If you can't find a spot that's dry - never mind.
If a sniper has you set,
And dents your parapet,
And all your troubles fiercer get - never mind.

LATE NEWS FROM A RATION DUMP

Three submarines mined on the Menin Road.
The Swedes have declared war, hence the shortage of turnips.
Jamaica threatens to go to war and will cut off all rum supplies.
The Germans have only 360,000,000 shells left.
Pay of permanent base Wallers to be doubled, owing to the increased cost of living.
Pay to be halved for men in the line, as they are not in a position to spend it.
Two Zeppelins forced down by one of our carrier pigeons.
The Pope is sending an army to stop the war.
The Russians crossed the River Bug for the twenty-third time.
German fleet bombarded Wapping Old Stairs and spoilt the carpet.

The world wasn't made in a day,
And Eve didn't ride on a bus.
But most of the world is a sandbag,
The rest of it's plastered on us.

The Swiss Navy have crossed the Alps.
There's five women to every man in Britain.
Stay-at-homes get £10 a week wages, We get 10 francs a fortnight if still alive.
Only one ship will be required to take the army home.

IN FLANDERS FIELDS

In Flanders fields the poppies blow
Between the crosses, row on row,
That mark our place, and in the sky
The larks, still bravely singing, fly
Scarce heard among the guns below.
We are the Dead. Short days ago
We lived, felt dawn, saw sunset's glow,
Loved and were loved, and now we lie
In Flanders fields.
Take up your quarrel with the foe;
To you from failing hands we throw
The torch, be yours to hold it high,
If you break faith with us who die
We shall not sleep, though poppies grow
In Flanders fields.

Lieut. Col. John McCrae

Glossary

CHATT : The louse. The word may be used in the singular, but the insect was found (or it escaped) in hordes. *Chatt* is given by Grose, who suggests it may be derived from *Chattell*, i.e. something personal, carried about. From this noun developed the verb, meaning to rid oneself of some of the parasites by searching uniform and underwear, especially along the seams, and cracking the lice between the thumb-nails. They squelched blood, not their own! Another and better method was to take off the garment and run the seams over a candle flame. A vivid crackling noise announced the death of both *chatts* and their eggs. *Chatts* were not fleas or bugs; they did not jump but crept. They were a pale fawn in colour, and left blotchy red bite marks all over the body except in the hair of the head. They also created a distinctive sour, stale smell. Living in the same clothes without a bath for weeks on end, it was impossible for a private soldier not to become *chatty*, and the most thorough *chattings* were little more than demonstrations of ill-will. A bath and a change of clothing at a *delousing station* (cf.) was the only remedy – and this happened rarely. (*Taken from "Dictionary of Tommies' Songs and Slang, 1914-18" – John Brophy & Eric Partridge*).

ESTAMINET: There is no equivalent in Great Britain. On the Western Front an *estaminet* was not a pub. Neither was it a café or a restaurant. It had some of the qualities of all three. It was never large and was found only in villages and very minor towns. It had low ceilings, an open iron stove; it was warm and fuggy; it had wooden benches and table. It sold wine, cognac and thin beer, as well as coffee, soup, eggs and chips and omelettes. The proprietress (a proprietor was unthinkable) had a daughter or two, or nieces, or younger sisters who served at table and made no objection to tobacco smoke and ribald choruses in English and pidgin French. No doubt some estaminets overcharged but in general they provided for the soldier off duty behind the line many and many a happy hour. The name had a magical quality in 1914-18 – and still has for those who survive. (Cf. *Eggs and Chips*). (*Taken from "Dictionary of Tommies' Songs and Slang, 1914-18" – John Brophy & Eric Partridge*).

FLIT: Depart.

O.PIP: Observation Post. It was often difficult to pass messages accurately over a field telephone and in order to differentiate similar sounds, a system was devised by which A became ack, B – beer, D – don, M – emma, P – pip, S – esses, T – toc, V – vic. This pronunciation was often taken into the general Army vocabulary. A Trench Mortar Battery would be referred to, for example, as a Toc Emma Beer. (*Taken from "Dictionary of Tommies' Songs and Slang, 1914-18"*).

POILU: French for an infantryman – hairy. In the first months of the War, French soldiers, of necessity, let the hair grow on their faces.

POTOMINE POISONING: Ptomaine poisoning. An obsolete term for food poisoning now known to be caused not by ptomaines – chemical compounds present in decaying foodstuffs – but by bacteria or bacterial poisons. (*Family Health Encyclopaedia*).

VAD: Voluntary Aid Detachment. More usually any trained but not professional nurse who volunteered for hospital service abroad or in England. Navy blue outdoor uniform.

(Cf. *W.A.A.C., Women's Legion, and W.R.A.F.*). (*"Dictionary of Tommies' Songs and Slang 1914-18"*).

VALISE (Private Soldier): The khaki canvas knapsack carried on the back in which were stored spare underclothing, overcoat, ground sheet, emergency rations, etc. (*"Dictionary of Tommies' Songs and Slang 1914-18"*).